Gender and
International Relations

Gender and International Relations

An Introduction

Jill Steans

Rutgers University Press
New Brunswick, New Jersey

First published in Great Britain 1998
by Polity Press in association with Blackwell Publishers Ltd.

First published in the United States 1998
by Rutgers University Press, New Brunswick, New Jersey

Copyright © Jill Steans 1998

Library of Congress Cataloging-in-Publication Data

Steans, Jill.
　　Gender and international relations / Jill Steans.
　　　　p.　cm.
　　Includes bibliographical references (p.　　) and index.
　　ISBN 0-8135-2512-8 (cloth : alk. paper) — ISBN 0-8135-2513-6
　(pbk. : alk. paper)
　　　1. International relations—Psychological aspects.　2. Feminism.
　3. Feminist theory.　I. Title.
　JZ1253.2.S74　1998
　327'.082—dc21　　　　　　　　　　　　　　　　　　97-41156
　　　　　　　　　　　　　　　　　　　　　　　　　　　　　CIP

British Library Cataloguing-in-Publication Data is available upon request.

Printed in Great Britain

Contents

Acknowledgements

This book would not have been possible without the contribution of a number of people. I have gained both support and inspiration from my involvement with the BISA Gender and International Relations Working Group. I would like to thank Roger Tooze and Margaret Law for reading and commenting on the first drafts of chapters one and two. I owe a particular debt of gratitude, however, to my colleague Andrew Linklater and to two anonymous reviewers. All three read the manuscript in its entirety and provided constructive and helpful suggestions as to how it could be improved. Many of these have been incorporated into the final text. Last, but certainly not least, I would like to thank Luke and Ria for their continuing encouragement and support.

Introduction

Until relatively recently little had been written about gender issues in International Relations,[1] despite the enormous amount of interest in gender in other areas of the social sciences. This can, in part, be explained by the way in which the subject has developed historically. International Relations has been largely concerned with the study of relations between sovereign states and it had generally been assumed that the kinds of issues raised by feminism did not arise because the processes and structures of interstate relations could be understood without reference to gender. Of course, not all International Relations scholarship has been concerned solely with states and interstate relations. However, even in works which have challenged this rather narrow view of the kinds of 'relations' studied, very little work has been done on gender in practice. Of late, however, the discipline has become less 'gender-blind' and rather more open to the kinds of issues raised by feminism.[2] This is largely due to the efforts of feminist International Relations scholars who have pointed out that, while frequently ignored, gender issues are deeply embedded in what is conventionally understood to be the 'mainstream' concerns of the discipline.

This book has three major aims. First, it is in a broad sense concerned to explore the ways in which 'gender makes the world go around'[3] and suggest ways in which feminist theories furnish us with conceptual and theoretical tools to construct knowledge about the world. It does not, however, attempt to construct a single feminist theory of International Relations, nor does it advance a particular perspective on how gender can best be understood in an international or global context. Rather, the approach adopted is in sympathy with the view that whilst partial in themselves, feminist theories have collectively produced a great many insights which contribute to our understanding of many of the concerns of International Relations as conventionally defined. For this reason, the organization of the book mirrors the conventional concerns of the discipline, for example, issues of political identity, conceptions of political community and citizenship, the nature of power, the state, violence, peace and security, global political economy and development. However, in adopting what could be regarded as a somewhat conventional approach to the subject matter of International Relations, the intention is to both rework the central concerns of the discipline in ways which demonstrate the relevance of gender and to show how foregrounding issues of gender encourages us to think about each of these areas in radically different ways.[4]

The second major aim of this book is to demonstrate how insights drawn from feminist scholarship, in both International Relations and other fields of study, can be used to challenge conventional or *orthodox* approaches to the discipline. Feminists have long pointed out that key concepts and ideas in social and political theory contain gender bias.[5] In the last ten years, feminist scholars have demonstrated that International Relations is also a profoundly gendered *ideology* or *discourse*.[6] Feminist critiques of International Relations have concentrated particularly on realist and neo-realist traditions of thought, and this concern with realism/neo-realism as the 'orthodoxy' in International Relations is reflected in this book. Feminist critiques have demonstrated how realism as a dominant theory of International Relations is not grounded in eternal truths about the *real* world. There is no *objective* social and political reality 'out there'. Our 'reality' is constituted by *intersubjective* understanding of a complex social and political world. The construction of meaning also involves the use of imagery and symbolism. Power is profoundly implicated in the construction of knowledge and the categories and concepts which are employed to construct our 'reality'. Feminist critiques are particularly powerful because by exposing the gender bias in key concepts in realism and highlighting the profoundly gendered imagery and symbolism employed in realist texts, they address the politics of knowledge construction in concrete ways.

Feminist critiques also encourage critical reflection upon the whole question of what 'theory' is and how theory relates to specific social practices. Feminist critiques of realism raise important questions about the *subject* of knowledge. In simple terms subjectivity refers to self awareness, consciousness or individuality. The conscious individual or subject positioning herself or himself politically, assesses the social and political significance of institutions and practices and infuses her or his actions with social and political meaning. Foregrounding issues of gender is in itself an effective way of putting 'political subjectivity back into the picture' in International Relations theory.[7] These rather complex ideas are discussed at greater length in the first chapter of this book where the interest in gender and feminism is located in the context of contemporary theoretical debates in International Relations.

A further reason why a powerful argument can be made for International Relations scholars to engage with issues of gender and feminism is because the so-called 'third debate'[8] in International Relations theory has itself opened up important questions about the activity of 'theorizing' and the politics of knowledge claims. The third debate in International Relations has raised questions about the social and political dynamics involved in the construction of knowledge. Somewhat belatedly perhaps, International Relations scholars have begun to think through the implications of the insight that understanding and explaining international relations does not simply involve identifying the structures and processes which will be the object of study, but also reflecting critically upon what can be said to constitute *knowledge* of the world. In the realist/neo-realist orthodoxy the state is frequently taken to be the main *actor* in International Relations. Furthermore, knowledge about the world is constructed from the 'point of view' of the *state as actor*. To challenge the orthodoxy in International Relations is, therefore, to challenge the notion that the state is the subject of knowledge.

The third debate has addressed the consequences of the dominance of realism in terms of how the field of International Relations has been mapped out conceptually. That is, of how categories for 'understanding' and 'explaining' international relations have been constructed and how this has served to delimit the scope of the 'legitimate' field of study. The influence of critical theories, in a broad sense,[9] has encouraged a transgressing of the boundaries between academic disciplines. This development has encouraged some International Relations scholars to draw upon insights developed in other fields of study, including the insights derived from feminist scholarship. In some respects, therefore, contemporary feminist theorists working in International Relations, while having their own distinctive agendas, share some common ground with other critical theorists. Concentrating specifically on gender in the context of contemporary theoretical debates in International Relations has the additional attraction of serving to introduce some difficult and complex issues in ways which ground the discussions in concrete concerns and easily understandable issues.

Since the end of the Cold War in 1989, a great deal has been written about the nature of the 'new world order'. However, what non-feminist commentators fail to notice is that the so-called new world order of the 1990s, while radically changed in some respects, remains a world of stark gender inequalities.[10] While there are differences between women across the world, there are also many commonalities; and while the pattern of gender inequality varies between regions, it is nevertheless a global phenomenon. In general terms, there remains a real dichotomy between economic and technological changes and social progress. Even in areas of the world where economic growth has been rapid, economic progress has not been matched by social progress in general terms and by improvements in the relative position of women in particular. Furthermore, ideas about the naturalness of gender roles and the 'private' and 'natural' roles of women, serve to render women's work invisible. This not only perpetuates unequal relations between women and men, but also distorts our understanding of many of the most pressing problems facing the world today. While this is not a book about the global condition of women as such, its third main aim is to show how focusing on women's lives provides important insights into many contemporary global problems.[11] These issues are addressed more fully in chapters 5 and 6.

Until quite recently, most feminist theory started out from the conditions of women's lives. This book draws upon feminist scholarship which is frequently concerned with *women* whilst recognizing that women's lives can only be fully understood in terms of prevailing *gender* relations. Some feminists have adopted the metaphor of 'feminist lenses'[12] or 'gender lenses'[13] to describe an approach to feminist analysis which brings into view the different dimensions of power and gender inequality. Gender lenses can be

used to challenge dominant assumptions about what is significant or insignificant, or what are central or marginal concerns in
International Relations. To 'look at the world' is to try to make
sense of a complex social and political 'reality'. Everybody engages in this process of trying to make sense of the world and in
this sense, everybody is a 'theorist'. It is in the nature of academic
inquiry, however, to make explicit our assumptions about the
nature of the world – what can be said to exist *ontologically* – and
about what is significant or insignificant or enduring rather than
ephemeral. Knowledge-building is seen to involve empirical research and theoretical debate within the academic community,
which is driven by a desire to establish a degree of consensus
about these matters. However, before the process of constructing
knowledge about the world can begin, the field of study has to
be mapped out conceptually. Thus International Relations
scholars in the realist or neo-realist tradition have identified
states as major actors and conflict as a major process, while liberals
have identified 'actors' such as states, transnational corporations
and international organizations and identified cooperation as a
major process. However, until recently International Relations
scholars had not included gender as a category of analysis or as an
approach.

To look at the world through gender lenses is to focus on
gender as a particular kind of power relation, or to trace out the
ways in which gender is central to understanding international
processes. Gender lenses also focus on the everyday experiences
of women as *women* and highlight the consequences of their unequal social position. The term 'lenses' is, however, preferred to
'lens', because it is recognized that gender relations are complex
and it is necessary, therefore, to draw upon a variety of feminist
perspectives to get a better understanding of a complex whole.
Looking at the world through gender lenses brings into focus the
many dimensions of gender inequality, from aspects of 'personal'
relations, to institutionalized forms of discrimination: from, for
example, the formal barriers to equality of opportunity, or the
underrepresentation of women in decision-making structures, to
gender inequality as an integral part of the structural inequalities
generated by operation of the global economy. Postmodern feminists do not make use of the *lens* metaphor, however, since, as
will be argued at greater length in chapter 1, postmodern feminism problematizes the notion that women can be seen as a

homogeneous group with common experiences, common interests and a common perspective.

The book is organized into seven chapters. Since little or no
prior knowledge of gender, feminism or International Relations is
assumed, chapter 1 introduces the central concept of gender,
outlines briefly the main strands of feminist thought and discusses
in more detail contemporary theoretical debates in International
Relations.

Chapter 2 concentrates on the consequences of realism/neo-
realism as the dominant approach or the 'orthodoxy' in International Relations for how the discipline has been 'mapped'
conceptually. It suggests that feminist critiques of the realist
orthodoxy demonstrate the profoundly gendered nature of key
concepts and ideas. Feminist critiques of the orthodoxy also raise
important questions about the processes of *inclusion* and *exclusion*
involved in the construction of theory.

Chapter 3 continues to explore the theme of *inclusion* and
exclusion by focusing on dominant constructions of political identity in International Relations. The chapter begins by considering
the implications of the privileging of the 'imagined community'[14]
of the nation-state as the single irreducible component of identity
and human attachment in realism and neo-realism. It goes on to
suggest that, consequently, the complexities of world politics have
been reduced to relations between *reified* sovereign nation-states.

By foregrounding gender in discussion about identity, this
chapter also explores the complex ways in which gender identities
are central to the construction of political identities. The example
of nationalism is chosen because there is an extensive feminist
literature which illustrates the way in which gender is central to
nationalist constructions of identity. In concentrating on the imagined community of the nation and nationalist constructions of
identity the intention is not – paradoxically – to reaffirm the
centrality of the nation-state in the study of International Relations. However, neither is it to claim that nationalism is not important in understanding world politics. Rather, the aim is to provide
a concrete, familiar and seemingly 'unproblematic' example of
collective identity in order to raise a series of questions about the
importance of power in the construction and ascription of
identity.

The construction of identity involves drawing a boundary between 'self' and 'other'. Within the orthodoxy, the nation-state is

seen as the fundamental territorial and political boundary which separates and divides human beings. For this reason, International Relations scholars have largely confined their interest in identity to the question of citizenship. Citizenship should not simply be understood as the means by which states confer rights and duties upon individuals within a particular nation-state, however, but also as a particular expression of identity, allegiance and belonging. Gender is central to the construction of the 'inclusive' and 'exclusive' categories which establish rights of citizenship. Feminists have pointed to the exclusionary practices involved in the demarcation of 'in' and 'out' groups. Historically women have been excluded from citizenship through masculinist constructions of politics and 'further excluded through the close association of citizenship with bearing arms'.[15] This has had important consequences for women who have historically been removed from the realm of justice, denied rights, and subjected to patriarchal forms of authority. It could be argued that the masculinized nature of politics and conceptions of citizenship has also profoundly affected the way in which the actual business of politics has been carried out. Focusing on gender and identity leads us to ask rather different questions about the social practices involved in the construction of those 'bounded communities' called nation-states which have so occupied International Relations scholars.

Having illustrated the complexity of issues of gender, identity and power in nationalist constructions identity, the final section turns to questions of how we might move beyond the territorial and conceptual boundaries of state and nation. It does this by focusing on issues of gender and identity in global perspective. By foregrounding questions of gender and identity, feminist scholars present a radical challenge to dominant conceptions of identity in international politics. Focusing on gender challenges the nation-state as the primary locus of political identity, while transnational feminist alliances serve to demonstrate how competing forms of identification, allegiances and expression of solidarity influence global politics.

Focusing on processes of inclusion and exclusion also highlights the way in which the concept of the *state as actor* in International Relations fundamentally shapes the way we come to understand ourselves and our relations with excluded others. The nation-state functions as a conceptual boundary in realism, a fundamental category for understanding relations between self (citizen) and other (foreigner) between inside (order) and outside (anarchy). Employing the nation-state as a conceptual 'boundary' might be justified on the grounds that nation-states are 'real' entities. Furthermore, it could be argued that the nation-state remains the dominant form of political organization. However, the nation-state is a dynamic entity which is *made* through practices which construct and police territorial borders, for example diplomacy and 'foreign' policy. These practices are important in carving out a distinctive political place, space and identity for the nation-state.

Nation-states are frequently made through war. Chapter 4 concentrates upon how gender is central to the processes involved in constructing the boundaries of the nation-states, specifically war. This chapter concentrates on the implications of the historic linkage between military participation and citizenship. Historically, this linkage has been one of the main justifications for the exclusion of women from the public realm and has provided a strong justification for the subordination of women. The chapter concludes by drawing out the broader implications of women's relationship to the state, the military- and state-sanctioned violence in terms of how we think about the security of individuals and collectivities.

The orientation of feminist critical theory towards an emancipatory politics and the postmodern feminist celebration of different expressions of identity and solidarity have in quite distinctive ways encouraged a radical rethinking of dominant conceptions of identities and boundaries in which traditional approaches to security have been framed. Chapter 5 starts out from the position that security for the individual cannot be adequately understood purely in terms of his or her membership of a given national community. Adopting feminist perspectives on security not only challenges the view of the military as a defender of a pre-given 'national interest', but also suggests that the degree to which people feel or actually are 'threatened' varies according to their economic, political, social or personal circumstances.[16] Thus militarism, poverty, inequality, mal-development and the denial of human rights or at least basic needs are important in understanding how secure or insecure people feel or actually are in terms of their race, ethnic identity, political status, class and, of course, gender.

It has been argued that by problematizing the fusion of 'secure individual identity' with 'secure state identity'[17] feminist approaches draw attention to the political subject as relevant to our understanding of security. Indeed, the achievement of security of identity varies according to 'the degree to which threats are perceived or exist on economic, political, social or personal grounds'.[18] Therefore 'the development of a complex understanding of political subjectivity inevitably implies recognition of the influence of political economy', because economic factors cannot be discarded when addressing issues of subjectivity and power.[19] Chapter 6 is concerned to explore further some of these issues through a discussion of feminist approaches to global political economy and development issues.

Chapter 6 is also concerned with the ways in which gender is an integral part of both the theory and practice of global political economy. It includes a discussion of the role played by the UN in 'bringing women into' the development process. However, women are not, and have never been, the passive 'victims' of global political and economic processes. While frequently ignored, 'women's work' makes an enormous contribution to the global economy. Furthermore, women have sought to influence debates about global political economy and development by taking advantage of the opportunities offered for both networking and lobbying, by, for example, United Nations conferences.

Chapter 7 turns to the question of whether approaches to studying the international/global realm can be developed which avoid the reductionism and silences of the orthodoxy. The first section of the chapter is explicitly concerned with 'reconstructive' projects, although for reasons which will become apparent, it does not attempt to construct a coherent feminist 'world-view'. The second section of the concluding chapter concentrates on what are, arguably, emerging as two of the three main approaches[20] to gender, feminism and International Relations – feminist critical theory and postmodern feminism. These two approaches offer very different responses to the question of whether or not it is either possible or desirable to construct a 'feminist International Relations'.

Chapter 1

Gender, Feminism and International Relations

This first chapter provides a broad overview of the different strands of feminist theory and of the historical and contemporary debates which have shaped International Relations. The chapter is divided into three main sections. The first section discusses briefly different approaches to gender. The second section outlines some of the main concepts and ideas found in different schools of feminist thought. The final section sets the interest in gender and feminism in the context of contemporary debates in International Relations theory.

What Is Gender?

Gender and gender differences are sometimes seen to be derived from differences in biological sex and are, therefore, thought of as 'natural'. Indeed in everyday usage, the terms 'gender' and 'sex' are frequently used interchangeably. However, gender refers not to what men and women are *biologically*, but to the ideological and material relations which exist between them. The terms 'masculine' and 'feminine' do not describe natural characteristics, but are gender terms. In all societies and in all cultures there are certain emotional and psychological characteristics which are held to be essentially 'male' or 'female'. Similarly, while sex and gender do not coincide naturally, individuals who are born as biological males or females are usually expected to develop 'masculine' or 'feminine' character traits and behave in ways appropriate to their gender.

In the 1920s and 1930s social scientists, regarded gender as a personal attribute and the study of gender was largely confined to the study of character traits and 'sex roles'.[1] This notion of sex roles was developed as a way of describing the social functions fulfilled by and seemingly appropriate to men and women. Social scientists generally speaking supported the 'common-sense' view that men and women had particular characteristics which made them particularly well suited to the performance of particular social roles. Thus, while social scientists did not see sex and gender as synonymous, they believed that they were closely connected. Connell has argued that in the 1920s the 'new' social sciences, including sociology and psychology, became interested in how the psychological differences between men and women were caused.[2] By the 1930s the use of personality tests to measure masculinity and femininity was widespread in the social sciences. Approaches which concentrated on personality traits were then synthesized with an analysis of the prevailing sexual division of labour and conventional sex roles. Early social scientists concluded from their studies that biological sex and gender characteristics were closely connected. It was also widely accepted that the prevailing sexual division of labour reflected the close correspondence between gender traits and sex roles. Those who were held to be insufficiently masculine or feminine were regarded as in some way abnormal or deviant.[3]

In the 1960s feminist analysis was brought to bear on questions of gender in ways which radically challenged this view. Feminists argued that sex roles were assigned by society. Furthermore, they argued that male-identified roles were frequently seen to be more important and deserving of greater social rewards than female-identified roles. For example, those performing the role of 'bread-winner', which was strongly male-identified, were usually accorded higher social status than 'housewives'. The status accorded to men and women within societies was not, therefore, equal. Feminists pointed out that rather than reflecting the personality traits of men and women, ideas about gender were used to justify unequal treatment and thus provided an important ideological justification for a specific form of social inequality. Historically, the idea that women possessed certain gender traits, for example that they were more passive, emotional and sensitive than men, and that men, by contrast, were aggressive, objective and logical, had been used to justify female subordination.

Feminists condemned the subordinate status assigned to women. They also argued that theories which explained women's particular status in terms of either their 'natural' or 'essential' characteristics were ideological, serving to legitimize an unjust social order which valued men more highly than women. However, feminists believed that the subordinate social position of women was, nevertheless, rooted in socially assigned sex roles. On the basis of this analysis, in the 1960s, feminists argued that the route to sexual equality and women's liberation lay in challenging conventional sex roles. By the 1970s, however, feminists had become aware that this was no easy matter. Sex roles were deeply entrenched. The ascription of gender involved a highly complex system of stereotyping which was in turn supported by a whole range of social institutions and practices. 'Women' and 'men' were not only created by society but conformity to the characteristics held to be specifically 'masculine' and 'feminine' was rigidly enforced. Individuals found themselves under a great deal of social pressure to conform to gender-stereotypical behaviour.

By this stage, feminists had become less concerned with gender traits and sex role functions and more interested in power relations. Feminist analysis was increasingly directed towards the ways in which biological differences became strongly linked to socially constructed 'masculine' and 'feminine' traits, and how these were then used to justify unequal relations between men and women. Gender came to be viewed as a socially constructed inequality between men and women.[4] At its simplest form this power analysis of gender 'pictured women and men as social blocs linked by direct power relations'[5] and this, in turn, led to the notion that women as a group shared a common interest in challenging the prevailing gender order.

Some feminists argued that gender roles followed rather than preceded a hierarchical division of labour between the sexes and transformed previously existing anatomical differences into differences relevant for social practice. Gender came to be understood in social and political terms as a relationship which had meaning within social practices which, in turn, structured and supported social institutions. This view of gender shifted feminist thinking away from a preoccupation with sex roles, to a concern with how gender was constituted by the structure of various social institutions and practices which tied gender into intricate patterns of domination. In the 1970s and 1980s radical feminists argued that gender should be seen as a collective phenomenon and not just an aspect of personal identity or personal relations. Radical feminists directed their attentions to the social dynamics which underpinned the creation and maintenance of 'sex–gender systems'.[6] That is, systems which institutionalized male control over women. Radical feminists saw men's overall social supremacy as being embedded not only in face-to-face settings such as the family, but also generated in the functioning of the economy and through social institutions such as the church and the media. Indeed, radical feminists argued that the state itself had to be seen as a patriarchal power. In some radical feminist analysis, the state came to be viewed as a *process*. That is, the state was not seen as a 'thing', an entity with an independent existence, but was actually a dynamic entity which was constantly being made and remade. The state was constituted by the very practices and processes it engaged in and, furthermore, patriarchy – male dominance – was embedded in the procedures and practices of the state. The implications of viewing the state as a process and also a patriarchal power for understanding International Relations are discussed at greater length in chapters 3, 4 and 5.

In recent years, there has been a move towards understanding gender as both an aspect of personal identity and an integral part of social institutions and practices. In contemporary social science, gender is frequently seen in terms of the interweaving of personal life and social structures. Such an approach is seen to avoid the pitfalls of *voluntarism,* that is, the idea that people exercise free choice over their actions, and various forms of *determinism,* which suggest that human behaviour is wholly conditioned by constraints – for example predetermined by biology or by existing social structures. Such an approach also allows gender to be seen in historical context, rather than as a transhistorical structure which arises out of the sexual dichotomy of the male and female body.[7]

The impact of postmodern thought both within the social sciences and feminist theory has also influenced approaches to gender. A number of postmodern feminist thinkers have found the work of the French philosopher Michel Foucault useful because he presented a theory of power and its relation to the body which could be used to explain aspects of women's oppression in ways which suggested that sexuality was not innate, but the effect of historically specific power relations.[8] Foucault's work on discourse suggested that the production of knowledge was bound up historically with specific regimes of power. According to Foucault every society produced its own 'truths' which had normalizing and regulatory functions. It was the task of the genealogist of discourse to trace out the ways in which these discourses of truth operated in relation to the dominant power structures of any given society. In this view, gender is seen as the *discursive* or the cultural means by which 'natural sex' is produced and established as pre-discursive or prior to culture.[9]

This insight gives feminism a useful analytical framework to explain how women's experience is impoverished and controlled within certain culturally determined images of female sexuality.[10] Connell has argued that gender should be seen in terms of social and cultural practices which construct gender relations by 'weaving a structure of symbols and interpretation around them and often vastly exaggerating or distorting them'.[11] In this view, 'to sustain patriarchal power on the large scale requires the construction of a hyper-masculine ideal of toughness, and dominance' and 'images of physical beauty in women'.[12] Thus the male or female body does not confer masculinity or femininity on the individual; it takes on meaning through social practices. This process has a power dimension in that 'meanings in the bodily sense of masculinity concern, above all else, the superiority of men to women, and the exaltation of hegemonic masculinity over other groups of men which is essential to the domination of women.'[13]

The above represents a brief overview of how gender has been understood historically. There have been, and continue to be, differences in perspective and emphasis. These differences are notably between those who argue that gender should be understood in terms of structural inequalities and those that argue that, while social institutions and practices are central to understanding how gender is constructed, analysis should focus on discourse and discursive practices. However, what is clear from this discussion is that gender is not synonymous with sex and is social rather than natural. Despite differences of emphasis and approach, there is widespread agreement that gender is best understood in terms of power.

Feminist Theories

Most definitions of 'feminism' or 'feminist' centre on the notion of equality between the sexes or equal rights. Feminism is frequently defined as a belief that women are entitled to enjoy the same rights and privileges as men. Feminism is also defined in terms of political activity. The 'feminist movement'[14] aims to bring about changes that will end discriminatory practices and realize equal rights for women in all spheres of life. However, focusing narrowly on the issue of equal rights can obscure the richness and diversity in feminist thought. The term 'feminism' covers a wide variety of perspectives and practices. In a general sense, however, such a definition does serve to capture the importance of viewing feminism as both a set of ideas and a social movement. Indeed for many feminists, these two activities can scarcely be separated. Being a feminist involves an ongoing struggle to live one's life according to feminist principles. Similarly, engaging in the activity of 'feminist theorizing' involves thinking about how in our everyday lives our activities either perpetuate or challenge the status quo. This in turn involves reflecting upon the complex linkages between gender relations and other forms of social inequality. It also involves making value judgements about the just or unjust nature of existing social arrangements and putting forward alternative models of how we might live. Feminist theorizing is not, then, purely an abstract academic activity, but an ongoing critical engagement with the world. Feminism is a point of departure, a position from which contending values and practices are assessed and evaluated and from which one's own actions are given social meaning and political significance.[15]

Gender as both a social category and an analytical category has been central to feminist theory until – arguably – quite recently. However, it is clear that beyond the common commitment to gender equality which gives feminism its core identity and distinctiveness, feminists hold very different views about how gender relations are constructed, how they can be transformed and how women can be 'liberated'. Furthermore, while feminist theories are centred around the concept of gender, it is difficult in practice to separate gender from other facets of identity and experiences and other forms of social inequality which are rooted in social class, perhaps, or justified by racist ideologies. For these reasons there are many 'feminisms'. Rather than try to identify the essence of feminism, or establish a set of core feminist values and beliefs, therefore, it is probably more useful to demonstrate the richness and variety in feminist theories and practices by sketching out some of the major ideas that have influenced the development of feminism as both a school of thought and a social movement. Rosemary Tong has outlined a useful classification which divides feminist thought into liberal feminist, radical feminist, Marxist feminist, socialist feminist, psychoanalytic feminist thought and existential and postmodern feminism.[16] For the most part, the following will closely follow Tong's classification and discussion.

Liberal feminism

Liberal feminism[17] is centrally concerned with equal rights. Liberals hold a view of human nature which stresses the capacity of human beings for rational thought. That is, human beings are seen to be capable of calculating the best means to achieve some desired end, or of having the capacity to comprehend rational principals. It is the individual's capacity for reason which allows him[18] to exercise autonomy and to make meaningful choices. Liberals also believe that all human beings have the capacity to think and act rationally. It is this capacity for reason which gives rise to the idea that human beings have innate *rights*. Liberals support the right of individuals to seek fulfilment and pursue their own interests, providing that, in so doing, they respect the rights of others.

In the eighteenth and nineteenth centuries, feminists used what were essentially liberal arguments to challenge the unequal treatment afforded to women. The argument that women were 'by nature' different from men was frequently used to justify different and usually unequal treatment for women. Rights were frequently denied to women on the ground that they were 'irrational' creatures and so less than fully human. Feminists found liberalism useful in challenging patriarchal authority justified by religious dogma. At the same time, however, feminists were logically compelled to argue for women's equality on the grounds that women, like men, were rational beings capable of making their own decisions and determining their own best interests. Written in 1792, Mary Wollstonecraft's *Vindication of the Rights of Woman*[19] was the first attempt to make the liberal case for equal rights for women. However, even at this early stage, feminists were arguing that the realization of genuine equality entailed more than the achievement of formal rights. Thus Wollstonecraft insisted that to achieve sexual equality and justice, women not only needed to be granted the same rights as men, but also needed to have equal access to education, and economic opportunities. Liberal feminists in the eighteenth and nineteenth centuries argued that as a result of different processes of socialization and discriminatory social and cultural practices women were afforded fewer opportunities than men to realize their full potential as human beings. Historically, women had been confined to the home and to the domestic service of their husbands and children. Therefore they had little opportunity to exercise their intellectual faculties or develop skills other than those deemed necessary for the performance of domestic duties. Over the years, liberal feminists have consistently advocated equal rights and equal opportunities for women. Many contemporary women's groups such as the National Organization for Women in the United States of America, continue actively to campaign around issues of rights and equal opportunities. Most liberal feminists also argue that in order to achieve genuine equality of opportunity it is necessary for men to share the responsibility and work involved in raising a family, and for the state to provide childcare facilities, thus recognizing that women still bear the burden of responsibility for childcare and this in itself is a significant barrier to genuine equality of opportunity.

The liberal feminist position has been criticized because it is reformist in character. Liberal feminists are, indeed, content to advocate reformist measures to address discrimination against women rather than demand revolutionary social and political changes. Nevertheless, as Zillah Eisenstein has argued,[20] liberal feminism involves more than simply achieving the bourgeois male rights earlier denied women. Liberal feminism is not merely feminism added onto liberalism. There is a real difference between liberalism and liberal feminism in that feminism requires a recognition, however implicit and undefined, of the sex–class identification of women as women. Early liberal feminists argued for individual rights of women on the basis that they were excluded from citizen rights as members of a sexual class. The ascribed sexual status of women prevented them from being included in individual accomplishments promised by liberal society. According to Eisenstein, it is in this recognition of women as a sexual class that the subversive quality of liberal feminism lies, because liberalism is premised upon women's exclusion from

public life on this very same basis. The demand for real equality of
women with men if taken to its logical conclusion, therefore,
would displace the patriarchal structures necessary to a liberal
society. However, it is frequently argued that liberal feminism
also ignores other major forms of oppression rooted in race, for
example, or social class.

Marxist feminism

To some extent, Marxist feminism[21] can be read as a critique of
liberal feminism. According to Marxist feminists, the oppression
of women as a social group is not a result of bias, or ignorance, or
the intentional actions of individuals; it is a product of the political, social and economic structures associated with capitalism.
Marxist feminists believe that ultimately it is the class system that
accounts for women's unequal status. Frederick Engels's work,
The Origins of the Family, Private Property and the State,[22] written in
1884, is often seen to be the starting point for Marxist thought
about the causes of women's oppression. Engels claimed that
women's oppression originated in the introduction of private
property. Private ownership of the means of production by relatively few people, originally all male, inaugurated a class system.
Capitalist society was characterized by a conventional split between the 'home' and the 'workplace'; the 'public' and the 'private' spheres.[23] According to Engels, the preindustrial era, while
still patriarchal, was nevertheless an age in which 'women's work',
which consisted of providing the everyday necessities of life, was
considered to be as important as men's work. However, with the
advent of industrialization and capitalism, production was transferred from the home to the workplace. At the same time, production came to be seen as constitutive of the world of freedom.[24]
With the transfer of everything which was deemed to be valuable,
worthwhile and essentially 'human' to the 'public realm', and the
valorization of production over reproduction, women came to be
regarded as either the private property of men, or, at a later stage
when women achieved formal rights, denigrated as second-class
citizens.[25]

Marxists continue to stress the sexual division of labour as the
root cause of women's inequality. Marxist feminist analysis, however, extends to a sophisticated analysis of how women themselves

contribute towards their own subjugation by unwittingly providing a 'support system' for capitalism. This consists both of women's household production, which, although not a formal part of the economy, is both economically significant and 'free', and of women's vital consumption function in their role as housewives. Marxist feminists also stress the role played by women in providing capitalism with a valuable 'reserve army' of labour which may be exploited at times of labour shortages or used to keep male labour cheap. In all of these ways women help to maintain and reproduce an exploitative economic and social order. Given the stress on the importance of historical analysis and economic and social structures, it is not surprising to find that Marxist feminists contest the view that women's equality can be achieved by campaigning for formal rights in a world which is necessarily hierarchical, exploitative and unequal. Marxist feminists reject the reformism of liberal feminism, but also criticize schools of thought which emphasize the general oppression of women by men. Many Marxist feminists have argued that women frequently have more in common with men of their own social class than women in general and that women's subordination can only be overcome if women join with men in overthrowing capitalism and its contemporary international manifestation: imperialism. According to Marxist feminists, socio-economic and sexual inequality are inextricably linked. They argue that it will be impossible for women to gain equality in class society. Women's liberation must be a part of a wider struggle against an exploitative capitalist system.

Radical feminism

Marxist feminism has been criticized precisely because it fails to explain how patriarchy works independently of capitalism and how men of all classes and races can derive particular benefits from a male-dominated social order. In the final analysis, Marxist feminists stress the importance of class in understanding systems of subordination. In order to understand gender inequality, Marxists begin from a historical analysis of the development of capitalism as a social and economic system. However, *radical feminism*[26] sees women's oppression not as a by-product of capitalism, but rather as the root of all systems of oppression. The central concept in radical feminist thought is *patriarchy*. Patriarchy, which means literally 'the rule of fathers', is a system which ensures male domination over women. Radical feminists argue that male power is also at the root of the social construction of gender. Radical feminists argue that gender distinctions, usually assumed to be natural, structure every aspect of our lives, including crucially the realm of sexuality and sexual relations. Some radical feminists have developed the idea of 'sex–gender systems' to capture the all-pervasive nature of patriarchal domination. Radical feminists were the first to articulate what is now generally regarded as the central insight of feminist thought: *the personal is political*. From this perspective, women's liberation does not only involve striving to achieve formal equality, access to public space and to the means of production, but also involves a thoroughgoing transformation in the most private and intimate spheres of human relationships.

Radical feminists are critical of liberal and Marxist feminism because they see both as offering a model of women's liberation which is based on male values, thus encouraging women to aspire to what are essentially patriarchal values. Liberal feminism, for example, valorizes the public realm and supports the male-identified values of competitive individualism. Marxism valorizes the male worker to the extent that it sees the male proletariat as the agent of social and historical change. Marxism also emphasizes the importance of productive rather than reproductive labour power. Some radical feminists have argued that rather than seek to emulate men, feminists should actively promote a counter-culture which valorizes female-identified roles and values. In this way the values derived from women's experiences can be used to create alternatives to patriarchal society. The work of Mary Daly[27] is particularly associated with the notion of a 'women's culture'. Radical feminism is also associated with the idea of 'women-centred' analysis, as a means of challenging all male-defined structures and values and finding alternatives to patriarchal society. However, radical feminist thought has been criticized on the grounds that it has an *essentialist* view of male and female nature. This is not necessarily the case, but it is probably fair to say that in their attempts to find a basis for solidarity among women and suggest alternatives to patriarchal society, radical feminists have rather tended to gloss over major divisions which exist between groups of women and groups of men.

Socialist feminism

Socialist feminism[28] is often presented as a school of thought which attempts to combine the insights of Marxist feminism, radical feminism and psychoanalytic feminist thought by, as Tong argues, weaving together the various strands of feminist thought into a coherent and comprehensive account of gender oppression.[29] Socialist feminists are committed to overcoming both class and gender oppression. Following radical feminists, socialist feminists argue that 'the personal is political', broadening the Marxist conception of the material base of society to include reproduction as well as production. In socialist feminism the oppressiveness of the '*dual systems*'[30] of patriarchy and capitalism is also emphasized. Both are viewed as distinct forms of social relations, representing distinct sets of interests which are dialectically related to each other.[31] Capitalism is viewed as a material structure or historically rooted mode of production/sexuality, while patriarchy is viewed as a material structure or historically rooted mode of reproduction/ sexuality. Juliet Mitchell,[32] in her pathbreaking work *Woman's Estate*, argued that Marxist feminist thought placed too much emphasis on women's productive and reproductive labour, while radical feminists arguably overemphasized reproduction and sexuality and liberals stressed socialization over and above all else. Mitchell argued that, while the insights of all of these schools of thought were useful, woman's status and function in all of these areas must change if she is to achieve liberation. In addition, woman's interior world – her psyche – must also be transformed.

Psychoanalytic and existential feminist thought

The psychological dimension of women's oppression has been further developed in both *psychoanalytic*[33] and *existential* feminist thought. In psychoanalytic feminism, the work of Sigmund Freud has been a central influence. According to Freudian psychoanalytic theory, single-sex parenting ultimately explained the different personality structures in boys and girls. Object-relations theory,[34] which will be discussed at greater length in chapter 2, draws upon this view of the consequences of single-sex parenting. At birth the human infant is not yet a 'self'. That is, the child is not able to distinguish between 'self', 'other' and the world. Nancy

Chodorow[35] has argued that the formation of gender identity is necessarily a different task for boys and girls. Since mothers usually assume primary responsibility for care during a child's formative years, this means that girls relate to a care-taker of the same sex throughout their formative years, while boys relate to a care-taker of a different sex. Boy children develop a sense of 'self' – of identity – through a process of radical differentiation from the mother and identification with a frequently absent father-figure.

According to this theory, to *be* a boy involved escaping the world of women and the home and entering the public realm of men. However, the formation of gender identity in girls involved closely relating to the mother-figure, developing an orientation towards the domestic realm and adopting passive and submissive behaviour patterns. These different developmental processes created a psychology of male dominance in boy children and submissiveness in girls. This pattern of gender identification forms the basis of a basically unequal social division between the public (male) world and private or domestic (female) realm.

Psychoanalytic theory has been criticized on the grounds that it contains both a Western cultural bias and a class bias. Nevertheless it has been very influential in feminist analysis. *Feminist standpoint* theorists, for example, take seriously the idea that the process of *psychic and social development* produce differences in views of the self as either fundamentally separate or connected. Others have combined the insights of psychoanalytic feminism with Marxist feminism. Nancy Hartsock,[36] for example, has combined a basically Marxist historical materialism, which posits that groups who share socially and politically significant characteristics also share a standpoint, with object-relations theory to argue that women's material life activity has important epistemological and ontological implications.[37] In the context of International Relations, Ann Tickner[38] has argued that adopting a feminist standpoint allows both a powerful critique of dominant realist approaches and a radically different perspective of a whole range of issues and areas central to the study of International Relations, for example the nature of power, conflict and cooperation and security.

Clearly, attempts to theorize from the position of women's lived experiences are problematic. One of the main objections is to the very idea that there is an 'authentic woman's experience' which

can serve as a basis for identification, political action and knowledge claims. The strengths and weaknesses of feminist standpoint
in the context of 'reconstructing' International Relations are discussed at greater length in chapter 7.

Existentialism, derived primarily from the work of the German
philosophers Hegel and Heidegger, is a radically different perspective on the 'internalities' of gender and identity. However,
existentialism also focuses on the relationship between the individual psyche and the social world and is also concerned with the
processes by which human beings develop consciousness of themselves as independent, autonomous beings. According to existential thinkers, the activity of establishing one's sense of being, or
subjectivity, is inherently conflictual because one develops a sense
of self only by differentiation from an '*Other*'. That is, one's sense
of self is achieved via a process whereby the *subject* comes to define
'Others' as *objects*. This occurs because of the basic dualism in
human consciousness which perceives a difference between the
'self' and 'Others'. This process of self-definition involves seeking
power over 'Others' who are thereby *objectified*. That is, they are
understood only in terms of their relation to the subject and
subordinated to the subject's wishes and desires.

Simone de Beauvoir's classic feminist text *The Second Sex*,[39] first
published in 1949, offered an existential explanation of woman's
situation. De Beauvoir argued that woman's oppression was
rooted in her 'Otherness'. Woman was the Other in all male-
dominated cultures. However, woman was not only 'Other' to
men, but to herself. Woman had come to accept her objectification and play out the role of Other as defined by man. Historically man had defined himself as the essential and woman as
the inessential. Woman was not perceived as, or allowed to be,
fully human. Woman was always 'Other' because she was defined
in terms of what she was not: woman was not man. Thus man was
the self, the free, determining being who defines the meaning of
his existence, while woman was Other, the object whose meaning
was determined for her.[40] In a world were men had power and
made rules, the sexual division of labour between men and
women came to be seen as natural. Furthermore, women had
internalized the view that man was essential, central and significant, whereas woman was inessential, marginal and insignificant.
If a woman was to become a self, a *subject*, she had to transcend the
definitions, labels and essences limiting her existence.[41]

Postmodern feminism

While there are important differences between each of these schools of feminist thought, all share a commitment to gender equality and advocate political strategies to achieve 'emancipation', although feminists differ as to what this means and how it is to be achieved. Liberal feminists start out from a commitment to political liberty, self-development and personal fulfilment. Marxist and socialist feminists share a similar vision of human progress and emancipation and have a clear sense of the contribution that feminism can make to bringing about a better form of human existence free from exploitation and alienation. Radical feminist thought has similarly attempted to suggest ways in which alternative social orders can be built which do not rely upon and perpetuate the subordination of one half of the human race; and, since patriarchal society is inherently conflictual, competitive and damaging, they have suggested that these will benefit and enrich human kind as a whole. Psychoanalytic and existential feminist thought similarly share a common desire to understand the 'internalities' of gender oppression in order to suggest ways in which people can be freed from repressive relations and from social constraints that impoverish their lives.

At the risk of generalizing and glossing over what are undoubtedly important differences between these schools of thought, all are rooted in a belief in the possibility of human progress and freedom. As such, they belong to the *Enlightenment* tradition. Feminists in this tradition understand the purpose of human knowledge as being to further an interest in human emancipation. In arguing for women's emancipation they implicitly, and sometimes explicitly, argue for the maximization of human potential and the expansion of the realm of human freedom. Feminism has arguably enjoyed a somewhat ambiguous relationship to this same tradition. Indeed, feminists have exposed the degree to which the Enlightenment tradition has in reality been characterized by gender inequality and oppression. However, feminists have argued for women's equality and freedom from within this same tradition. In so doing the various feminisms described so far have served to reaffirm the historical project of the Enlightenment. These different schools of feminist thought all agree that to some extent all women are members of an oppressed group, or, in the case of liberal feminism, a group which is subjected to unjust forms of discrimination. Some feminists also argue that women's experiences give rise to a common perspective or *standpoint.*

Postmodern feminism[42] is distinctive because it not only calls into question the Enlightenment project, but also challenges many of the values and beliefs central to other schools of feminist theory. Postmodernism[43] can be seen as growing out of a critique of the Enlightenment project. The point of departure for many postmodern thinkers is to note a paradox. That is, that while Enlightenment discourses have championed the values of progress and human freedom, historically the Enlightenment period has been accompanied by the widespread oppression of many peoples in the name of the 'advance of civilization' of 'progress' and 'freedom'. Postmodern thinkers have argued that the Enlightenment project which has sought to establish the *truth* about the human condition and establish the *universal* conditions for human freedom and emancipation has in reality been used to consign to the realm of the 'inhumane', 'uncivilized' and 'backward' whole societies and peoples who do not share the cultural characteristics of 'Enlightenment Man'.[44] While the Enlightenment has been presented as a period in which mankind has been liberated from ignorance, the whole process of rational and scientific *discourse* characteristic of the 'modern' age has been deeply entrenched with bias and has excluded the experiences of many groups. Discourse, which in simple terms means the language which is used to construct social meaning and *intersubjective* understanding, is never innocent. Those in positions of power are more likely to be heard. Their 'truths' are more likely to be accepted.

Postmodernism is concerned to expose the hidden presuppositions and assumptions that underlie all attempts to theorize or tell 'One True Story' about the human condition. Similarly they criticize all-encompassing visions of human freedom and emancipation and theories grounded in 'universal' truths. Postmodern thinkers also make use of the idea of 'Otherness'. The 'Other' is the experience which confounds that which is held to be 'universal'. It is the voice that is marginalized or silenced when the 'truth' is asserted. Postmodern thinkers argue that, by their very nature, schemes which try to provide universal 'truths' necessarily *centre* some experiences and, in the process, *decentre* or marginalize others. The 'truth' only serves to produce and reproduce a series of 'Others' which must be set aside or made invisible to maintain the coherence of the doctrine. Tong argues that, rather than seek universal truths, postmodern thinkers embrace and celebrate 'Otherness', which they see as not just an oppressed or inferior position, but a way of being, thinking and speaking that allows for an openness, plurality, diversity and difference.[45] This emphasis on the positive side of 'Otherness' is a major theme of *deconstruction*,[46] which seeks to expose the assumptions, presuppositions and biases which underpin universalist theories. Postmodern writers have argued that power is so deeply implicated in theorizing that one might view the whole process as a form of domination whereby the theorist comprehends and appropriates the *objects* of knowledge.

Postmodern feminist thinkers have, therefore, celebrated feminist discourses, because they are the discourses of the 'outsiders'. Feminism, in its many guises, has been born out of 'experiences of marginality, and as such unusually attuned to issues of exclusion and invisibility'.[47] As such, feminism exposes the cultural arrogance and class bias of 'universalist' theories. However, postmodern feminists simultaneously resist the notion of a uniquely female experience, because this involves making essentialist or universalist knowledge claims on the basis of experiences which are historical and culturally specific.

Mohanty[48] has argued that feminist analysis in the 1980s and 1990s has to be understood not only in terms of postmodernism, but in terms of the precise challenges posed by race and *postcolonial feminism*[49] to white Western feminisms. Even as liberal, Marxist and radical feminists were raising issues surrounding sexism in the 1960s and 1970s, black women were arguing that sexism had to be viewed in the light of the harsher more brutal reality of racism, thus challenging the rather trite assumptions made by some feminists that it was possible for black women to divorce the issues of race from sex or sex from race. As black feminism flourished culturally and politically during the 1980s, black feminists[50] began to problematize a particular tradition of white, Western feminism which had sought to establish itself as the only legitimate feminism in current political practice.[51] In this process, they argued, black women's experiences had been silenced. This in turn opened up an impassioned debate about what feminism was, or, rather, what 'feminisms' were – what was meant by 'women' or 'women's issues' – which led to calls for feminists to abandon 'universalist theories', to question the coherence of gender as a category and to promote cultural and historical specificity in feminist analysis.

The emergence of postcolonial feminism in the 1980s and 1990s expanded the debate about race, ethnicity and gender considerably, and in so doing both forced Western feminists to face up to their own exclusionary practices and exposed the pretence of a homogeneous 'women's experience'. Postcolonial feminists insisted that while ideologically sexism and racism were similar in that both constructed 'common sense' through reference to 'natural' and 'biological' differences, and that race and gender were both socially constructed, beyond that 'race' and 'gender' had little internal coherence as concepts.

Postmodern feminist thinkers argue that there is no authentic 'women's experience' or 'standpoint' from which to construct an understanding of the social and political world. Much feminist scholarship in the 1980s and 1990s has been characterized by a move 'from grand theory to local studies, from cross-cultural analysis of patriarchy to the complex and historical interplay of sex, race and class, from notions of a female identity or the interests of women towards the instability of female identity and the active creation and recreation of women's needs or concerns'.[52]

Furthermore, postmodern feminist thinkers reject the idea that gender identity is in some way fixed, or essential. Postmodern feminists see gender not so much in terms of identity, or social structures, but rather in terms of discourse. Postmodern feminists agree that gender inequality cannot be understood as 'natural', or 'universal' and, therefore, outside of history. However, gender is seen as 'a process in which the 'body' becomes objectified in discourse which takes for granted the reality of sexual difference and inequality'.[53] The idea that the 'body' is produced by power and is cultural rather than 'natural' avoids the problems inherent in advancing essentialist accounts of gender – that is, accounts which suggest that gender is directly related to biological sex. Foucault's approach to gender, discussed earlier, has proved attractive to postmodern feminist thinkers because it suggests that 'masculinity' and 'femininity' have been variously constructed and located in specific historical and social practices and discourse. This allows sexuality to be seen in political terms. It also allows for an analysis of gender inequalities without positing a single cause, because the 'body' can be worked upon by gender construction and other functions such as race, class and ethnicity which cut across gender historically.

Postmodern feminists who draw upon Foucault's work argue that discourse is set up historically and that there are differences in discourse besides gender. By highlighting the power/knowledge relationship, the existing links between power and knowledge are simultaneously weakened. In this way other forms of knowledge are validated. It is also helpful to feminists who want to explore the ways in which dominant ideologies and practices are resisted. Feminist discourses, for example, have a contested and radical status which can be used strategically to block the imposition of patriarchal 'truths'. However, while postmodern feminists accept that dominant or *hegemonic* discourses and structures are deeply imbued with patriarchal ideology and male dominance, they are sensitive to the degree that power operates at every 'site', including sites where emancipatory potential is explored.[54] Postmodernists thus seek a politics of dissent which disrupts and erodes the theory and practice of specific power regimes.[55] The coherence and order characteristic of Enlightenment discourses is eschewed, however, because this can only be maintained by the suppression of difference. Postmodern feminists are sceptical of the degree to which the experiences of one particular group of people called 'women' can be used to speak for other groups of 'women', not only because the circumstances, context and specific conditions of oppression are complex, but also because Western feminists have, historically, constructed non-Western women as 'Other'.

Postmodern feminists value the diversity in feminist thought and see the existence of many 'feminisms' as a reflection of the many ways of articulating the social and political experiences of 'women'. Postmodern feminism, it is argued, refines our sensitivity to differences and our ability to tolerate the incommensurable. Thus Lorde[56] believes that while 'there are very real differences between us of race, age and sex' it is the 'refusal to recognize those differences, and to examine the distortions which result from our misnaming them' which is divisive for feminism. The notion of generic 'woman' in feminist thought obscures the heterogeneity of women and prevents serious consideration of the significance of such heterogeneity for feminist theory and political activity.

Feminist critical theory

However, while postmodern feminists have been able to embrace and celebrate difference, many feminists express a deep concern that the emphasis on difference undermines the very possibility that 'woman' can exist. Critics of postmodernism in particular argue that a postmodern feminism can only be a negative feminism. If 'woman' cannot 'be', feminist practice can only be at odds with what already exists.[57] Feminists cannot make demands in the name of woman and cannot speak out against sexism if the category 'woman' does not exist. Others have argued that a feminist politics is not possible if one rejects the Enlightenment project of emancipation and progress or, indeed, the notion of 'truth'. From this perspective, feminist theory is rooted in an Enlightenment tradition which understands the purpose of human knowledge to be to further an interest in human emancipation.

Furthermore, while not denying that issues of where identity is 'centred' are highly complex, many feminists believe that the 'need for an analysis of culture and difference, must be balanced with a need for a politics of solidarity predicated on women's shared problems'.[58] From this perspective, the emphasis on difference in postmodernism also runs the risk of overstating the degree of fluidity in social relations and glossing over the degree to which we are involved in social relationships which are inherently unequal and in which some groups of people are consistently privileged at the expense of others.

Feminist critical theorists are trying to find a way forward which both retains gender as a category of analysis and retains the historical commitment to the emancipatory project in feminism, but which takes on board the postmodern and postcolonial critique of the exclusionary practices of Western feminism. A similar tendency is found in post-Marxist critical theory in so far as it recognizes the many silences of orthodox Marxist theory and the weaknesses of its own assumptions.[59]

The central insight of critical theory is, perhaps, that the activity of 'theorizing' is intimately connected with social practice. Critical theorists see part of the critical project as reorientating social theory to the understanding of the activity of the knowing subject and *moments* of reflection and self-understanding. Habermas,[60] for example, argues that all human knowledge is historically rooted and interest-bound. Epistemology should not be seen as *transcendent* but as a *moment* of emancipation. That is, there is no ahistorical, transcendental subject. History, social 'reality' and 'nature' are products of the constituting labour of the human species. Knowledge is created in the process of a person's efforts to produce her or his existence. Gramsci similarly argued that while 'reality' was, to a certain extent, independent of the processes of knowledge production, the 'truth' of social reality was intractable because it involved the thoughts, motivations and intersubjective meanings of individuals who had different forms of self consciousness and awareness as to the social nature of their actions.

Critical theorists agree, then, that there is no *immediate* knowledge of the world. Knowledge is created through a dialectical process. Conceptualization and conceptual frameworks are produced by concrete understanding of the significance of social 'facts' generated by the process of reflection and thought. The process of understanding and explaining the social and political world, according to Gramsci, involved understanding the centrality of the interrelationship between 'subjective' and 'objective' in historical development. This process was a dialectical one and was thus a part of the historical process.[61]

By linking a theory of knowledge production to a theory of identity and interests, critical theorists are able to show how 'theory is always for someone and for some purpose'.[62] 'Theory' is a means to make sense of one's life in a coherent and critical way, thereby developing a politics of coherent resistance to dominant ideologies and oppressive social relationships.[63] It is perhaps this linkage between identity and interest that appeals most to feminist critical theorists. Feminist critical theorists argue that feminism needs a theory of the subject or it would not be possible to account for resistance to forms of domination. According to Gramsci and Habermas knowledge arises in specific historical 'moments' and is an integral part of the human desire to escape from repressive social conditions. The express purpose of critical theory is to further the self-understanding of groups committed to transforming society.[64]

While critical theory has its intellectual roots in Marxism, contemporary critical theorists similarly look beyond the working class to a number of groups and to 'new' or 'critical' social movements or *counter-hegemonic*[65] forces who offer *sites of resistance*[66] to capitalism and can, potentially, act as agents of social change. Feminism has been described as 'one of the most basic movements for human liberty' and emancipation.[67] If therefore, as Nancy Fraser advocates,[68] one accepts 'Marx's definition of critical theory as "the self clarification of the struggles and wishes of the age" '[69] and as such, 'straightforwardly political',[70] the 'critical' credentials of feminism can scarcely be denied. Feminist theorizing is not a purely abstract activity, but a reflexive and critical engagement with the world. Feminist critical theory aspires to move beyond critique and construct 'knowledge' about the world in the service of an emancipatory politics. Feminist knowledge is understood as a *moment* of emancipation. The orientation to emancipatory politics in feminist critical theory and the stress on the importance of the political subject goes beyond the aim of 'bringing in' women or making visible gender inequalities; it involves empowering women as subjects of knowledge. Critical theory is characterized by a certain scepticism towards notions of essential 'truths', while simultaneously arguing that 'truth claims can be adjudicated'.[71] Critical theorists encourage dialogue by exploring the contradictions in existing bodies of thought and seek to gain a more complete understanding of a complex 'reality' through a continual confrontation of concepts with 'reality'. Similarly, feminism raises normative questions about the nature and purposes of human knowledge, while at the same time enjoying a 'dialectical relationship to dominant and influential traditions'.[72]

Feminist critical theorists draw upon the work of scholars both from the Marxian tradition of critical theory and from the long tradition of radical and Marxist feminist thought. Feminist critical theory explores the intersections between individual, or subjective, experience and institutional structures. For example the radical feminist notion of sex/gender systems has been used to refer to the *specific* social relations which organize patriarchal domination. This approach offers the opportunity for historically and culturally specific analysis but points to the relative autonomy of the sexual realm. As such, it enables the subordination of women to be seen as a product of the relationships by which sex and gender are organized and produced. Thus to account for the development of specific forms of sex/gender systems, reference must be made not only to particular modes of production but also to the totality of specific social formations within which each system develops.

In feminist critical theory, one's identity is taken as a point of departure, as a motivation for action and as delineation of one's politics. Women use their positional perspective as a place from which to interpret and construct values.[73] In this view, identity politics sides with Marxist class analysis, in that it combines identity politics with a conception of the subject as non-essentialized and emergent from historical experience, yet retains the political ability to retain gender as a point of departure. Feminist critical theory retains the notion of a political subject and so allows an analysis of how women are positioned in relation to dominant power structures and how this forges a sense of identity and a politics of resistance. Women use their position and experiences as a point of departure from which to reflect critically upon processes which have an impact on their everyday lives. While the need for a politics based upon a shared identity and solidarity is very much at the heart of this approach, feminist critical theory views gender in social and political terms. This allows an exploration of the interplay between gender relations and the institutional context in which they take shape.[74]

Sandra Whitworth[75] has argued that social forces and material conditions combine to reproduce social practices and that gender informs and is reproduced by the practices of actors, institutions and international organizations. Furthermore, gender is about knowledge. Gender relations are sustained by social practices and *ideas.* Critical theorists must, therefore, also address questions of the meaning given to the 'reality' that constitutes gender and ask how ideas about gender are expressed in social and political institutions. Whitworth insists that while gender relations must be seen in the context of inequalities rooted in social class or race, a feminist analysis must be able to demonstrate how institutions and practices embody patriarchal forms of power relations which allow men to exercise power over women. A feminist critical theory must also seek to understand how hegemonic structures and institutions are also deeply imbued with patriarchal ideology and male dominance.[76]

The challenges of constructing 'feminist International Relations' are further developed in chapter 7. At this stage, it is enough to note the richness and diversity in feminist thought and recognize that different approaches give rise to different insights which might be useful in the project of 'rethinking' International Relations. The next section of this chapter turns to the question of why feminists have argued that there is a need to 'rethink' in International Relations, and to the relevance of gender and feminism in contemporary theoretical debates.

Gender, Feminism and the 'Third Debate'

Since the late 1980s, International Relations theory has entered into its so-called 'third debate'.[77] This third debate has in turn opened up questions about the nature of 'theory' and the relationship between theory and practice which has served to challenge the assumption that gender is not useful in helping us to understand the world. Since International Relations was established as a distinctive academic discipline, it has been characterized by a series of debates about what constitutes its subject matter and central concerns. Early International Relations scholars believed that the purpose of the discipline was to understand the causes of war and suggest ways in which relations between states could be organized according to principles which would sustain an enduring peace. This so-called first phase of political *idealism* was displaced after the Second World War, when it was generally accepted that attempts to build a just world order had failed. Thereafter the study of International Relations became dominated by *realism*, which claimed to address the 'realities' of power in the international system. The purpose of the study of International Relations came to be seen as developing a better understanding of the problems and dilemmas that states faced in achieving security and realizing their interests in an 'anarchic' international order.

In the 1960s, however, students of foreign policy moved away from this narrow concern with security and 'national interest' and began to draw upon a range of theories adapted from other areas of the social sciences to help them understand both the decision-making processes of government elites and foreign policy 'outputs'. In the 1970s, realism was further challenged by a proliferation of works which were largely liberal pluralist. Here scholars drew attention to the qualitative changes in the nature of international relations which had been impelled by technological advances. They also argued that power was increasingly decentralized in the international system, and that International Relations scholars should expand their research agenda to study the

influence and activity of a whole range of non-state 'actors'. At
the same time Marxist perspectives were being brought to bear on
the discipline of International Relations, in order to explain the
enduring structural inequalities which existed in the world.[78]

The very existence of competing perspectives in International
Relations and the proliferation of approaches in the 1960s and
1970s provoked a serious debate about the implications of these
competing 'paradigms', or 'world-views'. International Relations
scholars understood that the existence of competing perspectives
on the nature of the world did not simply raise questions about
how competing theories or perspectives could be evaluated. The
existence of multiple approaches and competing paradigms
served to highlight the degree to which International Relations
lacked an established core and to demonstrate the existence of
multiple perspectives on the world in which we live. The profu-
sion of approaches and literatures in International Relations demonstrated that 'rather a lot happens in the world which might be
construed as "political"' and that 'ontological choices are affirmed by categories of inclusion and exclusion and judgements
about what is significant'.[79] International Relations scholars concluded from this that the pursuit of knowledge in International
Relations was not a matter of developing better theories through
thorough empirical research and testing, because all theories
were ideological; they simultaneously expressed the political
values of the theorist and shaped the world which was being
analysed.

The 'third debate'[80] has taken this insight further. In so doing,
it has opened up a general discussion about research methods in
International Relations and raised a number of complex ontological and epistemological questions. That is, it has opened up discussions about what we take to be the nature of the world we are
studying, what can be said to exist, what is significant and insignificant, and the nature and purpose of knowledge. In this way, the
third debate has opened up a space for a whole range of new
theories and approaches that explicitly recognize the ideological
nature of knowledge claims. Feminism is only one of a number of
new departures in the field. Others include post-Marxist critical
theory and postmodernism. While feminist scholars have their
own distinctive agendas and concerns, most share with other
'critical' perspectives a critique of the 'positivist' assumptions of
much International Relations theory. Put simply, positivism is the

idea that there are certain 'facts' about the world that can be ascertained through 'scientific' analysis. Most feminist scholars in International Relations adopt perspectives which draw upon the insights of postmodernism, or feminist critical theory, or adopt feminist-standpoint positions. There are important differences between postmodern and 'critical' feminism and feminist stand-point, which will be discussed at greater length elsewhere in the text. However, all criticize the idea that the theorist is simply an impartial observer whose role is to observe and explain an unproblematic reality 'out there'. Feminists also share a common concern with the degree to which power is implicated in 'claims to know' and recognize the intimate connection between knowledge and interests. The implications of *positivism* and the *post-positivist* debate for International Relations and feminist theorizing are further developed in chapter 2.

Since the mid 1980s, post-Marxist critical theory has emerged as a 'new departure' in International Relations, a departure which one scholar has claimed represents the 'next stage' in the discipline's evolution.[81] As was noted earlier, post-Marxist critical theory refuses to separate theory and theoretical understanding from practical activity and frames its research project with the explicit intention of furthering the aims of oppositional groups. Not all feminist theories adopt an explicitly 'critical' position on the relationship between theory and practice, nor insist on the intimate connection between power and knowledge claims. Indeed as was noted in the previous section, much Western feminist theory has been criticized because it is 'unreflective' in this respect. Furthermore, postmodern feminists, while noting the intimate connection between knowledge and power and between discourse and social practice, do not share the feminist critical theorists' desire to understand the world in order to change it. However, as was noted earlier, one feminist International Relations scholar has argued that post-Marxist critical theory and feminist theory share common ground.[82] Furthermore, a number of feminist scholars have argued that research should begin from the 'standpoint' of women's lives, because one cannot separate the process of theorizing from practical activity and interests.[83]

However, postmodern thinkers regard the central problem with International Relations theory, like any attempt to theorize or gain knowledge of the world, as being that it inevitably gives rise to an exclusionary perspective which asserts sovereign claims to shape human identities, construct linear histories and impose social and political boundaries, when truth and meaning are in doubt and forms of identity in question.[84] Postmodern thinkers also reject so-called 'reconstructive projects' because they are seen to rest on some form of foundationalism. Furthermore, as V. Spike Peterson has suggested all attempts to 'map' the discipline have a power dimension.[85] That is, all attempts to demarcate the sphere of International Relations as an academic discipline and establish its core concerns are the result of the ability of socially powerful groups to impose their definitions on others.

Postmodern thinkers, therefore, reject all attempts to 'reconstruct' International Relations theory because this will inevitably give rise to, marginalize and displace a range of other perspectives and agendas. So, while International Relations has been described by Walker as one of the most gender-blind and crudely patriarchal of all institutionalized forms of contemporary social and political analysis,[86] postmodern thinkers are sceptical about the 'reconstructive' project inherent in post-Marxist critical theory and many schools of feminist theory. Indeed, postmodern feminist scholars would, perhaps, argue that feminist critique and feminist theorizing bring into question the very possibility of 'International Relations'.

However, while there are important differences between feminist approaches to International Relations, scholars such as, for example, Cynthia Enloe, Christine Sylvester, Cynthia Weber, V. Spike Peterson, Ann Sisson Runyan, Marianne Marchand, Jan Pettman, Ann Tickner, Sandra Whitworth and Marysia Zalewski[87] would no doubt agree that feminist working in International Relations should refuse to be 'disciplined' in the sense of addressing only the so called 'big issues'. Feminist scholars would, perhaps, also agree that all 'post-positivist' approaches share a common objective of breaking down the positivist 'orthodoxy' and challenging the dominant conception of what is central and what is marginal in the discipline.

The final chapter of this book examines the possibilities and problems involved in constructing a feminist International Relations. However, what might be described as the 'first wave' of feminist scholarship in International Relations has been largely concerned with exploring the degree to which International Relations is a gendered discourse. Feminist theorizing in International Relations has frequently taken as the object of its inquiry the problems of exclusion, exploring the problems of bias and distortion which arise when knowledge about the world is only constructed by particular social groups who occupy a dominant position in society and exploring how these same biases and value judgements delimit the scope of what is considered legitimate inquiry in the field. For this reason chapter 2 concentrates on feminism as a critique of dominant or 'orthodox' approaches to International Relations.

Chapter 2

Feminism and Critiques of the 'Orthodoxy'

In chapter 1 it was suggested that one reason why International Relations scholars are now required to engage with the issues and concerns raised by feminism is because the 'third debate' has opened up important questions about the activity of 'theorizing' and the politics of knowledge claims. The central insight of critical theories, in a broad sense of the term, is that all social and political theory is conditioned by the social and historical context in which the activity of theorizing takes place. This chapter expands upon these issues through an extended discussion of the nature and purposes of *critique*. The chapter concentrates on critiques of realism because while there have always been competing perspectives, realism has dominated International Relations theory to such an extent that it might with justification be described as the 'orthodoxy'.

The chapter is divided into two broad sections. Starting out from the position that there are numerous perspectives on the world in which we live, the first section asks *why and how has realism established a hegemonic position in International Relations theory?* and *what does it mean to speak of realism as the 'orthodoxy'?* It explores the social and political dynamics involved in the construction of theory and draws out the consequences of the dominance of realism in terms of how we conceptualize the international realm, construct categories for 'understanding' and 'explaining' International Relations and delimit the scope of the 'legitimate' field of study. This section, however, draws upon the work of a range of critical thinkers rather than focusing narrowly upon feminist critiques. This is partly because one of the functions of critique is to demonstrate how theories which purport to be based upon universal categories, or which claim to be grounded in essential 'truths' about the human condition, are ideological. Feminist theorists have long pointed out that key concepts and ideas in social and political theory contain gender bias. However, the work of critical theorists on the nature of ideology and ideological mystification, and postmodern accounts of the intimate connection between knowledge and power and discourse and social practice, have also proved useful to feminist thinkers.

However, critical theorists and postmodern thinkers frequently overlook or disregard the degree to which International Relations is a profoundly *gendered* discourse. In the second section of the chapter, therefore, the focus turns specifically to gender issues and the uses of feminism as critique. In this context, feminist critique fulfils four functions. First, it exposes the profoundly gendered nature of key concepts in realist theory. Second, it suggests that realism draws upon male-identified roles as the basis for political identity while simultaneously claiming for itself a central insight into the human condition. Third, it demonstrates how the statecentric assumptions of realism serve to render gender relations invisible. Fourth, feminist critique demonstrates how, while ostensibly concerned with power, realism serves to disguise the degree to which power is implicated in 'claims to know'. As such, it raises ontological and epistemological questions: that is, questions about what can be said to exist, our 'being' in the world and what might constitute knowledge of the world. In all of these ways, feminist critique addresses in concrete and pertinent ways issues of exclusion and bias. This section also undertakes a feminist reading of influential realist texts, in order to expose the particularly masculinist bias in the concepts and categories employed in realism and explores the significance of the use of gendered imagery and symbolism in realist writing. Finally, the chapter concludes by drawing upon object-relations theory to suggest that 'abstract masculinity' has left its mark on realism and, in consequence, produced an incomplete and exclusionary view of international relations.

Realism as 'Orthodoxy'

It has frequently been noted that everyone who studies International Relations immediately confronts problems of conceptualization and theory.[1] The view that the proper object of knowledge in the discipline is the state and its power corresponds with the realist tradition in International Relations. The central assumptions which underpin realist thought are that states are the main 'actors', that there is a sharp distinction between foreign and domestic spheres, and that international relations is essentially a struggle for power among sovereign states. Realists frequently argue that the nature of relations between states can be understood in terms of human nature.[2] Conflict between states is seen to be inevitable because it is the nature of man to try to dominate and oppress others. Therefore it is prudent for the state to seek to preserve and, if possible, increase its power. In the realist tradition, the state is viewed as a self-sufficient and purposive 'actor' which pursues its interests in a largely anarchic environment, in which 'Reason of State' is the final arbiter of state conduct. The key concepts in realism are, therefore, state autonomy and power.

Early International Relations scholarship was very much driven by normative concerns. Its purpose was defined in terms of the need to promote respect for the norms of international society and devise institutions which would strengthen and uphold international law. However, the collapse of the League of Nations and the outbreak of the Second World War brought about a reaction to the idealism of the age – an idealism reflected in much early International Relations scholarship. It has been argued that this reaction possibly reached its intellectual peak in Britain with the publication of E. H. Carr's *The Twenty Years' Crisis* in 1939.[3] This powerfully argued text developed a realist critique of the core assumptions of what came to be labelled *political idealism* and called for a science of international politics.[4] However, it was perhaps Hans Morgenthau's *Politics among Nations,*[5] published in the United States in 1948, that attempted the first systematic and comprehensive account of state behaviour. Morgenthau insisted that the study of International Relations should be empirical and theoretical rather than centred on a normative concern with justice. *Politics among Nations* has been widely regarded as the first attempt to develop a 'scientific study' of relations between states based on a recognition of the realities of power.[6]

The nature of paradigms

Since the publication of this key work, realism has established itself as the dominant *paradigm* in International Relations. At this juncture it is useful to consider briefly the nature of paradigms because this goes some way towards answering the question posed in the introduction to this chapter: *why and how has realism established a hegemonic position in International Relations theory?*

A paradigm is a shared understanding and way of approaching problems which is accepted by a community of scholars and used to inculcate students with fundamental ways of 'knowing the world'. In *The Structure of Scientific Revolutions,*[7] Thomas Kuhn identified the construction of theory as a communal, or social, activity carried out by groups of scholars who share common assumptions about the nature of their subject matter. That is, the construction of theory was not an activity designed to establish 'truth'. Indeed, the central insight of Kuhn's work was that paradigms do not *describe* reality but rather *construct* reality. Kuhn argued that 'fact'-gathering in science was guided by the dominant paradigm. It was a prerequisite of all scientific inquiry that a paradigm focused on and magnified certain phenomena while allowing other phenomena to disappear from the picture. Such guidance was necessary because the world consisted of numerous phenomena which could only take on meaning to the extent that they could be conceptualized. Conceptualization was, therefore, a function of paradigm construction.

Kuhn was concerned to show how a paradigm was usually provided by a single work which was so unprecedented in its achievement that it became the 'exemplar' of scientific analysis in a particular field.[8] According to Vasquez,[9] once established, scholarship in the field was characterized by the extensive articulation of the paradigm by programmes that guided theory construction and empirical research. This constrained scholars to the elaboration of theories which did not violate the fundamental assumptions of the paradigm. Kuhn's analysis suggested that in the social sciences, as in the natural sciences, one had to be sensitive to how the discipline had developed historically, which paradigms had been widely accepted and the consequences of this. In a Kuhnian sense it was Morgenthau's *Politics among Nations* that provided the particular picture of the world, or paradigm, that permitted the International Relations community to develop a common research agenda. It quickly became the 'exemplar' for the study of International Relations and was, perhaps, the single most important vehicle for establishing the dominance of realism in the field.[10]

As was noted in chapter 1, alternative traditions of thought about the nature of international relations and alternative 'world-views' have existed alongside realism. Marxism, for example, has not only provided an alternative conception of the 'international realm', but has also challenged the realist conception of the state and notions of a 'national interest' by suggesting that particular social groups share common interests irrespective of their nationality. The study of foreign policy has drawn upon the insights of other areas of the social sciences. While in the 1970s and 1980s a number of works written from a broadly liberal perspective challenged many of the statecentric assumptions of realism, by stressing the degree to which technological changes had brought about increasingly complex forms of interdependence and increased the importance and influence of non-state actors. However, despite the existence of competing approaches, none succeeded in displacing realism as the dominant paradigm within the discipline.[11] That there have been different strands of thought historically, and there are a number of competing approaches today, should not detract from the degree to which realism represents the 'orthodoxy' in International Relations. According to Vasquez, since the publication of *Politics among Nations*, the International Relations literature had been fairly systematic and somewhat cumulative in articulating the realist paradigm.[12]

In the late 1950s realism faced a so-called 'behaviouralist revolt'.[13] However, behaviouralism only attacked the research methods of International Relations. It did not offer an effective substitute in terms of theory. It neither challenged the view that the central concerns of International Relations were state autonomy and power, nor the view that the best way to understand the world was through an analysis of the state and the underlying dynamic of the struggle for power among states. Behaviouralism provided realism with a 'scientific' methodology, insisting on a rigorous approach to the collection and analysis of data.[14] As such, it only served to clarify and systematize Morgenthau's concepts and explanations.[15] The legacy of the behaviouralist revolt can be seen in neo-realist approaches which claim to have a detached and disinterested view of the central actors and processes in International Relations and yet retain central realist assumptions about the nature of the world which forms the object of study.[16] The quest for rigorous and 'scientific' research methods in International Relations also served to displace the traditional realist approach which involved looking at the world from the perspective

of the statesman or diplomat,[17] with *positivist* epistemological assumptions. Put simply, positivism is the idea that there are certain
'facts' about the world which may be ascertained and understood
by thorough empirical research and through the rigorous testing
of theories. In this way the 'facts' can be established and our
knowledge advanced. The role played by the theorist in interpret-
ing the 'facts' and the possibility of bias or distortion of the 'facts'
is either not seriously addressed or it is assumed that, if rigorous
scholarly procedures are adopted, bias will be minimized or elimi-
nated. In this way positivism gives realism the aura of *truth* which
is often associated with scientific theories.

Problems of reductionism and reification

The historical development of International Relations has seen
the dominance of the realist paradigm. What have been the consequences of this? First, a vast amount of writing in International
Relations is statecentric. That is, it assumes that states exist as
concrete entities, have agency and are the main actors in international relations. Therefore, interstate relations should be the central focus of study. It has been argued that the notion that the
state is the central actor gives rise to *methodological individualism* in
the study of International Relations. That is, it is assumed that
there are certain 'facts' about the world that may be ascertained.
Furthermore, these 'facts' about the world can be explained in
terms of 'facts' about individuals, or more properly personalized
states as actors. This reduces complex international phenomena
to relations between *reified* sovereign states.[18] The notion of
reification, which is derived from critical theory, 'involves a process whereby social phenomena take on the appearance of
things'.[19] According to critical theorists like Lukács,[20] in capitalist
societies where production is *commodified* and orientated towards
exchange rather than use, people's productive activity 'appears
strange and alien to them'.[21] That is, the product of one's labour
appears to be a 'thing', an entity. Furthermore, reification perme-
ates all spheres of life, as social relations of all kinds are reduced
to 'thing-like' relations.[22] To reify the state, in this sense, is to
suggest that it has a concrete existence. The state is viewed as a
'thing' in itself, an entity which *acts.* A further objection to the
'state-as-actor' approach is that it is *reductionist* and disguises the

degree to which international processes can have an impact on specific social groups. It has been argued that statecentric approaches to the study of International Relations marginalize or render invisible unequal social relations and many contemporary problems which have an international dimension.[23]

The theory/practice dynamic

However, critiques of realism go beyond issues of methodological individualism, reification and the invisibility of internationalized social relations. One of the central themes of the third debate has been that the social practices involved in the production of theory must be studied in relation to the dominant social forces and practices of the age.[24] This is not to say that International Relations scholars have not recognized the importance of the historical and social context in which they worked.[25] However, the rather more reflective approach of scholars like Carr and, perhaps, Morgenthau has been missing from much realist scholarship and wholly abandoned in 'scientific' or 'structuralist' realist approaches based on positivist assumptions. It has been argued that when applied to the study of the social world, positivism denies the role of social practices in making and transforming social orders because positivist methodologies perpetuate a belief in the natural rather than historical character of real social and political relations and reify social institutions.[26] It has also been argued that positivism is a mode of thought which puts at a distance, objectifies and separates the 'knower' from the object of study. Human beings become the objects of study, the assumption being that it is possible to explain social phenomena without reference to the meanings which people ascribe to social situations.

The insight that there is no one unproblematic social reality 'out there' waiting to be explained, raises the question of why it is that some theories, or world-views come to be accepted as constituting knowledge of the 'real' world, while others are dismissed as idealistic, wishful thinking, ideological and 'unscientific'. Clearly 'knowledge' is intimately connected with social practices. The linkage between knowledge and social practice is a central theme in contemporary feminist theory. Stanley and Wise,[27] for example, have pointed out that there is no one social *reality*, but different ones which are negotiated and managed by members of any given society.[28] The linkage between knowledge, power and social practice is also central to the work of postmodern thinkers such as Foucault.[29] A number of critical theorists in the Marxist tradition have found the work of Pierre Bourdieu useful in understanding the linkages between knowledge and social practice. A brief discussion of Bourdieu's work is useful at this juncture because it provides one answer to the central question posed at the outset of this chapter: *what does it mean to speak of realism as the 'orthodoxy'?* Bourdieu's work is in part concerned with the way in which so-called 'objective' knowledge *constructs* social practice and representations of social practice and, in the process, presupposes that the social world is self-evident.[30] Positivism, according to Bourdieu 'detemporalizes' the subject, puts the subject outside of time, outside of history, and in so doing reifies practice. The structures which constitute a particular social order produce what Bourdieu calls a 'habitus'.[31] A habitus is *history* turned into *nature* which itself 'reproduces individual and collective practices and, hence, history in accordance with schemes engendered by history'.[32] According to Bourdieu every social order produces the naturalization of its own arbitrariness and 'from the individual family up to the largest political unit we have the cohesion of the habitus endlessly exalted by mythological ideology but capable of holding individual interests together'.[33] Thus, Maclean[34] argues that in realism the 'state', an abstraction, is made material or concrete in realist conceptions of the 'state as actor'. The result is a *reification* of categories. A scholarly convention becomes conceived of as a pre-existing historical phenomenon and explanations are validated in relation to a posited reality which is both the source of and the test of claims about reality.[35] This perpetuates a belief in the natural rather than historical character of real social and political arrangements. According to Bourdieu, it is only when oppressed groups come together to see the possibility of changing that order that the arbitrariness of existing social arrangements is exposed. Dominated groups have an interest in challenging the *orthodoxy* by pushing back the limits of the '*doxa*', the universe of possible explanation, to give voice to that which cannot be articulated because of the constraints of existing discourse.[36] Critiques of the orthodoxy serve a dual purpose, therefore, in both opening up spaces for the voices of the marginalized and excluded to be heard, and in breaking down the realist 'orthodoxy'.

────────── **A Gendered Discourse** ──────────

Gender has been denied salience as an issue in International Relations because the discipline has been seen as constituted by a system of states which relate to one another in a context of anarchy.[37] Realists assume that the proper way to understand the international system is via concepts of power and security, concepts that are ungendered and universal.[38] With respect to gender, International Relations theory grounded in realist assumptions has either been seen as neutral or assumptions about the position and status of women have not been made explicit. However, International Relations is a *gendered* discourse.[39] The invisibility or marginalization of gender issues in the study of International Relations is a consequence of methodological individualism which begins with a high level of abstraction, taking the state to be the key actor. The realist conception of the state as actor has been built upon the supposedly unproblematic figure of 'sovereign man'. Sovereign man is an abstraction which is underpinned by a conception of the warrior, Prince or modern-day practitioner of *Realpolitik*.[40] These same concepts and categories employed by realism make necessary the exclusion of women.[41] Indeed 'the whole theoretical approach to International Relations rests on the foundation of political concepts which it would be difficult to hold together coherently were it not for the trick of eliminating women from the prevailing definitions of man as the political actor'.[42]

The masculinized identity of the state

This view of the state as an autonomous entity or 'actor' has been influenced by the analogy of the state as a *purposive individual* more than any other device.[43] It has been suggested that the notion of the state as a purposive individual – sovereign man – is derived from the fusion of the territorially based nation-state with a nationalist construction of political identity. The significance of this fusion of 'state' and 'nation' is developed further in chapter 3. However, the intellectual heritage of realism stretches back to before the emergence of nationalism as a political force. The masculinized conception of sovereign man has been for the most part drawn from the 'intellectual fathers of realism',[44] Niccolò Machiavelli and Thomas Hobbes.[45]

Machiavelli was, arguably, the first thinker to shift the ground of political theory away from a central concern with justice to issues of power and autonomy. In what is perhaps Machiavelli's best-known work, *The Prince*,[46] he sought to advise the ruler who could not base his rule on traditional authority on how to get power and how to keep it. Machiavelli's ideas would later appeal to the sceptical mood of the post-war world and to scholars who believed that their role was to provide prudent advice to statesmen based on an understanding of the realities of power, rather than speculate about how the world *ought* to be organized. Machiavelli's thought was very much attuned to the conditions of his own time. It was an age when the existing social order was breaking down. This, in turn, encouraged political thought about the nature of power and how it was exercised.[47] Machiavelli was concerned to advise the Prince without traditional authority how to found his rule upon the support of the broad masses and speak to their specific interests and concerns.[48] The Prince was not to offer the citizen body a direct share in the exercise of power, but rather the reflected glory that came from the identification with great men. The role of the Prince, the founder of the political order, was to enhance men's sense of honour, to invite and encourage heroism and reintroduce *virtù* into the citizen body.[49] It would be more accurate to describe Machiavelli's thought as republican, rather than 'nationalist'. However, twentieth-century International Relations scholars seeking to understand both state power and the nature of nationalism would later find his ideas useful.

Hanna Pitkin has argued that Machiavelli displayed an understanding of self-government and citizenship which was intimately connected with his sense of what it was to be a man. To be a man one had to be self reliant, autonomous, avoid dependence on others. Similarly, what mattered for the security and glory of the state was autonomy and this was constantly referred back to psychic and personal concerns.[50] Similarly the founder of the Republic personified most completely the autonomous self-governing man. The founder, therefore, had to be seen to be the pure source of and not the product of law.[51] This idea would later find echoes in the realist conception of *sovereignty* and *sovereign man*. It was no accident, therefore, that the Prince could not be seen to be born of woman, but had to be seen as the embodiment of a

generative paternity.[52] Women were excluded from the citizen
body because they constituted a threat to men both personally
and politically. Women were both a sign of their original weakness
and a threat to their self-control. Women were a potential source
of conflict and division among men. More importantly, perhaps,
they represented competing values; they could draw men out of
the public realm. The male citizen had to be persuaded that all
that was of value depended upon the willingness of the citizen
body to defend the state.[53] In Machiavelli's work women were thus
presented as dependants, but also potentially subversive of the
male-dominated political order. The exclusion of women was thus
both necessary and desirable.

The realist conception of political community and the relationship between citizens and excluded 'Others' is discussed further
in chapters 4 and 5. However, at this stage, in tracing out the
historical origins of realist thought, the aim is to demonstrate how
key concepts and ideas in realism are not universal but contain a
specific gender bias. It is possible to identify a particularly Machi-
avellian strand in much realist thought. The state is conceived of
as a purposive individual who has a particularly masculinized
identity. Whilst many realists acknowledge that the state is an
abstraction, the state is, nevertheless, viewed as more than a defined territory or set of institutions. The state has an *identity*.
Sometimes the reader is presented with a view of the (male)
citizen body enjoying a collective freedom and glory. Carr saw the
personification of the state as a device designed to encourage the
exaltation of the state at the expense of the individual. The state
was associated with pugnacity and self-assertion. Through the
state the individual sought strength through combination with
others. According to Carr, for the individual his national community meant 'the expression of a transferred egoism as well as
altruism'.[54] If a man was strong he could play a leading role, while
'if he was weak he could find compensation for his lack of power
to assert himself in the vicarious self assertion of the group'.[55]
Carr, unconsciously perhaps, made the linkage between power,
honour, self-assertion and masculinity in his observation that 'the
faint doubt about Italy's status as a great power is due to the fact
that she has never proved her prowess in a first-class war'.[56]

Morgenthau similarly believed that since in a society only a few
will realize the aim of power and domination, the majority must
seek to achieve their ends indirectly through identification with

the state.[57] According to Morgenthau 'when we are conscious of being members of a powerful nation we flatter ourselves and feel a great pride'.[58] Social institutions might restrain aspirations for individual power but 'the nation encourages and glorifies the tendencies of the greatness of the population' and 'the emotional attachment of the nation *as the symbolic substitute for the individual* then becomes ever stronger'.[59]

Morgenthau insisted that 'politics' had to be seen as a relatively autonomous sphere of action, because without this separation it would be impossible to distinguish between political and non-political acts and thus impossible to delimit the field of study of 'international politics'. These are the choices of 'inclusion' and 'exclusion' which are made prior to the process of theorizing relations between states. However, the distinction relies upon a prior distinction between 'private' and 'public' realms. Once this distinction is made, gender relations are removed from the field of inquiry and it is now possible to speak of the state as a purposive individual whose masculinized identity is disguised.

The state, power and patriarchy

A familiar theme in realist writing is the disorder and lawlessness, fear and insecurity that exist in an international environment which lacks a central sovereign power. Realists see international relations as a struggle for power amongst unequal sovereign states. States operate in an environment where their security and autonomy are constantly threatened. Relations between states are inherently conflictual and fear and insecurity are endemic because it is in the nature of man to enslave and dominate others. The work of Thomas Hobbes has also been a key influence on realist thinkers. Like Machiavelli, Hobbes's thought has to be seen in the context of an age characterized by great social change and political instability. The development of modern science and the emergence of capitalism were both major influences on Hobbes's political thought. Modern science both implicitly challenged the idea that sovereigns ruled by virtue of Divine Right and the notion that the social and political order reflected a unified moral order. In order to explain the origins of the state and sovereign power, Hobbes posited the existence of a 'state of nature' in which all enjoyed a natural liberty, but in which life was nasty, brutish and short because of man's desire to dominate and oppress others.[60] Hobbes argued that all human beings were essentially self-regarding hedonists who sought to achieve their own ends with little regard for others. Only the desire for self-preservation allowed the setting up of a sovereign body that would secure the conditions necessary for civilized life. However, while men might be persuaded to give up their natural liberty for the protection of the sovereign, the international realm would remain a war of all against all, since the conditions which forced men to give up their natural liberty for security in the 'state of nature' could never be realized in an international context.

However, while Hobbes is often presented in realist texts as having described the condition of human beings without government, the state of nature is 'a strange world where individuals are grown up before they are born . . . a world where wives, sisters and mothers do not exist'.[61] Hobbes's state of nature is structurally sexist, denying the historic role played by women as child-rearers and -bearers. Hobbes's thought must be viewed in the context of profound social changes which led to the progressive loss of power by women.[62] Hobbes recognized that the political order was patriarchal, but justified male rule on the grounds that commonwealths were erected by fathers not mothers.[63] That is, men erect a sovereign power and in so doing institutionalize their advantage. Rights were accorded to citizens, but women and children were outside the realm of justice, could not exercise power nor provide for their own defence. The social and political order was inherently patriarchal.[64]

In realist texts the patriarchal nature of the social and political order is seldom made explicit. As was suggested earlier, realists either assert that the concepts and categories employed are neutral, or assumptions about gendered relations are not made explicit. For this reason, it is necessary to reread realist texts with an eye to what is not directly discussed, but rather implied. In *Politics among Nations* Morgenthau argued that the starting point for theorizing about international relations was the 'nature of man'.[65] Morgenthau based his theory upon a distinctly Hobbesian view of human nature. Morgenthau proceeded from the central belief that man's behaviour was essentially driven by bio-psychological drives to create society. The drive to live, propagate and control were essentially power struggles. Morgenthau did not discuss gender relations as such but he did argue that the tendency to dominate is an element in all human associations from the family, which is necessary for the propagation of the species.[66]

Such an argument suggests that the subordination of women is an inevitable consequence of the unequal power struggle and is also 'natural' in so far as it is deemed 'necessary'.[67] While Morgenthau made no explicit reference to women, one might infer with justification that he assumes politics to be a male-dominated activity. Since he also believed that all social institutions including the family were necessary to channel the natural aggression of man, one might infer from this that in his view patriarchy was necessary for social order. In Morgenthau's view, politics is anything which establishes the control of man over man.[68] Morgenthau left undiscussed sexual relations and parent–child relations, but since he argued that all relations were essentially based upon self-interest, presumably he thought that women would submit to male rule because it was prudent to do so. This wholly perverse portrayal of human relations finds echoes elsewhere in realist writings.

The realist portrayal of human relations as a struggle for power is modified to some extent. Morgenthau acknowledged that political man alone would be but a beast.[69] However, the political order and political institutions are seen to be inherently fragile. They are supported by a carefully constructed hierarchical order reinforced by social institutions and symbols of national honour, unity and strong leadership. Just where women fit into the realist conceptual universe is not made clear. Presumably male citizens are seen to defend the state, while women contribute nothing directly to their own security or the security of others; a rather perverse portrayal of the 'natural order of things' since the assumption of a patriarchal family is inherently problematic and, in the first instance, men are largely dependent on women for their survival.

Teasing out the hidden assumptions about gender in realism is undoubtedly useful in exposing the social conservatism of realist thought; but beyond that, does it matter? Realists would no doubt respond to criticisms by arguing that the patriarchal nature of state power is not discussed explicitly because it is not relevant to understanding relations *between states*. Furthermore, given that women have historically been excluded from political power and today remain heavily underrepresented in the 'high politics' of statecraft, it could be argued that realism does in some senses present an accurate picture of the world. The masculinized imagery and language of realism is, after all, often quite explicit. Inis Claude argued that realism was a test of the intellectual virility and manliness of the field.[70] The realist could look at the grim realities of power without flinching, while one who rejected this reality was 'cowardly' or 'soft'. According to Claude 'a self-respecting realist can advance the proposition that the balance of power contributes something virile and vigorous like the protection of the national interest, but would be embarrassed to state that it contributes to something as lacking in intellectual masculinity as peace'.[71] Once the 'maleness' of international politics and the patriarchal nature of state power is acknowledged, is it not the case that realism presents an accurate picture of the *real* world?

There are, however, a number of issues which are raised by feminist critiques. For example feminism raises the question of whether or not the patriarchal nature of state power matters for the way that the business of international or interstate relations is actually carried out and whether, therefore, the inclusion of women would lead to less conflictual relations. This is discussed at greater length in chapters 4 and 5. A second issue is to do with the kind of knowledge claims that are made by realism. It is clear from the earlier discussion of the social and political dynamics involved in the construction of theory, that realism does not simply describe the world as it is but is rather a powerful ideology. The ideology or discourse of realism, constructs a particular model of the world which then serves to justify and perpetuate the kind of social and political order it describes.

Feminist critique, therefore, goes beyond the unspoken assumptions about the position and social roles of women and men in realist theory to deeper analysis of the ways in which ideas about gender are constructed and used to legitimize and perpetuate inequalities. By exposing the particularly masculine bias in realist writings, feminist critique also raises fundamental challenges to realist knowledge claims. That is, it raises deeper issues about what might be said to constitute *reality* and the real *world*. If theories are constructed from particular perspectives and are always conditioned by the social, political and historical context in which the theorists operate, this suggests that at the very least there are multiple 'realities' and multiple perspectives on the world. Furthermore, if there are indeed multiple realities and perspectives on the world this poses further questions both about the purposes of theory and about why and how some theories are generally accepted and other rejected. In this way feminist critique addresses issues of bias and exclusion in concrete ways.

Epistemological and ontological considerations

The gender bias in International Relations runs much deeper than use of male-identified roles in the model of 'state as actor'. While realism rejects the idea that knowledge can be based on specific identities and interests, at the same time it implicitly draws upon male-identified roles as the basis for political identity. In this way, feminists argue, realism employs a distinctly masculinist way of 'knowing the world'. The critique of sovereign man which is central to all critical or 'post-positivist' approaches goes beyond questions of reductionism and reification to the status of the knowledge claims made about bounded communities called nation-states. For the purpose of theorizing, realism invests the state as 'purposive individual' with particular characteristics. Sovereign man is a rational choice-making individual able to legitimize violence.[72] Sovereign man is in some sense held to embody the 'truth' about international relations. Discussions about international relations are framed in terms of ideas about rationality and the pursuit of instrumental interests. The idea of sovereign man is placed firmly at the centre of the conceptual universe. In this way, sovereign man becomes the *subject* of knowledge. International relations are understood as relations between him, the state as both actor and knowing subject, and a series of marginalized and displaced others.

The idea that the study of gender is not part of International Relations because the subject is about the study of the state and its power is premised on orthodox ideas about what counts as knowledge. Nancy Hirschmann[73] argues that an important difference between the social construction of 'maleness' and 'femaleness' has been power. Men have historically dominated women and had control over how they construct both themselves and women. However, this has not only resulted in institutions which socially and politically privilege men over women, but it has also affected the structure of meaning and reality by pervading our categories of knowledge. Hirschmann argues that modern epistemologies affect the kinds of questions asked and the particular modes of inquiry that are considered legitimate. The perspective of a

socially constructed 'masculine' experience is then epistemologically validated and imposed on women, thus preserving male
privilege and the social practices and structures that enable men
to consider their own experiences the *human* experience.[74] That
is, 'the assertion that epistemology and ontology are entirely separate is granted the status of objective truth and epistemology
comes to be defined as excluding ontological considerations'.[75] In
this way 'by explicitly ignoring gender while implicitly exploit-
ing a distinctly masculine meaning of knowledge seeking these
epistemologies are able to mask their own bias'.[76]

This is not to say that realism reflects in any straightforward way
what *all men* think, but that the categories and concepts reflect
historically and culturally conditioned ideas about 'masculinity',
and ways of 'knowing' the world which are identified with a distinctly masculine experience. Feminists are concerned to address
the implications of representing a male experience as the *human*
experience. The concept of 'man' employed in realist writings
must depend on the denial of any distinctly 'feminine' experience
because it is necessary to the methodological individualism characteristic of realism. The image of the state as a 'purposive individual', the state as subject, presents a particular way of knowing
the world and relating to the world which excludes other possible
ways of knowing. Feminist critique demonstrates how the male
bias in realist theory presents an incomplete and exclusionary
view of human relations, including international relations.

Feminists have pointed out that the use of gender in the imagery in realist texts is highly significant. The realist conception of
the autonomous state is frequently juxtapositioned against images
of anarchy or a disorderly international 'state of nature'. The use
of such imagery must be seen in terms of a deeply rooted fear of
the 'feminine'. In realist texts, the political community can be
seen as a community of men whose power is based upon the
domination of those 'outside'. Once again much of the gendered
imagery and symbolism in realism is derived from political theory.
While Machiavelli did not explicitly personify nature, it is clear
that the masculine world of human agency in history and autonomy is juxtapositioned against the world of women and relations of dominance and dependence.[77] In Machiavelli's work, the
male world of order, law and liberty is constantly threatened by
fortuna, a force which threatens the overextended state or ambitious ruler; and *fortuna* is a woman.[78] Pitkin argues that the mascu-

line world of order and *virtù* is haunted from behind the scenes by female forces of great power. The 'feminine' in Machiavelli represents the 'Other', that which is opposed to the masculinized world of order and discipline. Women represent the 'Other', a force that not only threatens the political order, but men's very sense of self. Machiavelli's notion of autonomy is misogynistically defined. It leads to relations which must be seen in terms of dominance and dependence.[79] Hobbes's conception of anarchy and order is also profoundly gendered. However, the female force which appears in these writings, which had to be mastered, is no longer *fortuna*, but the 'state of nature'.

Scholars of international political theory who are interested in the influence of Hobbes and others, have long recognized that knowledge is constructed and this process involves differentiating between the world of human knowledge and interests and the 'natural realm'. For example, Cornelia Navari has argued that both Machiavelli and Hobbes understood that knowledge was derived from power.[80] Hobbes recognized that what constituted knowledge of the world arose from the immediate concerns of men. Hobbes's *Leviathan*, the ultimate sovereign power, expressed the need for a 'validator'. Since 'knowledge only arose in the context of a state or society, nature took on the feel of that which was discontinuous with and alienated from social settings and was increasingly relegated to what was "outside"'. Navari has argued that in the absence of an institutionalized framework relations between states similarly came to be as relations as in nature, nature being that which is 'outside' and separate from self.[81] However, it is highly significant that the forces of nature are associated metaphorically and, indeed, metaphysically with the feminine.

Geneviève Lloyd has argued that modern science profoundly influenced the political thought of Hobbes.[82] Early attempts by a modern state theorist to impose categories on the world involved a process whereby the powers of reason were to control and dominate nature which was identified with the 'female'. Science heralded a new relationship between the 'knower' and the 'known'. Knowledge was associated with the control or subordination of nature. It is highly significant that nature was identified metaphorically with the 'female'. The issue of gender bias is not then 'simply the absence of women', but the persistent association of the 'masculine' with the 'objective, scientific, asexual' and the way in which the construction of 'scientific' knowledge is a process which involves the domination of nature; nature being ubiquitously female.[83] Peterson argues that having divided the world into 'knower', mind, subject and 'knowable' nature/object, scientific ideology further specifies the relation between knower and known as one of distance and separation.[84] The so-called objectivity of science, then, presupposes a scientific mind and modes of knowing rigidly set apart from what is to be known – nature – and the 'masculine' by association comes to connote autonomy, separation and distance.[85]

Di Stefano claims that Hobbes's thought is characterized by a distinctly masculinist outlook, by dualistic thinking, a need for a singular identity, a denial of relatedness and a radical individualism.[86] One is presented with an image of the world in which the solitary subject confronts a dangerous world in which autonomy, agency and knowledge are viewed in opposition to dependence and 'nature', and identified metaphorically with the female. One is presented with a picture of atomized individuals who relate to each other in entirely impersonal ways and where the image of self/other distinctions is strongly enforced. This 'fully encapsulates both Machiavelli's and Hobbes' ideas of autonomy but it is a theory which constantly distances subject and object'.[87] Benhabib has argued that one must see in Hobbes's thought the reflection of an early bourgeois world characterized by a division between 'reason' and 'sentiment' and in which reason is male-identified and associated with 'knowledge'.[88] In Hobbes's thought, Benhabib argues, one sees the freeing of the male ego from all bonds of dependence and the male- and female-identified dichotomies reified as essential to the constitution of the self.[89] Benhabib argued that the denial of being born of a woman frees the male ego from the most basic bond of dependence. This is then reflected in epistemologies which embody a white, male, ruling-class perspective which divides the world up in ways which put the omnipotent subject at the centre of the conceptual universe and construct a series of marginal Others seen as sets of negative qualities.[90]

'Abstract masculinity' and object-relations theory

Feminists have critiqued the sovereign rational subject which is privileged in realism because it cannot represent women epistemologically or politically. Feminist critiques have argued that the concept of the sovereign state employed in realism has been built upon a model of 'abstract masculinity', characterized by a need for a singular identity, for separation and a denial of relatedness. The image of the autonomous state is juxtapositioned against images of a disorderly international state of nature which is often identified metaphorically with the female. When the identity of the state is constructed around a notion of 'abstract masculinity', characterized by a separation of subject and object, it has profound consequences for how relations with others are conceived. The experience of the mind/body duality is reflected in a series of dualisms characterized by rigid dichotomies; self/other, culture/nature, male/female, national/international. In this way, in realism the identity of the nation-state is defined in terms of what it opposes.

A number of theorists have drawn upon object-relations theory, discussed briefly in chapter 1, to explain why human relations are constructed in this way. The central concern with autonomy is seen to stem from the male infant's struggle to establish a sense of separate identity. The move towards separation and autonomy and the development of a sense of self which occurs in childhood can lead to over-rigid ego boundaries where other people are perceived as a threat to be controlled or dominated. Chodorow argues that given the initial relationship between child and mother and the absence of the father for most of the period of a child's primary care, boys tend to achieve their identity as males by differentiating themselves from their mothers. The boy must *be* what his mother is not. Masculinity must be attained by means of opposition to the concrete world of daily life, by escaping from contact with the female world of the household into the masculine world of politics and public life.

The male experience is reflected in epistemologies which embody a particular conception of the world conceived of and, according to Hartsock,[91] in fact, inhabited by a number of fundamental 'others' with whom one must construct relationships in order to survive. This leads to a conceptualization of the world in which the self, or in this case the state, is seen to operate in an environment where its integrity is threatened by a series of hostile others. Hirschmann argues that a significant part of this bias is the dichotomy between epistemology and ontology.[92] Hirschmann suggests that positivist epistemologies revolve around the concept of objectivity. Objectivity as a means of classifying the world derives from the objectification of the woman/mother, a central task in masculinist development that is undertaken as a means to escape the mother and solidify masculine identity. The notion of objectivity is based upon a need to control and dominate others and this is clearly associated with males. To be male 'requires not only self reliance and self control, but control over other people and resources'.[93] These characteristics are so completely associated with males that it would be difficult to think about gender except in terms of this dichotomy. Furthermore, it is assumed that these definitions reflect a universal trend, departures from which are instances of abnormality.[94]

Hartsock has combined the insights of Marxism with object-relations theory to show how power is gendered. While she denies that psychoanalysis can explain the totality of human relations, she suggests that it is useful in understanding how the masculine but not the feminine experience replicates itself in both the hierarchical dualisms of Western class societies and in their cultural construction of sexuality. Material reality as experienced by the boy in the family provides no model and is unimportant in the attainment of masculinity, which becomes an ideal which must be achieved. The experience of two worlds, the public and the private, lies at the heart of a series of dualisms – mind/body, self/other, culture/nature, ideal/real – which are overlaid by gender. On the first side of each lies the male. Dualism, along with the dominance of one side of the dichotomy over the other, lies at the heart of phallocentric social and political life and, one might add, realist International Relations theory. However, unlike the experience of the ruling class where persons seem related only indirectly through the medium of things, the experience of the ruling gender is one in which participants confront each other directly, share no common interests and experience the other as a threat to their existence.[95]

Object-relations theory has proved useful to feminists who are trying to understand why power is gendered and why a particularly masculine experience is presented as the 'human' experience. It has also proved helpful in understanding why human relations are in consequence presented as 'zero sum games', as in realism. Feminist critique does, however, rather raise the question of whether or not the experiences of the female could serve as a standpoint from which to reconstruct International Relations – a feminist standpoint which draws upon psychoanalytic feminist thought, radical feminism and, in Hartsock's work, Marxist historical materialism.

However, the first achievement of feminist theorizing in International Relations has been to problematize gender. Theories which have assumed as the norm, the universal and the human, a gendered identity have produced an incomplete and exclusionary view of the nature of human relationships of all kinds. Feminist critique thus dereifies male reason and objectivity by demonstrating its material and ideological exclusivity.

Chapter 3

States, Nationalisms and Gendered Identities

In the introduction to this book, it was suggested that the activity of 'theorizing' involves an initial process of conceptual 'mapping'. In chapters 1 and 2, it was further suggested that realism has been the dominant perspective in International Relations and this has had important consequences for how what is undoubtedly a complex social and political world has been understood. The realist construction of the 'state as actor' involves a process whereby the state is given a concrete identity through the fusion of the sovereign state with a nationalist construction of political identity. Critics of the orthodoxy argue that the state should be seen in dynamic rather than static terms. The boundaries of the nation-state do not embody eternal truths, but are made and remade by state practices, through powerful representations of 'national interests', and through received narratives of political space and place. Similarly, the interest in citizenship extends beyond the issue of the rights and duties of individuals within the polity and their obligations to excluded others, to citizenship as a prism for investigating processes of inclusion and exclusion.[1] In this view citizenship is conceived of as 'a space within a discourse on politics that institutionalizes identities and differences by drawing boundaries, in terms of both membership and the actual political practices associated with membership'.[2] This chapter continues to explore some of these issues.

The chapter is divided into five main sections. The first section focuses on the ways in which International Relations has conventionally understood identity. The second section highlights gender issues in nationalist constructions of identity. In so doing, the aim is to explore the complex ways in which gender identities are central to the construction of political identities. Gender is also central to the construction of the 'inclusive' and 'exclusive' categories which establish rights of citizenship. Focusing on gender and identity leads us to ask rather different questions about the social practices involved in the construction of those 'bounded communities' called nation-states which have so occupied International Relations scholars.

However, highlighting gender as a factor in understanding forms of both personal and collective identification further illustrates why the assumption of stable and homogeneous identities which underlies the use of the nation-state as the basis for political identity in International Relations is highly problematic. Having illustrated the complexity of issues of gender, identity and power in nationalist constructions identity, the final section turns to questions of how we might move beyond the territorial and conceptual boundaries of state and nation. It does this by focusing on issues of gender and identity in a global perspective. It suggests that taking the nation-state to be the single irreducible component of identity, disguises the increasingly complex ways in which identities are formed and transformed. In so doing, it returns to the theme of the theoretical challenges to International Relations that arise when issues of identity are problematized. It suggests that International Relations needs to develop new approaches to conceptualize and theorize relations in a global age, because it is only by 'looking beyond the boundaries that we erect by thinking about the world through the privileged concepts of state, nation and citizen' that we will develop 'alternative concepts and greater understanding of the problems facing people across the world';[3] a theme which is further developed in chapter 5.

State, Nation and the Logic of Identity

The received idea that questions of identity in International Relations are confined to identification with the nation-state is in part due to the ways in which accounts of identity in International Relations have been linked to the notion of organized space and the creation of boundaries, most obvious in the process of state building.[4] Historically, the creation of state boundaries in Europe was closely linked with the rise of nationalism as a powerful ideology and political force. Furthermore, nationalism was seen as a progressive force, closely associated with the process of 'modernization' and secularization. The nation-state was seen as a form of political organization which allowed for the creation of 'centralized political institutions supported by a homogeneous national identity' and as such establishing 'a reasoned stable space for human improvements'.[5] In this context, the conflation of 'state' and 'nation' can be seen as mutually reinforcing in an orderly and hierarchical system. The realist orthodoxy sees the state as not only a unit of political organization, but also embodying the collective identity of the nation and so of moral worth. However, beyond the boundaries of the nation-states lies the 'anarchy' and disorder characteristic of human life in the absence of government, and where the rule of law gives way to the dictum that 'might makes right'.

It is perhaps because the nation-state continues to function as the irreducible component of identity that gender, along with class, race or other facets of identity, continues to be rendered invisible in International Relations. Certainly, the orthodoxy within International Relations continues to privilege the 'nation-state' as the primary locus of collective identity. A great deal of work on security in International Relations defines its purpose in terms of understanding how the distinctive identity of 'human collectivities' can best be protected.[6] Deeply ingrained in this type of analysis are ideas about the moral worth and distinctive identity of human collectivities called nation-states. The idea of the 'national interest' as a central organizing concept in International Relations relies upon the assumption that our identification with the nation overrides all other dimensions of social and political identification. The national interest is in essence about the preservation of the political expression of the nation, the sovereign state, and defence of the nation from 'foreigners' who threaten its political and territorial integrity and its distinctive identity.

The assumption that the state in some senses embodies the collective identity and will of 'the people' reduces all aspects of social relations which play a role in shaping identities, including violence and conflict for example, to relations between sovereign states. This idea of state autonomy and view of the state as a purposive actor relies wholly upon the assumption that the nation-state can be viewed as the irreducible component of identity. By investing the state with an identity it is possible to suggest that our identities are stable and homogeneous, that we identify first and foremost with the nation-state and that our relations with others are mediated through the state. The notion of the autonomous, sovereign state expresses the need for singular identity as a first stage in theorizing relations between states. Employing the device of state as purposive actor thus allows International Relations to draw distinctions between international and domestic politics. This device also reinforces the idea that there are clearly demarcated boundaries between what is 'inside' and what is 'outside' the state. This in turn allows International Relations to impose a logic of identity on world politics.

Raising issues of identity in International Relations is disconcerting because it moves the observer away from the comfortable sanctity of orthodox theory and understanding by focusing on new types of boundaries and divisions at previously hidden sites of repression.[7] Exploring issues of identity from feminist perspectives forces a critical reassessment of 'the theoretical and practical processes of inclusion and exclusion in the way that International Relations scholars have sought to understand individual and collective attachments and feelings of belonging'.[8]

Feminists are also sceptical about the possibility of speaking on behalf of the nation-state because 'feminist awareness makes anyone wary of seeing France or Japan as naturally cohesive on the world stage because feminism has revealed how few women in any country actually get to make these policies so glibly labelled "national" policies'.[9] Throughout the world, politics is a male dominated activity.[10] The feminist emphasis upon gender and identity serves to critique the received wisdom within the International Relations 'orthodoxy' that the nation-state is the only significant source of political identification and allegiance in the world. However, feminist perspectives have more to contribute to our understanding of issues of identity in International Relations than a mere critique of conventional or orthodox approaches to identity. Feminist analysis goes beyond critique and helps us understand the complex ways in which gender and identity are relevant to understanding the world. By focusing on issues of gender and identity, feminism both critiques the idea of stable and homogeneous identities embedded in the fusion of state identity and nationalist political identity and offers alternative conceptions of collective identity which are not tied to the territorial or conceptual boundaries of the nation-state. In this way, by foregrounding questions of gender and identity, feminist critique serves to expose the ideological exclusivity of the orthodoxy in International Relations and highlight what is lost, marginalized and excluded in the construction of the nation-state as actor. Feminist analysis also highlights the complex ways in which gender identities are central to the construction of political identities and, in so doing, raises questions about how identities are formed and transformed. In this way, feminist analysis raises questions about power in the construction and ascription of identity.

Gender is one of the most obvious facets of our identity. It is clear that in an important sense our view of ourselves, how we relate to others and how we understand our world and our place in it are all coloured by our perception of ourselves and others as gendered individuals. The ways in which we experience gender and the ways in which we come to understand ourselves as gendered are undoubtedly influenced by other factors such as social class or ethnicity which cut across gender historically. However, while we might identify with a particular ethnic group, or our experience of gender might be influenced by the cultural context in which masculinity and femininity is defined, at the same time our identification with a particular culture, or our sense of ethnic or national identity, is profoundly influenced by gender. Gender as a central facet of human identity is politically significant because ideas about gender have been used historically to justify different and usually unequal treatment between men and women. Gender identity becomes politically significant when traditional ideas about gender are challenged by those who have an interest in breaking down the existing gender order.

Gender, Nationalisms and Identities

The importance of gender, social relations and power in understanding how political identity is constructed is now explored in relation to nationalism and nationalist articulations of 'national identity'. According to Scholte, the 'world-wide process of decolonizations which occurred in the Post-Second World War period saw a 'renewed privileging of the nationality principle above alternative constructions of political identity in terms of small-scale locality, larger-scale religion, religious faith, class, race, gender, sexual orientation, age and so on'.[11] This process seemed to

reaffirm the nation as the 'terminal community'[12] and demonstrates the continuing power of appeals to the 'nation' as the
primary source of collective identification. However, in concentrating on how gender is relevant to understanding both aspects
of nationalist struggle and nationalist articulations of identity, the
aim here is to highlight the ways in which power operates in
political struggles and influences the construction and ascription
of identity. Feminist scholarship in these areas can be used to
explode the myth of homogeneous identity which underpins
dominant conceptions of the nation-state as actor.

Addressing issues of identity in an international context,
Zalewski and Enloe make the observation that identity is not just
a question of self-identification. Identities are constructed by
others who have a stake in making up certain social categories and
in trying to make people conform to them.[13] Thus when we think
about identification we need to be sensitive to the operation of
power in the ascription of identities. This can clearly be seen in
the context of nationalist struggles which involve the assertion of
national identity, culture and traditions and the mobilization of
people in the cause of national independence. Gender is central
to understanding the way the 'nation' is constructed. Gender also
plays a role in influencing the strategies and goals of participants
in nationalist struggles.

Nationalist ideologies are based upon the idea that the imagined community of the nation is 'natural' because, irrespective
of difference, there is a natural bond between members of the
national group.[14] However, the nation is not a natural entity but
is constructed. In his influential book *Imagined Communities*,
Benedict Anderson[15] argued that identities were not 'essential',
homogeneous and stable, but rather constructed. Nationalist
consciousness was created by appeals to symbols and imagery.
Essential in the process of establishing a sense of identification
with the nation and inculcating a nationalist consciousness was
the telling of a particular *story* about the nation and its history.
Feminist scholarship has shown the relevance of gender relations
in our understanding of the construction of the nation and shown
the significance of women, sexuality and family as symbols in
the reproduction of the nation and its boundaries. They have
also explored the significance of gendered symbolism and imagery which is employed in story-telling about the nation and its
history.

Nira Yuval Davis and Floya Anthias have noted a 'janus-faced' quality in nationalist discourse.[16] On the one hand, it presents itself as a modern project which melts and transforms traditional attachments in favour of new identities. Nationalism by its very nature challenges traditional cultural and political values and in so doing opens up a degree of fluidity in social relations and transforms political identities. By opening up a degree of fluidity in social relations nationalist struggles often create the conditions that allow women to challenge traditional gender roles and create spaces for women to create new identities and imagine new possibilities for themselves.[17] In the context of nationalist struggle, challenges to existing gender relations often involve a radical reinterpretation of the cultural traditions of the nation. In so doing, the participation of women is often a direct challenge to the privileged position of men within the social order.

On the other hand, nationalism draws upon cultural values drawn from some imagined past. The search for national identity may involve harking back to a national culture destroyed or suppressed by the experience of foreign domination. Thus while nationalism may reconstitute the political order on a radically different basis, women cannot be the total negation of tradition. It falls to women to become the guardians of national culture, indigenous religion and family traditions and these same traditions and values are used to justify imposing particular constraints on women's activities, thus keeping women within boundaries prescribed by male elites.[18] For example, in her discussion of struggles to establish Indian national independence, Jayawardena argues that the view that Eastern women were 'more spiritual', were the 'heirs to wisdom and tradition' and 'custodians of the past', served to keep women within boundaries prescribed by men, even though women played an active role in nationalist struggle.[19] These 'vagaries' of nationalist discourse are 'frequently reflected in changing portrayals of women as victims of social backwardness, icons of modernity or the privileged bearers of cultural authenticity'.[20]

Benedict Anderson's account of nationalism emphasizes the importance of kinship. The nation is held to be something to which one is naturally tied. Indeed, it is not uncommon to find that the nation is depicted as the 'motherland'. The power of nationalism lies in its appeals to a sense of belonging – of being *at home.* The association of women with the private domain of the home and family, reinforces the powerful imagery involved in merging the idea of national community with that of the selfless/devoted mother. This automatically triggers the response that one should ultimately be prepared to come to her defence or die for her.[21] Mosse has suggested that the sense of belonging and attachment is actually centred on male bonding. As such, it has special affinities for male society. This special affinity for male society legitimizes male domination over women.[22]

The rhetoric of nationalism is heavily sexualized and gendered. Not only is nationalism couched in terms of 'love of country', but within this image of the nation, women serve as the repository of group identity. National identity is equated with ideas about gender, parentage and skin colour. Women not only bear the burden of being the mothers of the nation, but their bodies may also be used to reproduce the boundaries of the national group, transmit its culture and become 'the privileged signifiers of national difference'.[23] It is because women embody the symbolic values of chastity and motherhood that incidences of rape in the armed conflicts that frequently accompany independence struggles have to be seen as political acts through which the aggressor attacks the honour of other men and through this breaks the continuity of the social order which it is women's responsibility to uphold.[24] Women might even constitute the symbolic configuration of the nation. It is not uncommon to find that the nation is depicted as a woman. This deeply ingrained image of the homeland as a female body whose violation by foreigners requires citizens to rush to her defence is a powerful image in nationalist ideology.[25] This depends upon an image of woman as chaste and dutiful.[26]

The privileging of nationalist constructions of collective identity is problematic for feminists because, as Massey and Jess have argued, 'nationalist constructions of political identity are in a sense always reactionary'.[27] Nationalism fuses the identity of state with the 'nation' through a profoundly gendered conception of 'kinship' and 'home'. In this way, Massey and Jess argue, the 'mother' of the nation is the unchanging point of reference, which is grounded in a complex net of social conventions, structures and practices.[28] The idea of the nation is constructed out of an invented inward-looking history,[29] a cult of origins. In this way, the fusing of nationalist political identity and the nation-state confers on women a 'place' within the social and political order, but it is a place which takes women prisoner.[30]

Kandiyoti has argued that because national identity is articulated as forms of control over women, to a great extent this can infringe upon women's lives as enfranchised citizens. Where women's rights are achieved during struggle, they can always be 'sacrificed on the altar of identity politics in another'.[31] The contradictions in nationalist projects might even limit women's claims to enfranchised citizenship. For these reasons, the integration of women into the modern state often follows a different trajectory to that of men.[32] In the process of carving out a distinctive political space and identity for the nation-state, the nation-state is actually being *made.* This involves, however, the institutionalization of gender differences. Women are controlled in different ways in the interests of demarcating identities. States are involved in regulating what are often held to be 'private' decisions, concerning, for example, whom one can marry and the legal status of children. In this way the boundaries of the national community are drawn and reproduced.

Where nationalist ideologies are explicitly racist, the consequences for women in terms of the policing of their sexual activity and control of their bodies are especially profound. The construction of women as 'dependants' who are identified only in terms of their relationship to men, as wives and mothers, plays a role in limiting rights of citizenship. Citizenship is frequently denied to the husbands and children of women who have married 'out'. Certainly, 'no nation state in the world has granted women and men the same privileged access to the resources of the nation state and claims to nationality frequently depend upon marriage to a male citizen'.[33] As Yuval Davis and Anthias point out, there are undoubtedly dangers in linking the interests of male subjects with the 'national interest'. To do so raises epistemological and empirical difficulties even where the problematic notion of interests is accepted.[34] It is clear that women themselves may directly benefit from practices that exclude people from particular ethnic groups from rights of citizenship, so it is important to avoid the reductionism which either sees national processes as fundamentally class processes or representations of generic sexual divisions and conflicts. Similarly, nationalist aspirations for popular sovereignty might stimulate an extension of citizenship rights, clearly benefiting women and so the modern state can serve in this sense to facilitate progressive gender politics.[35] Nevertheless, it is clear that nationalism has a special affinity for male society and legitimizes the dominance of men over women.

Power and the Construction and Ascription of Identity

Feminist scholarship has shown that gender plays a role in both the construction of national identity and in defining 'woman's place' within the national order, but women as a group are not *excluded* from the nation in the way that other groups defined by their skin colour or ethnic origin might be. Furthermore, it is clear that women, like men, frequently have a very strong sense of identification with the nation. While the assertion of national identity in nationalist struggle can lead to violent xenophobia, the celebration of national identity can also be seen as giving 'insiders' a positive source of strength and security. However, while we might identify with a particular national group, the way in which we identify is undoubtedly influenced by gender.

When gender relations are introduced into the analysis of nationalism, it encourages us to reassess nationalist political movements and to ask whether nationalism is 'progressive' or 'liberating' and, if so, from whose perspective? As the forces of nationalist struggle have drawn and redrawn the political map of the world this century, carving out political spaces and demarcating the boundaries between 'insiders' and 'outsiders', what has motivated women who have participated in nationalist struggles and what have been the consequences for the world's women? To what extent have women achieved lasting changes in their status? Asking questions of this kind raises further questions about how power relations operate and how existing social and economic conditions constrain the possibilities for achieving advances in the status of women as a group. In chapter 4, the relationship between masculinity, participation in armed combat and citizenship is explored in some detail. At this point, however, the aim is to demonstrate how the mobilization of people in the cause of national liberation can open up spaces for women to challenge dominant conceptions of national tradition and culture and create new

identities for themselves. However, at the same time, it demonstrates how the existing power relations limit the possibilities for
long-lasting change.

[Despite the emphasis on the 'naturalness' and organic unity of
the 'national family', groups participate in nationalist struggles
for very different reasons. In the context of African nationalism,
different groups participated in struggles for different reasons
according to class position, gender and even generation.[36] Feminist scholars have drawn on a wide variety of postcolonial nationalist struggles to illustrate the ways in which gender interests have
shaped the aspirations, and strategies of women. For example, in
the case of the struggle for Zimbabwean independence, married
women were partly motivated to support ZANU[37] because cadres
punished men who were found guilty of inflicting violence against
women.[38] In other examples drawn from Africa, women frequently participated because they wanted to gain access to education, or employment or mobility.[39]

However, when participating in struggle, women not only desire emancipation from foreign domination; they also, often implicitly, sometimes explicitly, challenge many of those same
'authentic' cultural traditions which have historically legitimized
patriarchal relations and the subordination of women. According
to Callaway and Ridd, the experience of struggle often challenges
and transforms the very authentic identities it seeks to preserve, by
opening up new arrivals, transforming identities and legitimizing
new roles and new identities.[40] The Nicaraguan revolution of 1979
opened up many opportunities for women to expand their horizons and this in turn had an important effect in legitimizing new
roles and identities for women. Women were 'no longer silent
drudges' but found spaces to create new identities and saw 'doors
opening on the world'.[41] The Nicaraguan experience was unique
because women themselves pressured the Sandinista regime to
move from a position of subsuming women's specific interests to
what were seen as military and economic priorities, to incorporating women's demands as an intrinsic part of the revolution.[42]
Women also played a central role in the FSLN.[43] The symbol of
the Nicaraguan Women's Association included a profile of a woman's head crossed by a gun, illustrating the central role played
by women in the struggle. Women also provided vital civilian
support, hiding Sandinistas, setting up first-aid posts, carrying
messages, gathering information, providing food, sewing

uniforms and providing transportation. Participation gave women confidence and a sense of worth, and as women took part in public life they gained consciousness of their oppression.[44]

India provides an interesting example of how both 'internal' and 'external' factors play a role in shaping the goals of the independence movement and within the context of that broader struggle prompt demands for women's emancipation. According to Jayawardena,[45] the struggle for national independence coincided with moves towards secularism and a broader concern with social reform. Jayawardena has argued that in India movements for emancipation took place against a background of nationalist struggles aimed not only at achieving political independence and asserting national identity, but also at 'modernizing' the country. As nationalist aspirations grew, the local bourgeoisie struggled against both imperialism and internal pre-capitalist structures. The bourgeoisie appealed to people in terms of both cultural identity and in terms of its desire to promote reforms aimed at education, scientific, technological and industrial advancement. In this context women's emancipation struggles became an essential and integral part of nationalist struggle, because the status of women became a popular barometer of 'civilization'. Jayawardena suggests that while efforts were made to 'Westernize' and educate women within the confines of patriarchal traditions, women often made their own demands. It was impracticable to launch slogans that claim to be universal and to mobilize around these banners for political causes without oppressed groups taking up issues on their own behalf. Women wanted emancipation from certain social customs that were detrimental to them. Women demanded equality, entered the professions and demanded suffrage.[46]

According to Callaway and Ridd, at times of conflict it is not unusual to find that tensions open up as women find spaces to create new identities and new opportunities for themselves. There will also be some degree of fluidity in social relations unless steps are taken to prevent this.[47] The implications of this are that we cannot assume that members of the collectivity of the nation share the same interests and goals. We need to understand, therefore, the way power relations operate both in times of struggle and in consolidating the social and political order in the post-revolutionary period. Callaway and Ridd have noted the curious paradox that conflict in itself, however orientated towards

achieving change, can be inherently conservative.[48] Nationalist
revolutions are certainly not watersheds for women. Even where
women's emancipation has been openly declared to be integral
to revolutionary struggle, change is often short-lived. It seems
that the degree to which women achieve significant and lasting
changes in their status or conditions of life depends in part on
other factors, particularly class. Harris argues that in the Nicaraguan case the revolution certainly changed the idea of what
middle-class women should be, and quite clearly some women saw
their lives as transformed. However, in the post revolution period,
some women saw no difference in their day-to-day lives from what
they had experienced under the previous Somozoa regime.[49]
However, this may be because of the ways in which women are
mobilized in support of nationalist movements. Harris's study of
Nicaragua suggests that, despite women's role in the struggle, the
male-dominated army saw that women needed to be better edu-
cated because they were needed to fulfil administrative and
logistical positions, rather than because it was a means to achieve
general and lasting changes in their status.[50]

Where women play an active role in struggles, it is usually seen
as a supportive role. This raises the question of why and how
women's interests can be subordinated to a greater collective
interest or 'national interest' as articulated by male elites. Political
conflicts are often about redefining social reality. At times of great
change and transformation whose definition prevails? Existing
power relations undoubtedly affect this process. Chatterjee has
argued that the relationship between the 'women's question' and
nationalism is inherently problematic. The problem arises when
one politics is taken over and spoken for by another.[51] When the
imagined community of the nation is authorized as the most
authentic unit of collective identity, men are often in positions of
power and so able to define its meaning. This may even extend to
the ways in which women's contribution to nationalist struggle is
recorded. As Helie-Lucas has argued, 'if a man carries food to
armed fighters over long distances he is acknowledged as a
fighter, while if a woman does it she is "helping" the man in her
natural way of nurturing'[52] and even in 'times of struggle, women
are confined to the kinds of tasks which will not disturb the future
social order'.[53]

Indeed existing power relations and the power of men to interpret the meaning of actions may even extend to how the struggle

to redefine women's place is interpreted. It is not unusual to find that women who actively campaign for women's rights are stigmatized and accused of betraying the nation. The desire to achieve changes in the position of women can easily be portrayed as a betrayal of cultural or national identity. The struggle for changes in the position and status of women that flow from the fluidity in social relations and changing identities can be portrayed as being based upon a 'foreign' ideology – feminism – that alienates women from 'their' religion, 'their' culture and 'their' family responsibilities, on the one hand, and from revolutionary struggle on the other. Calls for 'women's liberation' are frequently and conveniently described as a product of Western capitalism and of no relevance to women involved in national struggle in the non-Western world. However, where there are marked inequalities between women, this can be used to reinforce the view that feminism is a middle-class ideology of no relevance to poor women. At times of conflict when the nation is held to be under attack it is particularly difficult to counter the accusation that women are betraying their cultural traditions and the greater interest of the national good. In the case of Algeria, for example, 'the overall task of women during liberation struggles was symbolic'.[54] Faced with colonization, 'the people had to build a national identity based on values of one's own traditions, religion, language and culture' and 'women bore the heavy role of being the keepers of this threatened identity and they paid a heavy price for accepting this role, because it is difficult to criticise the nation at times of struggle'.[55]

Gendered Practices

Feminist scholarship has shown that gender is important in shaping the goals of women and men in nationalist struggles. Existing gender relations constrain the possibilities of realizing far-reaching changes in the social position of women as a group. Gender relations are, however, deeply embedded in wider power relations. Women's sense of identity and allegiance is also strongly influenced by class and ethnic and cultural differences. Furthermore, women's protest must be seen in the context of pre-existing political organizations and socio-economic structures. The armed conflict which frequently accompanies nationalist struggle often

politicizes women. However, women do not alway try to change
the existing gender order and will often deliberately give priority
to their children, men and the wider society. Part of their reason
for doing so undoubtedly lies in the enormous pressures
women are under to consolidate and stabilize new orders. That is,
women's so called 'normalizing' role which women are expected
to play to reproduce the devastated nation, and the pressures
which women face from men who might accuse them of betraying
the nation. However, the experiences of women in a range of
otherwise quite different nationalist struggles bears out the importance of understanding how power and existing social hierarchies limit and constrain the possibilities of change in gender
relations.

All political practices derive from the collective interests and
needs of those who participate in them. While each political
movement has its own means of developing consciousness and
solidarity, the activities and practices of such movements work to
reinforce the relationship between the political activities of the
movement and the social and economic activities of participants.[56]
A collection of essays on gender and political struggle in Latin
America produced by Westwood and Radcliffe[57] demonstrated
how women in political movements find it difficult to undertake
roles not related to their own socio-economic experiences and the
kind of issues they find politically important. Women frequently
have a 'domestic orientation' to a lifestyle devoted to the home
and family relations. Men, on the other hand, have a 'public
orientation' to a lifestyle concerned with extra-domestic matters
of economic, political and military import.[58] This domestic/pub-
lic dichotomy is commonly treated as a natural function of the
physical differences between men and women, although in reality
it is no more than a man-made device. Furthermore, the distinction between domestic and public orientations should not strictly
be seen as a distinction between political and non-political
spheres of activity.[59] Women are not without power in their non-
public roles, nor are they non-political beings. Their ascribed
identities within the national order accord women a key role
which they can exploit to utilize what influence they have. However, women's power is more diffused and individualized outside
the bureaucratic structures of society, while men's power is more
coordinated within an institutionalized framework.[60]

Women's 'protests have to be understood not only in terms of

pre-existing political organizations and socio-economic structures, but also in terms of the 'internalities' of political protest. In
many ways women's own political powers may be derived from
their 'domestic orientation'. Thus, motherhood can come to be
seen as a national duty and act. This seems to be especially true of
older and less-educated women. Where women assert themselves
in a political role *as women* they may be well received, even hon-
oured, but once they step outside the boundary of the home and
domestic roles they are subjected to rough treatment by male-
orientated society.[61]

Maxine Molyneux makes a useful distinction between *strategic*
and *practical* gender interests.[62] Practical gender interest derives
from women's ascribed roles in the sexual division of labour.
These are shaped by class and ethnicity. For example, low-income
women will usually rally around health, housing and unemployment issues. In general, women as a whole are more responsive
than men to socio-economic issues which relate to both the public
and private spheres, because women are involved in a variety of
activities which span the arbitrary divide between production and
reproduction and have many modes of generating income. The
participation of women arises from the social bonds which are
created via these activities in local communities through which
they organize themselves and from which the political contexts of
such movements are developed. Molyneux suggests that practical
gender interests can be politicized and transformed into strategic
interests which involve challenging the subordination of women
and the struggle for equality. At this point, strategic gender interests cut across class and ethnic divisions.

However, in practice women have had relatively little success in
translating demands which arise from their immediate practical
gender interests into strategic demands. This is because women's
movements do not occur in a vacuum but are determined by the
goals and methods of wider social movements and wider power
structures. The pursuit of 'interests' implies access to institutions
that already in some sense embody male dominance and patriarchy. Callaway and Ridd have argued that institutionalized power is
for the most part controlled by men and that where women enter
the public domain they generally do so within a male-ordered
framework.[63] For these reasons it is extremely difficult to politicize
the 'women's question', and consequently it is easily and co-
ercively spoken for by the discourse of nationalism.[64]

————**Gender and Identity in Global Perspective**————

Work which has its focus on nationalism and the construction of collective identity is helpful in thinking about how gender plays a role in the construction of boundaries. Gender is also central to the construction of the boundaries between the 'public' and 'private' realms, a process which has been central to the exclusion of women, historically, from citizenship. Concentrating on gender in this context, therefore, helps us understand how citizenship has been defined to include and exclude certain groups and how relations between citizens and excluded 'others' have been constructed. The centrality of ideas about gender in the construction of the identity of the national group and the use of women's bodies to demarcate the boundaries between 'insiders' and 'outsiders' is perhaps a useful starting point for thinking about the powerful social and psycho-sexual processes central to the construction of nationalist political identities. Furthermore, it allows some insights into how gender is relevant to understanding the process of state-making, which involves the construction and policing of boundaries and, in the process, the carving out of a distinctive political space and identity for the state. Some of these issues are discussed further in chapter 4.

However, the social processes involved in the construction of collective identities and the sources of political mobilization, do not necessarily coincide with state boundaries. Similarly, the processes involved in the shaping of social relations are increasingly complex. The privileging of nationalist constructions of identity is also problematic because it renders invisible the multiplicity of identities which coexist within this particular 'political space' and the transnational dimensions of political identification. By fusing nationalist political identity with the territorial nation-state, International Relations imposes a logic of identity on world politics. Much contemporary scholarship in social theory contends that identity should be understood in terms of 'hybridity'.[65] That is, identity is fluid and multilayered rather than stable and homogeneous. Massey, for example, argues that while the specificity of place must be recognized, in a global age it is more useful to think about the nation-state as a particular territorial and political space in which 'a distinct, mixture of wider and more local social relations – layer upon layer of different linkages, local to world wide'

– exist and in which different social groups have different experiences of place, space and identity.[66] By foregrounding questions of gender and identity, feminist scholars present a radical challenge to dominant conceptions of identity in international politics.

In some senses we are influenced by events happening well away from the immediate context of our day-to-day lives.[67] At the same time, transnational movements and ideologies play a role in shaping social and political identities. In some ways, our sense of ourselves as gendered and the social meanings attached to gender are influenced not only by factors specific to our immediate locality or indigenous culture, but also by global influences, for example transnational ideologies and transnational economic activity. Even the global media plays a role in shaping gender identities and gender relations by, however crudely, promoting ideas about sexual equality or, conversely, presenting women in stereotypical roles.

International Relations scholars who adopt what might broadly be described as 'critical' approaches and perspectives have begun to challenge the statecentrism of the discipline, precisely because of the way in which it renders invisible the globalized nature of social and economic activity and the complex ways in which this shapes world politics. The reductionism of statecentric approaches and the assumption that the nation-state remains the only significant locus of political identity and allegiances, prevent us from appreciating other expressions of political community and other expressions of solidarity.

Furthermore, globalization is affecting how 'political space' is conceptualized. In an age when transnational companies, global financial institutions and, increasingly, people travel around the globe and seemingly have no fixed 'home', the relevance of the territorially bound nation-state and the claims of nationalism are increasingly being called into question. Similarly, technological advances such as the Internet have made it easy for people to engage in political activities across territorial, geographical, class, gender, ethnic and racial boundaries. It has even been suggested that the implications of these changes are so profound that the discipline of Inter-national Relations should be renamed 'world politics', or 'global politics' perhaps.[68] Rather than taking identification with the nation-state as a given, there is a need for International Relations scholars to understand the ways identities are formed and mapped into wider symbolic and political identifications and the ways in which both local and global processes influence this process. As Scholte contends, nationalism and attachment to the nation-state may complicate the process of identity construction,[69] but it should not be privileged as the primary source of identification and allegiance.

The growing significance of transnational politics and social movements does not just raise new *issues*, but demands that particular *identities* be recognized.[70] In recent years, there have been attempts by critical theorists to understand the phenomenon of transnational alliance politics not simply in terms of issues and social forces but also in terms of expressions of collective identity.[71] Globalization has also made our sense of place much more uncertain as people engage in numerous social interactions which tie people together across state boundaries. At the same time transnational and supranational institutions are playing a role in shaping social and political identities. However, the impact of globalization is uneven. People are affected quite differently according to a whole range of factors – for example geographical location, social class, race, ethnicity and, of course, gender. Globalization certainly should not be conflated with 'world unity' or growing homogeneity. Furthermore, globalization may generate feelings of uncertainty and vulnerability and throw people back into a 'cult of origins' and extreme forms of nationalist identification.

Nevertheless, in a world where 'after decades of spreading, deepening and generally accelerating globalization' our sense of self and community is characterized by 'greater fluidity, multidimensionality, uncertainty and perplexity'.[72] In many respects, feminist interventions serve to highlight the problematic character of identity in the world.[73] Feminist critical theorists and postmodern feminists each in their own distinctive way open up questions of identity and encourage us to think about these issues in a global context. The intervention of critical theories in International Relations also has profound implications for how we conceptualize social, economic and power relations in a global context, and for our understanding of forms of identification, attachment and allegiance in the world. Indeed postmodern thinkers argue that in a world in which all 'certainties' are being challenged identities might be thought of more as 'inter-relationships of difference marked by translation and negotiation'.[74]

The same processes that are shaping and reshaping identities are changing the nature of global politics and creating the conditions for different forms of political action and alliance. In this context, inequalities of power, gender relations and questions of identity have assumed a new significance in understanding the dynamic between the global and the local and between the competing claims of collective identities. While focusing on the significance of gender in the nationalist constructions of identity is useful in illuminating the ways in which issues of identity are intimately connected to social and economic processes and deeply embedded in power relations, increasingly these processes need to be understood in a global context. That is, our sense of both personal and collective identity is not only influenced by a whole range of factors specific to the immediate social and cultural context in which we carry out our day-to-day activities; it is also influenced by the social changes impelled by global economic activity, by transnational ideologies and even the powerful ideas and images disseminated by the global media industry.

The global dimension of gender relations, the ways in which global processes influence gender and the significance of gender and identity in understanding the global are of particular interest to feminist scholars of International Relations. The impact of global forces, transnational movements and ideologies needs to be explored in relation to how individuals develop a sense of who they are, their sense of belonging and political allegiance. The expansion of capitalism as an economic and social system to global proportions has transformed social orders and created the conditions for different forms of alliances. This is changing the nature of feminist politics. For example, as will be argued in chapters 6 and 7, the feminization of poverty is a global phenomenon and is intimately connected to the wider processes of global economic restructuring. The same processes are producing many and varied sites of resistance. At the same time, feminist movements have increasingly recognized the need to view the problems of women in particular localities in a global context. Processes of structural adjustment, the reform of GATT, and privatization have all become global gender issues and been addressed in international forums in recent years.[75]

Gender analysis is powerful because it challenges the constraints inherent in statecentrism and because it allows us to imagine other possibilities. Critical thinkers argue that radical new thinking is needed to meet the global nature of the many

problems and challenges facing the human race as a whole. However, the impact of global processes, technologies and ideas is
specific. While globalization may be bringing people together in
one sense – by, for example, bringing about a reordering of time
and distance in our lives – its impact is uneven. Feminist analysis
of the complex ways in which gender informs nationalist struggle
is valuable in demonstrating how indigenous women's movements grow up in times of change. However, what they also demonstrate is the degree to which gender identification is shaped by
the social, cultural and national context in which these movements are formed. Clearly, while gender is undoubtedly a major
influence on this same sense of identity, it is affected by a whole
array of social, historical and cultural factors, and other divisions
(such as social class, race or ethnicity) which cut across gender.
While recognizing the importance of specificity and difference,
feminists are attempting to develop approaches to thinking about
gender in an international or global context that avoid
reductionism and avoid marginalizing or rendering invisible the
experiences of different women. These are discussed at greater
length in chapter 7.

Chapter 4

The 'Warrior Hero' and the Patriarchal State

It was suggested in chapter 3 that the struggle to create nation-states involves the institutionalization of gender differences. Indeed national identity is frequently articulated as a form of control over women. In the interest of demarcating identities and constructing boundaries states routinely engage in practices which have profound implications for women's citizenship. This chapter, which is divided into four main sections, explores the masculinized nature of state power and militarized conceptions of citizenship and politics.

The first section of this chapter explores the historical linkages between conceptions of political community, citizenship and military participation. In the West masculinity, virility and violence have been linked together in political thought through the concept of the 'warrior hero'. Historically, the rights and duties of citizenship have been closely linked with the ability to take up arms in defence of the polity. Indeed, historically this linkage has provided one of the main justifications for the exclusion of women from the public realm and citizenship, and has provided a powerful justification for the subordination of women. The second section of this chapter explores the implications of this male dominance of the state apparatus generally and the military particularly. The military is, of course, only one manifestation of state power. However, it is a central arm of the coercive apparatus of the state and it is here that male dominance is most striking. In the third section, the focus is directed towards the implications of the near male exclusivity of combat roles in the military. In exploring this area the aim is to open up some interesting questions about the social practices which underpin the exercise of state-sanctioned violence. The fourth and final section considers the radical feminist claim that there is not only a connection between masculinity and the military, but a crucial linkage between the construction of 'masculinity', 'femininity' and male violence in all its manifestations.

Citizens and Warriors

Citizenship and the bearing of arms have been linked in Western political thought since Aristotle. The discourse of political community and citizenship in Western political thought has been heavily militarized and profoundly gendered. Indeed, Hartsock sees the entire history of Western thought about politics and citizenship as being dominated by the themes of masculinity, the warrior ethic and death. Hartsock claims that eros and power have been connected since the ideal of public virtue first took theoretical form in ancient Athens in an all-male political community. In Greek thought the battlefield was inhabited only by men who achieved either glorious victory or death.[1] However, while recognizing this historical connection between citizenship, masculinity and the 'warrior ethic', the continuing male near exclusivity of the military attracts little attention from non-feminist political theorists and International Relations scholars. Nor does it provoke curiosity about the gendered nature of the social and political order which underpins the life of the citizen body.[2]

There is a growing body of literature which considers the historical experience of women both in terms of the exclusion of women from political community, justice and rights of citizenship and in terms of how contemporary citizenship might be 'engendered'.[3] However, relatively little has been written about the significance of militarized conceptions of citizenships and the relationship between militarized citizens and excluded 'others'.[4] In recent years in the United States of America, as the women's movement has challenged gender stereotypes, demands for the integration of women into combat roles in the military have grown. These have come from both feminist activists and women already serving in the military in some capacity, who, while not necessarily identifying with the feminist cause, have argued that there is no good reason to continue to debar them from active participation in combat. The debate over the Equal Rights Amendment in the United States has in turn revived debates in feminist circles about the relationship between the construction of 'masculinity', 'femininity', citizenship and combat. It has also led to debates about the degree to which participation in combat roles can be used as an effective tool to advance the position of women.

Advocates of women's 'right to fight' are most frequently found amongst liberal feminists. Liberal feminists have not simply seen the issue in terms of extending rights and privileges to women. Those at the forefront of the 'right to fight' campaign have recognized that equal rights entails equal obligations. The state has historically granted to its people whatever rights they possess. In return the state makes certain demands upon its population, one of the most important of which is to require, or compel, citizens to play an active role in the defence of the state. Epstein has argued that the commitment of feminists to equal rights must entail a willingness to shoulder equally the responsibilities which stem from this.[5] Rights feminists argue that the differences between men and women which have been used to justify the exclusion of women are either non-existent or transitory. If fighting is needed to defend values, then these same values should be seen as female as well as male, or as 'human' values. Liberal feminists argue that, despite the acquisition of formal political and legal rights, women still do not enjoy the same rights of citizenship as men. This can in part be explained by the exclusion of women from combat roles in the military. Stiehm has argued that there are different categories of citizenship, the young and old men (who constitute ex-protectors or future protectors), those banned from service on the grounds of homosexuality (who constitute the 'despised'), the dishonest, and women.[6] Because women are forbidden from playing a full part in the armed services they are likened to the despised and the dishonest. They are also always 'the protected'. If women's citizenship is seen as in some sense imperfect, the answer must be to pursue a strategy which will lead to the realization of 'first-class' citizenship.[7]

If reflected upon at all by non-feminist commentators, male dominance in the military is usually seen as a reflection of the sexual division of labour and the *natural* scheme of things. How-

ever, for feminist theorists it raises important questions about how
the social construction of masculinity and femininity plays a role
in supporting social and political orders which perpetuate gender
inequalities. As Connell suggests, for liberal feminists working out
strategies to challenge male privilege, the idea of equality through
participation in the public domain on a par with men is associated
with a strategy which involves scaling a number of hierarchical
ladders. Women's equality can be achieved by firstly gaining the
vote, then gaining equal opportunities in education, in social
institutions and in the workplace, to gradually achieving equality
of representation in the edifices of the state of which the armed
forces are a central pillar.[8] The feminist cause can, therefore, be
furthered by achieving the participation of women in the military
on the same terms as men. Liberal feminists view the state as a
neutral arbiter between competing interests in an open and plu-
ralistic society. However, liberal feminists also recognize that, historically, the state has not been equal and impartial in its
treatment of women. Furthermore, liberal feminists recognize
that historically the relationship of women to the state has not
been direct but mediated through a male 'head' of the family. For
liberal feminists, however, the problem of male domination is
largely one of historical circumstance and accident. Liberal feminists largely accept the view that the state provides the conditions
for civilized life and human advancement and so view the state as
a vehicle for progressive gender politics.[9]

In this view the state can, perhaps, be seen as a 'hireling' of
patriarchy.[10] Men have 'captured' the state, so the strategy must be
for women to take it back. If 'men at present run bureaucracies,
governments and armies, then the solution is more access, pack-
ing more and more women into the top levels'.[11] The National
Organization for Women (NOW) in the United States of America
has played a central role in pressing for the advancement of
women in American public life. The 'right to fight' campaign has
attracted widespread support among liberal feminists actively involved in NOW. Quite apart from issues of citizenship and women's rights to equal treatment and equal opportunities, liberal
feminists have pointed out that economic and other benefits
accrue to men who serve. In the United States these benefits
range from state-supported livelihoods to advanced education,
free medical care and cheap loans. Many NOW activists argue that
women should have these things too.[12]

However, critics of the 'right to fight' campaign have accused liberal analysis of being theoretically rootless and the NOW campaign as misguided. Liberal analysis suggests that the exclusion of women is basically a consequence of bias and outmoded attitudes about the social role of women. The argument that participation in the military is a route to first-class citizenship rests on the assumption that patriarchy is an accident. The liberal feminist approach does not theorize gender – that is, the significance of the social construction of gender and the way in which ideas about gender are used to institutionalize male dominance. Liberal theory sees the citizen as an unsexed individual abstracted from his or her social context. Liberal feminists fail to explore the significance of the linkages between war, militarism and the social construction of gender. While the argument for admission to the military on the same terms as men makes feminist sense in terms of the politics of access, it might be at odds not only with the strategic interest which feminists have in challenging the role of the military, but also with conventional ideas about the nature of war and dominant conceptions of security.

Some commentators have suggested that the construction of male identity involves an ongoing battle to prove that one is not a woman. For example Hartsock argues that men's fixation with war arises from their need to affirm their manhood, a process which requires an ongoing and constant effort to distinguish themselves from women.[13] In the contemporary Western world the gender carried by power continues to associate masculinity with domination and thus fuses sexuality, violence and death. Heroic action is itself a construction that consists of deliberately facing the cessation of existence.[14] Jean Elshtain has also demonstrated how a feminist *reading* of the dominant discourse of war reveals the political identity of a virtuous male citizen, defined by the bearing of arms. Elshtain uses the term 'just warrior' to 'capture the male identity inscribed and reinscribed in the discourse of armed civic virtue'.[15]

Critics like Hartsock and Elshtain, while starting from very different theoretical positions, agree that the NOW strategy involves seeking equality by attempting to emulate men rather than criticizing 'male values'. Some radical feminists argue that the notion of 'rights' is itself a male value. Women can struggle for the right to enter into the public domain, but this is a space in which masculine values are valorized. In entering, women inevitably lose aspects of the identity and experience they formally embodied. In this view, the liberal politics of access may, therefore, ultimately only serve to further privilege and perpetuate masculine values. According to Elshtain 'in its deep structure, NOW's legal narrative is a leap out of the female/private side of the public/private divide basic to Machiavelli's realism and straight into the arms of hegemonic man whose sex linked activities are valorised thereby'.[16] Paradoxically, 'NOW's repudiation of "archaic notions of women's role" becomes a tribute to archaic notions of men's role'.[17]

Liberal feminists have also been criticized because they have failed to analyse the connections between the male domination of the military and male domination of other structures of state power. Historically, in Western political discourse the state has been sharply distinguished from 'civil society'. Feminist political theory has concentrated on how the delimitation of the state's proper sphere involves the active codification and policing of the boundaries of the public and the private. Some non-feminist political thinkers have also recognized that the 'citizen' must be supported by a functioning patriarchal household.[18] If this is the case, what are the implications for women as citizens? Furthermore, if citizenship is gendered, might not rule also be gendered? Is the state a patriarchal power?

The 'Patriarchal' State?

Perhaps the most neglected aspect of liberal feminists' analysis is the military's intimate relationship with the state and the laws, institutions and ideologies that sustain its authority. In her influential book, *Towards a Feminist Theory of the State*, Catherine MacKinnon boldly states that 'feminism has no theory of the state'.[19] This is not entirely accurate. However, it is the case that there is no general consensus among feminist political theorists on the degree to which the state can be seen as either an inherently patriarchal power or, alternatively, relatively autonomous and therefore potentially a vehicle for women's emancipation. As was noted in chapter 3, feminist scholarship on nationalism has highlighted the ways in which citizenship can work to institutionalize male privilege. However, there are empirical and theoretical problems involved in linking the state directly with male 'interests'.[20] Mary McIntosh has argued that the state does play a role in the oppression of women, 'not directly, but through its support for a specific form of household: the family dependent largely upon a male wage and upon domestic female servicing.[21] Other feminists have, as Dahlerup notes, engaged in theorizing about women's oppression in ways which 'tend to deal with the relation between the family and the sphere of production, almost forgetting the existence of the state'.[22] Kathleen Standt has argued that the feminist theorist should be interested in the ways in which male privilege has been institutionalized in state structures. However, her work has largely been concerned with the development process.[23] Certainly there has been relatively little feminist analysis of the relationship between state power and the military.

However, 'states destroy on a mass scale' and 'to do this requires masculine toughness which becomes institutionalised'.[24] Connell's[25] work draws upon earlier feminist analyses of the state. He argues that it can scarcely be denied that military thinking is imbued with masculine values. The creation of armies and empires has involved the historical embedding of violent masculinity in the state.[26] Connell argues that it is often difficult for us to see beyond individual acts of violence – or in this case beyond the individual acts of violence committed by personalized *states as actors* – to a structure of power. Yet all acts of violence are deeply embedded in power inequalities and ideologies of male supremacy. The connection of violence with ideology points to the multiple character of social power. Violence appears as part of a complex that also involves institutions and the way they are organized.[27]

According to Connell, the ability to impose a definition of a situation, to set the terms in which events are understood and issues discussed, to formulate ideas and define morality, is also to assert hegemony and this is an essential part of social power.[28] Thus state violence in the discourse of political theory and 'orthodox' International Relations theory is legitimized through the use of such key concepts as 'autonomy' and 'national interest', concepts which in turn rely upon masculinized notions of rationality as a technique of control. If 'authority is defined as legitimate power, then the main axis of the power structure of gender is the general connection of authority with masculinity',[29] though, as

Connell stresses, this is complicated by the denial of authority to some groups of men. He goes on to argue that the institutionalization of gender is central to state power. The personnel of the state are divided in visible, even spectacular, ways. Not only does the state arm men and disarm women, but also the diplomatic, colonial and military policies of major states have been formed in the context of ideologies of masculinity which put a premium on toughness and force.

In the 1980s the feminist anti-war movement often treated the state's military apparatus, especially nuclear weapons, as an expression of male aggression and destructiveness. In the nuclear defence establishments a 'language of warriors', a 'techno-strategic rationality' is shared by armers and disarmers, chiefs of staff and chief negotiators.[30] War is about masculinity and heroism; 'wimps and women'.[31] Sara Ruddick has pointed out that both the practices and ideology of the state are strongly masculinized.[32] Furthermore, as Cynthia Enloe has argued, state power is exercised through a range of institutions and practices which not only involve decision makers and law enforcers.[33] Across the world it is men who predominate as police chiefs, spies, judges and governors who construct a peace-time order guaranteed by the threat of violence.[34] Ruddick argues that not only is the world of generals, negotiators and chiefs of staff still a man's world, it is usually men who make battle plans, invent weapons and supervise their construction.[35] Carol Cohn's influential work has demonstrated the significance of the highly gendered symbolism and imagery employed by defence intellectuals,[36] while an important collection of essays edited by Cooke and Woollacott has emphasized the profoundly gendered nature of war talk.[37]

However, hegemonic masculinity does not just manifest itself in the military and the inner core of the security establishment; the state engages on a day-to-day basis in ideological activity on issues of sex and gender, from birth control to the criminalization of homosexuality. Ruddick points out that, states, both 'emerging' and 'established', routinely engage in practices ranging from the policing of sexuality and support for heterosexual marriage, to forms of labour legislation and taxation, which institutionalize gender relations.[38] Connell concludes, however, that the state should not be seen as inherently patriarchal, but more as a 'set of power relations and political processes in which patriarchy is both constructed and contested'.[39]

The Military System

Camp followers

If, as Connell argues, the state can be seen as a site where patriarchy is both constructed and contested, then perhaps the liberal strategy of utilizing the state in the cause of emancipatory gender politics is well conceived – particularly if, as some liberal feminists suggest, what at first sight appear to be limited objectives have great transformative potential. The historical evidence, however, would seem to suggest that ultimately this strategy will fail. While the distinction between the battlefield and the domestic arena has been central to political discourse, in reality this distinction has never been clear-cut. Indeed, the very idea of the 'home front', which has been very much part of the language of twentieth-century warfare, is indicative of the industrialization of war. This in itself transformed the earlier distinction between the 'front' and the domestic arena.

Furthermore, historically, women have always participated in the 'military system'. Women, unlike men, were never compelled to join the armed forces, but 'the same social and economic forces moved women as men'.[40] In the sixteenth century women played a vital role in armies throughout Europe. Women provided indispensable support services, though they were frequently dismissed as mere 'camp followers'. The military revolutions of the sixteenth and seventeenth centuries had far-reaching effects that sharply constrained women's military role. Revolutionary changes in technology and the art of war also set in motion a series of social and economic changes which affected both societies and states. Indeed, Roberts has argued that many traits of the modern nation-state that emerged in the seventeenth and eighteenth century can be traced to military institutions. As larger armies emerged, they ceased to be hybrids of public and private enterprises and became more clearly defined agents of the state. Because large standing armies were expensive, states started experimenting with financing, taxation and economic policy-making, measures that had far-reaching effects. As states altered to meet the needs of their armed forces, societies changed to meet the new demands of the state. According to Roberts military discipline became the model for a well-ordered civil society and the state began to intervene into areas of life once regarded as 'private'.[41]

As the armed forces changed it became more difficult for women to follow armies. At the same time, official policy statements made it clear that women were regarded as a disruptive influence, a diversion that jeopardized male loyalty and obedience. Where women were attached to companies, usually in their capacity as soldiers' wives, they were deemed to have a moral obligation to subservience to both military institutions and to individual men. Beevor argues that the official relationship between the British Army, for example, and soldiers' wives was developed in the late nineteenth century when long periods of overseas service changed camp-following practices and 'regimental harlots and seamstresses were dragooned into married respectability providing they conformed to patterns of behaviour prescribed by the officers' wives and the chaplain'.[42] Today, the wives of servicemen often organize to protect their interests. For example in Britain, the Federation of Army Wives was set up for this purpose. However, this organization, 'leans over backwards to avoid offending male sensibilities'.[43] Army wives feel obliged to declare loyalty to the army. In the army, the idea that a woman wants her own life or career is controversial because of the far-reaching implications. Senior officers fear women's careers, house purchase outside of the military barracks and family life, generally, outside the military environment, because these things threaten to 'civilianize the army'. At the same time, wives who do not aspire to these things, nevertheless often feel trapped and complain that their life is controlled by the army.[44]

Enloe claims that contemporary wives and other women who provide vital support services for those involved in roles, are the modern-day 'camp followers'. Furthermore, these women are deliberately kept ideologically marginal to the essential function of the military, which is combat. If women can be made to play the roles of wives, mothers or sweethearts and if men can be persuaded that the safety of women depends on their bravery, then women can be an invaluable resource to commanders. But women can only perform this function if they remain marginal to the military's core identity. According to Enloe, debates in the media and legislature over women in the military are nothing less than arguments over how to make use of women's labour without violating notions of femininity, masculinity and the social order itself.[45] Throughout history militaries have directed social and technological change, and they have in particular played key roles in making and keeping women subordinate within this same order. Although women sometimes perform important military functions, the basic fact remains that subordination defines women's relationship to armies. Military institutions arose from the fraternal interest groups of pre-state societies and persist in shaping the patriarchal form which states and societies invariably assume.[46] Historically women have played a role in the military system. Women have also participated in combat, but as the examples from nationalist armed struggles, discussed at some length in chapter 3, demonstrate when the task shifts from war-fighting to state-building, women again revert to their 'proper place'.

Nor, it seems, has the servicing of the war industry played a decisive role in improving the status of women.[47] Historical studies show that prejudices surrounding women and attitudes towards their role at home and work remained remarkably consistent over the first half of the twentieth century. In Britain in both the First and Second World War periods, conventional sex roles were put under strain, as women did far more 'men's jobs', although they were not permitted to fire weapons.[48] It is frequently asserted that there was a relationship between women's involvement in supporting the war effort in the earlier part of this century and gaining the franchise. However, Braydon and Summerfield argue that, despite participating in much greater numbers and in a wider variety of roles in the workforce during wartime, women in Britain did not achieve lasting changes in their economic status and social roles,[49] although, undoubtedly women's participation was an important instrument of radicalization and served to delegitimize, to some extent, dominant norms.

It seems, however, that when it came to organizing women's employment both government and the trade unions were careful to ensure that women's incursion into men's jobs was not permanent and would not shake up family life after the war.[50] According to Braydon and Summerfield the war made men think again about what women could do at work, but it did not alter their belief that women alone were responsible for the home life of the nation. As men enlisted, women were drafted into the labour force. Women were also desperately needed in munitions factories. However, trade unions were reluctant to welcome women into skilled trades and while there was a desperate need to increase the supply of women to the labour force, at the heart of government there was a reluctance to introduce any policy that would change the conventional role of women, even at the height of war.[51]

'Real men' . . .

It could be argued that the exclusion of women from combat preserves the patriarchal state by justifying the rule of men – on the grounds that only they have the requisite courage and honour to defend the state. Certainly dominant notions of politics and public life have served to exclude women from decisions governing war-making and peace-making historically, making them an almost all-male affair. However, the key to understanding how women are excluded lies not in understanding the innate characteristics of men and women as such, but in understanding gender as a set of cultural institutions and practices that constitute the norms and standards of masculinity and femininity. That is, 'masculinity' and 'femininity' are built around a set of ideals to which few men or women can measure up in practice, but to which all should aspire and by which all are measured. This is not to suggest that all men and women conform to gender stereotypes. Furthermore, few men who take part in war can be said to 'make war'. Often most are foot soldiers and workers in the service of grand campaigns they did not design, about which they are not consulted and which they rarely comprehend.[52] It is probably the case that women's peacefulness is as mythical as men's violence. Women have never absented themselves from war. Indeed, wherever battles are fought and justified, women support the military engagements of men.[53] There are numerous examples of forceful women who have led the troops into war in a symbolic, if not physical, sense. Nevertheless, gender is a 'system of meaning', a way of thinking that shapes 'how we experience, understand and represent ourselves as men and women'.[54] It is a system of meaning that affects us all. Thus a man who cries easily cannot avoid in some way confronting that he is seen as less than fully manly.[55] Similarly, an aggressive and incisive woman cannot avoid having her own and other's perceptions of such qualities being mediated by the discourse of gender.[56] If ideas about gender have played a central role in excluding women from participating directly in the frontline, it seems that the masculinity of war is largely a myth.[57] However, at the same time 'myths' about gender seemingly play a vital role in sustaining both women and men in their support for violence.[58]

It has been argued that the military plays a special role in the ideological structure of patriarchy because the notion of combat plays such a central role in the construction of 'manhood' and justification of the superiority of men in the social order.[59] In the armed forces there is a deliberate cultivation of a 'dominance-orientated' masculinity. A boy is not born a soldier, he becomes a soldier. Becoming a soldier means learning to control fears and domestic longings that are explicitly labelled feminine.[60] The army seems to engender in men an infantile sexuality.[61] 'Effeminate' young soldiers are also frequently the victims of bullying, because of the intense loathing of homosexuality that exists among both the officer corps and regular soldiers.[62] Militarists use the myth of war's manliness to define soldierly behaviour and to reward soldiers. Ruddick argues that boot-camp recruits are 'ladies' until trained in obedient killing.[63] Only then do they become *real men*. Misogyny is a useful element in the making of a soldier as boys are goaded into turning on and grinding down whatever in themselves is 'womanly'. This 'dominance-orientated' masculinity is 'cultivated in the rigours of basic training and in the manners of the officer corps'.[64]

However, 'masculinity' is not all of a kind. The violent masculinity of the squaddie would not be acceptable in the officer. Connell argues that gender is central to the armed forces, and the state apparatus works to construct particular forms of masculinity and regulate relations between them, not as incidental, but as a vital precondition of them.[65] However, one needs to make distinctions between particular kinds of 'masculinity'. Homosexual men, for example, are despised and excluded because they represent a direct challenge to the dominant conception of what it is to be manly. According to Connell, the key to understanding how this gendered system functions and how different masculinities are linked together lies in understanding the gendered pattern of emotional attachment that exists amongst men.[66]

The exclusion of women from combat is not, then, a historical accident. It is necessary because women are a symbol of insufficient masculinity. If, as Enloe argues, combat is uniquely male, sharing this role with women would challenge the identity of the soldier as a masculine creature.[67] To allow women into the central core of the military – combat – would throw into confusion all men's certainties about their male identity and thus claims to privilege in the social order.[68] Enloe suggests that for these reasons the notion of liberation through participation must be seen as 'a cruel hoax'. It suffers a deep flaw in seeking to attain equal rights in a military system which remains unchanged. Some radical feminists go further, arguing that the military teaches men to kill the woman in them. The consequence would be a more militaristic and, almost by definition, a more sexist society.[69]

The argument for women's inclusion in combat roles has not just been made in terms of equal rights and a desire to secure for women a greater share of the economic and social benefits that accrue from participation. Stiehm has argued that in order to persuade men of the need to fulfil the protector role strong appeals are made to their sexual identity.[70] Therefore, when women do not challenge their exclusion from combat, they assist policy-makers to describe some behaviour as 'manly' and other behaviour as 'unmanly'. Stiehm argues that in so far as women's enlistment is permitted, not permitted or manipulated by male decision makers, women are being used by men to manipulate other men. The social and political order depends upon appeals to masculinity. This can only be achieved by differentiation from a female 'Other' who must be portrayed as inferior and subordinate, and, indeed, excluded. Paradoxically she is also highly valued. It would not be possible to reconcile these two contradictory images unless women were assigned a particular role which did not threaten male political control.

Stiehm also contends that women's entry in equal numbers and as full equals would change the military. It would not be infused with feminist values, but it would lose some of its coercive power.[71] Stiehm argues that women and men should share the risks and responsibilities as 'defenders', because in this way the asymmetrical relation between protector and protected, and the ideology of violence which this permits, will be broken down. Her argument is not addressed to pacifists. Nor does she claim that she is offering a solution to the problem of war. Rather she is proposing what she believes to be a better position for women. However, Stiehm also claims that women's direct participation might reduce the acts of violence carried out by the male military with an 'on-behalf-of mentality'.[72] This would not exist if all were defenders and all bore equal responsibility.

... and 'feminine' soldiers

Ironically, the view that the inclusion of women into combat roles would change the military as an institution is also held by conservatives who continue to resist any such development. The feminist conception of the military as a profoundly gendered institution helps us to understand, perhaps, why there has been so much resistance to women in combat roles. In a British context, Beevor has documented the profound unease that most military men feel about the participation of women in combat.[73] It would appear that it is not just the British military who express doubts about the desirability of the incorporation of women into combat roles. The resistance to women in combat roles has often been couched in terms of threats to military preparedness or on the grounds that they are in some way unsuited to the rigours of military life. It has also been argued that women are 'weaker' or in some way physically unsuited to the task of fighting, or unable to bear the harsh conditions of military life. It has been claimed that women are in some way incapacitated by childbirth, or even menstruation. When the physical-weakness argument is challenged, the argument that women's 'socialization' makes them unable to endure physical distress and discomfort is sometimes put forward as a reason for their continued exclusion.[74] The justification for excluding women from combat roles has also been legitimized on the grounds that they are instinctively unable to kill, although there is little or no evidence to support this contention. Women are, of course, capable of violent acts, though women in general perpetrate far fewer violent crimes than men. Women have also been shown to be prepared to take life in self-defence. Furthermore, reports have shown that a large number of male recruits cannot bring themselves to fire weapons even when under attack.[75] It has also been argued that men's 'natural' inclination to protect women will distract them from the task in hand of defeating the enemy; or that women will disrupt the male-bonding process vital in developing trust among comrades in the face of battle.[76]

Many of the examples of resistance to women in combat roles so far are drawn from the British and North American context.

However, a similar debate has opened up in other countries where the women's movement has gradually challenged the male exclusivity of the armed forces. Where women have entered the bastions of male privilege in militaries they have frequently found that the myth that military women need protection has made it easier for men to be persuaded of their 'protector' role, and this in itself has made it difficult for women to gain acceptance on the same terms as men.[77] According to Stiehm, this myth seems to be the most certain proof of the necessity of maintaining the all-male nature of warfare. It also means that it is always possible for the moves to incorporate women to be reversed at a later stage. In 1978 the British Women's Army Corps was disbanded amid moves to integrate women, but this process was later reversed because women were seen to disturb the male-bonding process.[78] The Israeli defence force's about-turn was even more marked. They found that the performance of men in battle deteriorated if women were with them and suggested that this was because the male soldiers' instinct was to protect women rather than fight the enemy.[79] It seems that even when admitted to the inner core of the military, women are either held to threaten the discipline and male-bonding process necessary for rapid mobilization or are deemed to be some kind of threat because they continue to represent competing values and loyalties.[80]

Enloe argues that so long as women can be represented as inherently or intrinsically non-combative, and so objects of protection, their labour can be mobilized by governments and strategists without fear that such mobilization will shake the social order in which 'women are symbols of the hearths and homes that the armed forces claim to be defending'.[81] Historically women have usually been omitted from armed service even at times of total war. In Britain during the Second World War, women were not allowed to join even the home guard, so strong was the ideology of the male defender of women and children and the antipathy to women bearing arms.[82] Where women have been admitted to the military in wartime, usually in response to manpower shortages, it has been in the face of strong resistance. The evidence repeatedly shows that such moves provoke great fears that war, by necessitating the mobilization of women on an unprecedented scale, might undermine the established male-dominant sex/gender system. Men frequently lamented the compulsory war service of women because of its more immediate threat to conjugal relations.

In Canada, for example, women were admitted to the military during the Second World War in response to manpower shortages and because there existed a reserve of 'women power' embodied in a Canada-wide paramilitary movement of women volunteers. Pierson has argued that the very entry of women into the armed forces sharply challenged conventional views of women's nature and place in Canadian society.[83] One of the least examined and most unshakeable notions of the time about women was that subordination and subservience to men were inherently female characteristics that dictated women's place in society. One source of disapproval was the fear that women would risk their femininity by joining up. Men had no desire to tamper with existing gender relations.

Nevertheless, Canada's mobilization of women for the war effort necessitated violating the social ideal of women dedicated to home and family. Women's participation in the military prompted some talk of emancipation, equality and overcoming tradition, but recruitment propaganda sought to minimize the degree of change required and often stressed the expectation of a return to 'normalcy' at the war's end. It seems that the armed forces could persuade a male recruit that it would 'make a man' of him, but had to convince the female recruit that it would not make her less of a woman. Enlistment slogans suggested that the function of women in the forces was to subserve the primary purposes of the armed forces, the provision of an armed fighting force. The prevailing view was that men were by nature adapted to danger and high-risk jobs, while women were naturally adapted to monotonous tasks. Thus the contradiction between the armed services' need for women in uniform and the ideology of women's place being in the home or a paid job so long as it was sex-typed was bridged through a redefinition of some jobs as 'womanly'.[84] Pierson argues that the outward expression of women's place in the system could be summed up by the term 'femininity' and that 'through dress, deportment, mannerisms, expression, "femininity" both signified and maintained women's difference from, deference towards and dependence on men and prevailing definitions of womanhood'.[85]

Feminist scholars have provided numerous historical and contemporary examples of how women are incorporated into the militaries without challenging the ideology of gender roles. For example in South Africa there were frequent injunctions to women not to allow their role in the SADF[86] to contaminate their femininity.[87] Women were encouraged to combine non-traditional jobs with their domestic responsibilities as wives and mothers; while in the Israeli army the role of women has been seen as primarily to raise the morale of men and make the army a 'home from home'.[88] This would suggest that while it might be thought that the linkages between masculinity and the military would be eroded by the increasing incorporation of women directly into the armed services, in reality their incorporation preserves the ideology of gender roles and that 'the definition of femininity is expanded rather than fundamentally reworked'.[89]

Sometimes women are explicitly told not to lose their 'femininity'. Beevor records that at Sandhurst women, like men, receive lessons on dress and behaviour, but for women this includes warnings against outspoken feminism which might 'provoke' men.[90] Women in the armed forces are frequently subjected to harassment and slander campaigns by being labelled as lesbians or whores. This is debilitating on a strategic level because it makes it harder to recruit women and to integrate them in an effective way.[91] Arguably, the importance of the 'maleness' of the combat role combined with the injunction to women to stay 'feminine' reinforces and perpetuates the socio-sexual order within militaries and reinforces the masculinity of military roles. The military is, of course, much more than those actively engaged in combat. The numbers officially employed in militaries are usually disproportionately engaged in administration or a variety of support services. It is usually the case that women in the armed services are heavily overrepresented in support roles. The ways in which women have been incorporated into the military suggest that it has been done in a way that does not challenge the view that the military is a predominantly male institution. As long as women continue to accept or fail to resist these narrow images and definitions of womanhood and manhood, they will not be able to challenge the gender ideology upon which the military is built.

Patriarchy and Violence

As a discipline born out of the experience of war, violence has been at the heart of the study of International Relations. However, most International Relations scholarship has concentrated not on the problem of violence as such, but rather on direct acts of violence by and between states which occurs when 'states in a situation of social conflict and opposed find that the pursuit of incompatible or exclusive goals cannot be confined to non-violent modes'.[92] That is, the study of violence in International Relations has been largely confined to the study of war as an instance of state-sanctioned violence.

Those working from within the assumptions of the orthodoxy, do not make gender an explicit part of their analysis of war. However, it is clear that there is a crucial linkage between the construction of masculinity, femininity and the making of war. Chapter 3, in part, touched on the way in which struggles to carve out a place and identity for the imagined community of the 'nation-state' involve practices which demarcate the boundary between 'insiders' and 'outsiders', 'citizens' and 'foreigners'. War is central to the process of carving out political spaces and identities. War has been understood in social and political terms, resulting from social conflict and intimately connected to constructions of national identities and the pursuit of 'national interests'. However, radical and psychoanalytic feminist thinkers have argued that this process of constructing identities and boundaries can be seen as but one manifestation of an underlying psychosexual drama in which masculinity is forged, affirmed and reaffirmed. In this view, therefore, if, as Clausewitz maintained,[93] war is the continuation of politics by other means, it has been constructed out of hostility towards the female 'other'.

Interestingly, as was suggested earlier, viewing war in social and political terms in itself served to break down the distinctions drawn between the battlefield and the domestic sphere.[94] However, a clear distinction between war and other forms of violence is still made by International Relations scholars because the construction of inter-national relations continues to rely upon a division between 'domestic' and 'international' realms, and upon a view of states as 'bounded communities' which share a common identity and a common interest in survival. Indeed, security has been understood largely in terms of the protection of national communities from the violence – actual or potential – of excluded 'others'.

The image of the state as 'protector' is particularly powerful in realism, although realists do not regard the gendered distinctions between the 'protected' and 'protectors' as interesting in themselves. However, the conventional distinction between 'protected' and 'protectors', has long been challenged by feminists. The reason for challenging this distinction is partly because it obscures the degree to which women are involved in war. Not only are women frequently participants in war, but ideologies about masculinity and femininity are necessary for the conduct of war.

However, the distinction between 'protectors' and 'protected' also disguises the particular ways women suffer in wars. Both internal conflicts and international wars cause displacement among civilian populations. As carers, the lives of women are greatly complicated. Women are often left with sole responsibility for the welfare of the elderly and disabled relatives as well as children. Women and children constitute on average 80 per cent of refugee populations, although the smaller percentage of male refugees frequently gets disproportionate access to food, clothes, land, jobs and legal identity papers, water, livestock and tools. Decision-making structures within refugee camps are also male-dominated which has important consequences for the protection, or lack of protection, for women against sexual and domestic violence in this context too.[95]

While most commentaries on war concentrate upon the political or strategic objectives, or the heroics of the battlefield, feminist researchers have strived to uncover the unknown testimonies of women who have suffered greatly in war but whose suffering is unrecorded. By listening to women's testimonies and post-war stories, feminists have also come to understand the 'unboundedness' of war – unbounded in the sense that wars have no neat beginnings and endings. Women who bear the burden of picking up the pieces at the formal cessation of hostilities have come to see that wars do not simply 'end' with the signing of peace treaties. Women are left to deal with the task of rebuilding the physical infrastructure, along with men, but also they must also cope with the terrible consequences. Women must deal with the aftermath of war; the physical, psychological and emotional damage which people suffer.

A feminist analysis of war thus emphasizes the connections between war as an instance of state-sanctioned violence and other forms of violence. Seeking a feminist understanding of violence in warfare, particularly war rape, 'pushes us back to the connections between proving manhood and nationhood, between masculinity, militarism and violence'.[96] It facilitates an understanding of why the 'core identity' of the military is necessarily male. Furthermore, as Stiehm argues, 'protectors usually control those whom they protect';[97] and, as Jan Pettman notes, 'the protector/protected relationship makes women vulnerable to other men's/states' violence'.[98]

Women are frequently the targets of sexual violence from the enemy in war. The availability of women after the battle was the traditional prize for Greek warriors. The idea that women are part of the 'spoils of war', according to some feminist thinkers, remains a part of the militaristic concept of the soldier's 'right to women'. Rape in warfare does not occur as an isolated incident. Feminists involved in the peace movement have long argued that rape should be viewed as an accepted part of the code that governs the fighting of wars rather than as an individual act of wrongdoing. Furthermore, some feminists have argued that in warfare it is always difficult to distinguish between rape and war prostitution.[99] However, rape and sexual violence against women in wartime is not only a crime perpetuated by 'the enemy'. The distinction between the protectors and protected has also been challenged by feminists because it obscures the connection between war and other forms of violence. The likelihood of women being subjected to rapes and beatings from their own men increases at times of heightened aggression.

Radical feminists claim that so long as the privileging of masculinity is inherent in the political system women will face the consequences, while at the same time being seen as part of the 'innocent', the 'weak' and the 'protected'. As such, 'war' for women will be inherent in the system. In this view, to continue to draw an absolute distinction between war and other forms of male violence without recognizing the linkages obscures the real problem, which is patriarchy. The links between domestic violence and war go deeper than soldiers, brutalized by their experiences, beating their wives. Rather, there is an intricate relationship between the construction of masculinity and patriotism and violence. War and domestic violence are, in a symbolic but still meaningful sense, linked.

Many radical feminist thinkers involved in the peace movement believe that the insights that arise from women's particular relation to violence mean that issues of war, peace and security can be approached from a feminist standpoint. That is, the particular experiences of women can be used as a point of departure from which to construct an understanding of violence that makes gender central to the explanation, not because of women's 'traditional roles' or 'essential biology', but because women stand in a relationship to violence which is unique among oppressed groups. Feminist peace activists claim that for women the 'oppressors' are found among immediate family or lovers, and that terror for women is the quiet pervasive ordinary terror which happens in the home.[100]

In this view, not only is war part of women's daily existence, but war, violence and women's oppression all grow from the same root. Military institutions and states are inseparable from patriarchy. War is not then, as realists and neo-realists would hold, rooted in the *nature* of 'man' or the anarchy of the international realm. However, the hegemony of a dominance-orientated masculinity sets the dynamics of the social relations in which all are forced to participate. Some feminists argue that patriarchal societies have an inherent proclivity towards war because of the supreme value placed on control and the natural male tendency towards displays of physical force.[101] Though primarily concerned with the *discourse* of war, politics and citizenship, Hartsock argues that the association of power with masculinity and virility has very real consequences. She argues that 'it gives rise to a view of community both in theory and in fact obsessed with the revenge and structured by conquest and domination'.[102] Furthermore, according to Hartsock, the opposition of man to woman and perhaps even man to man is not simply a transitory opposition of arbitrary interests, but an opposition resting on a deep-going threat to existence. She argues that we re-encounter in the context of gender, as in class, the fact that the experience of the ruling group, or gender, cannot be simply dismissed as false.[103] This raises the question of how we conceptualize and understand not only the 'patriarchal state', but also the relationship between the patriarchal nation-state requiring in the context of competitive struggle with other states militarism and internal hierarchy.[104]

If liberal feminists are correct in their view of the state as a 'neutral arbiter', rather than a patriarchal power, and if women's inequality is largely a consequence of bias, it is possible that attitudes towards women in the military would change over time as women proved themselves, just as they have in other spheres from which they were once excluded. However, for many feminists the proper question to ask is not how women's status can be furthered by participation in the military, but how women and other 'outsiders' might focus their opposition to military institutions and strengthen institutions to build peace-orientated communities. As Stiehm acknowledges, even if women were to participate in combat roles, and were accepted, it would not solve the problem of their relation to other states' 'protectors' and 'protected', a relationship which feminists should be concerned to problematize. It seems that, while recognition of the close linkages between citizenship and participation in combat is an obvious starting point for feminists in their quest for gender equality, it may be that 'NOW's brand of equal opportunity or integrationist feminism' could merely function to 'reinforce the military as an institution and militarism as an ideology by perpetuating the notion that the military is central to the entire social order' and thereby perpetuate a gendered order which damages both women and men.[105] Human survival may depend upon breaking the linkage between masculinity, military capacity and death. It is for feminists and others committed to peace to provide new thinking about the nature of politics, to redefine 'political community' and our ideas of 'citizenship' and, in so doing, confront the 'barracks community' directly with its 'fear of the feminine'.[106] Feminist challenges to dominant conceptions of citizenship, political community and security and feminist 'revisions' are the subject of chapter 5.

Feminist Perspectives on Security

In the concluding section of chapter 4, it was suggested that, while feminists disagree about whether the state is inherently patriarchal or a site where patriarchy is both constructed and contested, they agree that the military is an integral part of the institutions and practices of the state. Violence should not, therefore, be viewed as a specific and limited act, but as part of a complex which involves institutions and the way they are organized. A feminist analysis of the military and the patriarchal state raises questions about the validity of continuing to view the state as the mainstay of security and of assuming that security for the individual is adequately understood in terms of her or his membership of a given national community. This is because adopting a feminist perspective challenges the view of the military as a defender of a pregiven 'national interest'.

Feminist approaches also offer radical new ways of thinking about the problems involved in achieving security. As was suggested in the introduction to this book, the orientation of feminist critical theories towards emancipatory politics and the postmodern feminist celebration of different expressions of identity and solidarity has encouraged a radical rethinking of dominant conceptions of identities and boundaries in which traditional approaches to security have been framed. Furthermore, feminist analysis of the military and the state raises questions about the validity of continuing to view the state as the mainstay of security – an approach which assumes that security for the individual is adequately understood purely in terms of his or her membership of a given national community. Adopting a feminist perspective not only challenges the view of the military as a defender of a pregiven 'national interest', it also demonstrates that the degree to which people feel or actually are 'threatened' varies according to their economic, political, social or personal circumstances. Thus, poverty, inequality, militarism, mal-development and the denial of human rights or at least basic needs are relevant to understanding how secure or insecure people feel or actually are, in terms of their race, ethnic identity, political status, class and, of course, gender.

This chapter is divided into three main sections. The first section outlines briefly how realists and neo-realists have understood the nature of security. It then draws upon a number of critical perspectives to build a critique of the *discourse* of state security which constructs a hostile 'Other' to legitimate state power. The second section turns to feminist critiques of dominant conceptions of national security. It begins by suggesting that there are a number of distinctive ways in which feminists have challenged the idea that the nation-state is the fundamental referent of security – first, by assessing the impact on women of military expenditure justified in the name of national security; and secondly, by analysing the gendered power structures, social institutions and values that underpin the 'national security state'. This section of the chapter includes, therefore, an extended discussion of feminist critiques of militarism. Militarism is relevant to any discussion of security because militarism is both rooted in and fosters a refusal to recognize the humanity of others. Rethinking security means recognizing the common humanity and worth of all human beings. The section concludes with a discussion of alternative conceptions of political community. The third section concludes the chapter with a discussion of new approaches to thinking about security which do not centre on the state and the citizen. Here the affinities between feminist approaches to security and both human-rights and 'people-centred' schools of thought are explored.

The State and 'National Security'

Realist and neo-realist approaches

Despite the central importance of security in International Relations, scholars have found the concept difficult to define. Like so many of the central concepts used in the study of International Relations, 'security' is essentially contested. A broad definition of security might be 'a state of being secure, safe, free from danger, injury, harm of any sort',[1] but few International Relations scholars would accept such a pervasive definition. Indeed, many would argue that such a state of being is neither possible nor desirable, pointing out that an element of danger will always be part of human existence.[2] In practice in International Relations, realist and, latterly, neo-realist, assumptions and perspectives have dominated debates about security. Security has been seen in terms of the overriding need to ensure the survival of human collectivities called nation-states.[3] Security has, therefore, been defined as a guarantee of safety which necessitates 'political arrangements which make war less likely, provide for negotiation rather than belligerence and which preserve peace as a normal condition among states'.[4] In traditional realist thought state security was thought to depend ultimately upon military power, because 'national security' denoted 'all purposes of defence, in effect the preparation for belligerence in order to defer or deflect it'.[5] Indeed, power was seen as the essence of security in times of intense conflict.

As was argued in chapter 3, realists and neo-realists tend rather to take it for granted that the nation state is the primary source of identity and allegiance for individuals and there is a strong sense in realist writings that national security issues, particularly in times of war, offer a sense of shared political purpose. As Tickner argues, it is, perhaps, for this reason that military budgets are least likely to be cut and contested by politicians of all ilks.[6] Most realists would no doubt concur with the view that the rights and privileges of citizenship have historically been tied to an obligation to defend the state. Certainly, from a realist perspective, it is for 'national security' that citizens are willing to make sacrifices. Realists and neo-realists would no doubt support the conservative view that whatever the shortcomings of the nation-state, it is the best form of political community that human beings have devised in the modern age. From this perspective, then, the nation-state is also of moral worth.

Realists and neo-realists usually define peace in negative terms. That is, peace is seen as an absence of war. In classical realist thought, peace and security were seen to be achieved by shifting alliances which preserved a balance of power among states. Since states were seen to be operating in an essentially 'anarchic' international political system, in the final analysis state survival and international order could only be secured through a stable balance of power.[7] Some neo-realists have argued that hegemonic states dominate international institutions and, in this way, 'manage' international security. Neo-realists understand that the security order is ultimately built upon and reflects the realities of power in the international system, although, as Barry Buzan has argued, in a 'mature anarchy'[8] states, secure within themselves might recognize and uphold international norms of behaviour and this strengthens international security.

From a realist or neo-realist perspective, the state is the mainstay of security. The state provides for the security of the individual by virtue of her or his membership of the national community. The security of the individual is thus 'inseparably entangled with that of the state'.[9] Therefore, from this perspective, individuals are not the appropriate starting point for thinking about security, because most threats to individuals arise from societal issues and the principal role of the state is to protect and preserve the social order and protect individuals from 'the invasion of foreigners and injuries to one another'.[10] Realists have also recognized a degree of interdependence between states, arising from historical associations or geographical proximity. Interdependence can give rise to 'security complexes' or 'security subsystems'[11] in which the security of one state is closely, inextricably even, linked with the security of other states. Realist and neo-realist thinking about security, therefore, involves a fairly sophisticated analysis of the connections between the individual, the state, the region and the global. However, the nation-state is the central linkage in this chain of security.

While International Relations scholars recognize the many dimensions of security, realists are generally sceptical about efforts to achieve security through disarmament, development and respect for human rights. It is perhaps, from a realist point of view, a laudable but ultimately utopian aspiration. Similarly, realists recognize that attempts to achieve military security by building up levels of armaments can fuel the fears and suspicions of neighbouring states and so encourage a 'spiral of international insecurity'.[12] Realists and neo-realists have also recognized that military strength incurs costs to society and that these might not be distributed equally among individuals or social groups. Furthermore, realists and neo-realists also acknowledge that the state may in some circumstances constitute a threat to the people living within its sovereign jurisdiction. Buzan, for example, has argued that the 'maximal state' might oppress its citizens, while the 'minimal state' might be weak and fail to resolve disputes between citizens and so fail in its duty to protect and uphold societal order.[13] However, realists argue that ultimately the problem of security is rooted in man's aggressive nature, or in the 'anarchy' of the international realm.[14]

Critiquing the orthodoxy

Recent critical interventions in International Relations and the openness of current theoretical debates have combined with the changed political circumstances of the post-Cold-War world to encourage a radical rethinking of approaches to security. As was noted earlier, alternative approaches to security had been advanced by International Relations scholars long before the so-called 'third debate' alluded to in chapter 1. Furthermore, in the Cold-War context, when the discourse of security was heavily coloured by the ideological conflict between the 'superpowers', most military conflicts took place in the Third World. Furthermore, increasingly it is difficult to distinguish clearly between 'domestic' and 'international' conflicts. For these reasons, too, a number of commentators have called for approaches to understanding conflict which are not subject to the limitations of state centric analysis.

Critical approaches to International Relations criticize the state centrism of realism, not only because it is inherently reductionist, but also because it presents a view of the state as a concrete entity with interests and agency. Not only does the state *act*, but the state acts in the *national interest*. Those who adopt critical approaches view the state in dynamic rather than static terms,[15] as a 'process' rather than a 'thing'. The 'state' does not exist in any concrete sense; rather it is 'made'. The state is made by the processes and practices involved in constructing boundaries and identities, differentiating between the 'inside' and the 'outside'. Andrew Linklater has recently argued that critical approaches to the study of International Relations centre around understanding the processes of 'inclusion' and 'exclusion', which have in a sense always been the central concerns of the discipline.[16] However, as Linklater contends, critical theorists understand that these processes have also worked to 'include' and 'exclude' people on the basis of race, class and gender.[17] In the 'making' of the state the construction of the hostile 'other' which is threatening and dangerous is central to the making of identities and the securing of boundaries. Indeed, David Campbell argues that the legitimation of state power demands the construction of danger 'outside'. The state requires this 'discourse of danger' to secure its identity and for the legitimation of state power. The consequence of this is that threats to security in realist and neo-realist thinking are all seen to be in the external realm and citizenship becomes synonymous with loyalty to the nation-state and the elimination of all that is foreign.[18] Jean Elshtain has argued that the problems of war and the difficulties of achieving security in the so-called 'anarchy' of the international realm, should not be seen as problems which are not rooted in the compulsions of interstate relations as such.[19] Rather, they arise from 'the ordering of modern, technological society' in which political elites have sought to control the masses by the implementation of 'the mechanism of the perfect army'.[20] Elshtain argues that to see war as a continuation of politics by other means, is to see a continuation of the 'military model' as a means of preventing civil disorder.[21]

In critiquing dominant conceptions of security in International Relations, feminists have, to some extent, echoed the arguments of non-feminist critical thinkers, but have been concerned to show what is lost from our understanding of security when gender is omitted. As was noted in chapter 4, feminist political theorists have demonstrated that in much Western political thought the conception of politics and the public realm is a 'barracks community', a realm defined in opposition to the disorderly forces which threaten its existence.[22] This same conception of politics is constructed out of masculine hostility towards the female 'Other'. One sees in the development of this political discourse a deeply gendered subtext in which the citizen role is in all cases identified with the male.[23] Hartsock believes that this sets a hostile and combative dualism at the heart of the community men construct and by which they come to understand their lives.[24]

Furthermore, as Ann Tickner has argued, the provision of national security has been and continues to be an almost exclusively male domain.[25] As was discussed at length in chapter 4, some feminists have argued that women should serve in combat roles in the armed services because this would give women a stake in national security. However, the liberal 'right to fight' campaign has been criticized because it advocates the politics of access while accepting uncritically a profoundly gendered conception of security which legitimizes state violence. They have also failed to address the degree to which the military plays a central role in justifying a social order and value system which, in the name of 'national security', privileges men and masculine values. Rather than argue for the 'right to fight', therefore, many feminists have argued that the cause would be better served by challenging militarized conceptions of security and offering alternative visions.

National Security/Women's Security

An 'impact-on' approach

Frequently, the starting point for this feminist rethinking of security is a critique of militarized notions of 'national security'. However, this critique has many distinctive strands. One of these 'strands' is an 'impact-on' approach. Some feminist economists have been concerned to demonstrate that military expenditure imposes particular costs on women as a group. Since one of the most prominent feminist strategies has been to push women towards equal economic opportunities, access to jobs, equal wages, similar career possibilities and equal economic protection in the form of pensions, unemployment insurance and so on, it is pertinent to ask *what impact does military expenditure have on women in all of these areas?*

During the 1980s, at the height of the second Cold War, perceptions of 'threat' from the hostile communist 'Other' dominated national security debates, and billions of dollars were poured into the United States military. In the United States of America between 1980 and 1985, increased military spending had a big impact on welfare and social spending as domestic social programmes, which provide support to low-income families, were drastically cut. In the 1980s in the US, the feminization of poverty became a significant phenomenon with 34.6 per cent of all women-headed households falling into the official category of 'poor'.[26] This figure increased to 50 per cent among black and Hispanic women-headed families.[27] In 1984 there were approximately 200,000 women in the US military involved in active duty forces. In 1985 42 per cent of all enlisted women were black. That is four times the proportion of all American women.[28] It is clear that women who joined up did so because they saw it as a way of improving their social position and benefiting from the economic rewards attached to military service. However, feminists have argued that the statistical evidence could be read in a completely different light. It could well be that the militarization of American society was, on the one hand, opening up new opportunities for women to enter the military but, on the other hand, was increasing the vulnerability of precisely those women who were precariously positioned in the economic system.

Feminist scholars have been concerned to show how women as, for example, low-paid workers and single mothers are less likely than working-class men to derive benefit from increased military spending. Outside of the number of people directly employed by the military, military expenditure has an impact on the number of people hired to work in factories which produce military hardware. Military expenditure also has an impact on the amount of resources diverted from other areas of the economy since, some economists have argued, expenditure on weapons does not have the same 'multiplier'[29] effect or transmit economic growth to other areas of economy in the way that expenditure on other goods does. The renewed arms race in the early 1980s also exacerbated the economic insecurity of women.[30] Even where women found employment in the 'military industrial complex' they were frequently paid less and had less job security.[31]

At that time, military spending constituted a large and growing component of both the US and the world economy. Feminists were quick to point out the costs, not only to American women, but to women across the world. Feminist economists argued that increased expenditure on the military, either directly or indirectly, was defeating the aims of the wider feminist movement to improve the status and position, health, welfare and security of women as a group. Beyond the United States, it was even more evident that high spending on militaries, arms and military research was a gender issue. At an international level, rising military expenditures put countries under severe strain. The Worldwatch Institute reported that in 1984 the global trade in arms exceeded the trade in grain for the first time.[32] In 1985, $980 billion was spent on arms worldwide; a figure that was more than the combined incomes of the world's poor.[33] The higher the levels of military expenditure worldwide, the less resources were spent on food and welfare. Feminist economists argued that this illustrated the need for a broader social analysis of the effects of military expenditure on women as a whole.

Feminists also argued that the transfer of resources from the military to the civilian sector of the economy would in all countries reap social and economic benefits for all people, but especially women. Resources devoted to arms expenditure could be spent on health, education, development, and in this way the most vulnerable people would derive immediate benefits. For example, the amount of resources devoted to the research and development of weaponry, all in the name of national security, also strongly affected the overall pattern of scientific research. It was argued that women's health needs in particular would be better served by biological and scientific research concerned with the development of nutritional supplements and safe methods of family planning than on armaments. Furthermore, the massive use of resources and capital to fund the military depleted the resources available to support social, medical and education spending.[34]

Gender and militarism

While this form of 'impact-on' analysis has proved useful in placing the impact of military expenditure in a broad social context, rather than thinking about it simply within the narrow confines of 'national security', some commentators have argued that it rather takes for granted the idea that men are the natural actors.[35] That is, women are only considered in so far as military expenditure has specific effects on them as a group. As such, it fails to address the ideological and social processes at work in supporting and justifying high levels of military expenditure. It could be argued that the 'impact-on' approach is a necessary but not sufficient basis of analysis.[36] What is needed is a feminist analysis of militarization or militarism. However, as Enloe concedes, militarism poses a special problem for feminist analysis, because it has wide-ranging effects on many different groups and so evokes various explanations.[37]

Before outlining the basic ideas underpinning both feminist and non-feminist analysis of militarism, it is necessary to define the term. This in turn involves distinguishing between the military as a social institution and a set of social relationships organized around war and preparation for war. Militarism can be defined as an ideology which values war highly and, in so doing, serves to legitimize state violence. Alternatively, militarism can be viewed as a social process which involves the mobilization for war through the penetration of the military, its power and influence, into more and more social arenas.[38] Militarism can be defined as the subordination of the civil society to military values and the subordination of civilian control of the military to military control of civilians.[39] Militarism is frequently associated with so-called 'unstable' Third World states where the military either forms the government or has enormous influence over civilian government. However, during the Cold War a great deal of analysis drew attention to the degree to which militarism was a characteristic of both 'advanced' communist states and Western capitalist states.[40] Furthermore, as Enloe points out, militarization occurs during periods of war and peace. Militarization occurs when any part of society becomes controlled by or dependent upon the military or military values. In this way virtually anything can become militarized, toys – marriage, scientific research, university curricula, motherhood.[41]

Non-feminist analysis of militarism can be broadly divided into two distinctive approaches. One sees militarism as a product of capitalism. The second suggests that militarism is a consequence of, or caused by, the inherent inclinations of the state regardless of the economic system. The first approach rests on the underlying conviction that capitalism is the moving force behind the military's expanding influence. Government officials may be motivated by a desire to enhance the status, resources and authority of the military but, ultimately, this is in order to protect the interests of private capitalist enterprises at home and abroad. At the root of militarism, therefore, are major business interests. In this view, an increasing number of workers in all affected countries become dependent on military spending for their own livelihoods. In contrast, according to statist approaches to militarism, state elites rule by coercion and threat and have always engaged in vast military enterprises.[42] In more recent times, however, technological changes have given rise to the growth of militarism as a social phenomenon, as the influence of the military has spread to more and more social institutions. It is not 'capitalists elites', but the existence of a number of large interest groups and statist bureaucracies that encourage the growth of militarism. The strength of statist approaches, which place the emphasis on the characteristics of state bureaucracies, lies in their ability to explain parallel developments in countries with very different political and economic systems.[43]

Enloe points out that for a distinctly feminist analysis of militarism to be persuasive it must demonstrate that both capitalism-centred and statist explanations are inadequate or misleading. It is necessary to demonstrate how militarism as a social process depends upon patriarchy and simultaneously promotes and sustains military values. What is distinctive about feminist theorizing about militarism is that it posits gender – that is, the social construction of masculinity and femininity – as a critical factor in the construction and perpetuation of militarism and therefore the possible reversal of the process. Feminists have argued that it is not capitalism, nor the state alone, but masculinity that links the military and industry. Male employees in weapons factories may work against their own class interests because they perceive themselves as doing important 'men's work'. The patriarchal assumption that they really are doing men's work then reinforces the militarization and the hegemony of the 'military industrial complex' in ways that may be crucial for the maintenance of such a militarizing alliance.[44]

Connell has argued that the structure of gender power works to privilege men at the expense of women in general. He has identified a 'core' to gender power. This core has four components. First, the hierarchies that work through the forces of institutionalized violence, found in the military, the police forces and prison services, which Connell calls the coercive arms of state power. As feminists have long pointed out, one of the most striking characteristics of militaries is that they are almost exclusively male. This is a result of quite self-conscious political policies which suggests that state officials create an explicit link between the presumed properties of maleness and the institutional needs of the military.[45] Foot soldiers, who are often drawn from a relatively powerless strata of society, are bound together by alleged common bonds of masculinity to reduce all too obvious class and ethnic tensions. The social construction of masculinity is the key to understanding this process.[46]

Second, Connell points to the hierarchy of the labour force in heavy industry and the hierarchy of high-technology industry; third, to the planning and control of the machinery of the central state; and, fourth, to the working-class milieux that emphasize physical toughness and men's association with machinery. Connell argues that the first, second and third components of the 'core' are connected through the military industrial complex, from which women are largely excluded. They are tied together through the ideology of masculinity, authority and technological violence. However, Connell argues that the connection with the fourth component is the crucial link in understanding the sexual politics of the whole, because it is this connection that gives a mass base to militarist beliefs and practices.[47]

Analysis which makes gender a central factor in understanding militarism is particularly powerful, because it can explain how militarism takes root in different societies. There may be disagreements over how integral militarism is to masculinity, but the importance of the construction of 'masculinity' and conceptual distinctiveness from 'femininity' in understanding how militarism works can scarcely be denied. Enloe argues that whether tracing militarization or demilitarization as social processes, one must chart how women and men in any particular historical setting comprehend what it means to be 'manly' and what it means to be 'womanly'. Government and military officials are affected by their own perceptions of 'manliness' and 'femininity' and design policies to ensure that civilians and soldiers relate to one another in gendered ways that ease the complicated process of militarization.[48]

So far the discussion has concentrated largely on the importance of understanding how ideas about masculinity foster and support militarism. However, a gender analysis has to understand not about masculinity or femininity as such, but rather the *relation* between the two. Women contribute to the militarization of society in both material and ideological terms. Women play a vital role in encouraging men to 'act like men'. Women have been incorporated into war in many roles: as a pretext for war, as wives and prostitutes who provide for warriors, as entertainers, as victims, as sympathetic nurses, spies or castrating bitches.[49] But in all these many and varied roles the incorporation of women has served to reinforce the masculinity of war and justify militarism. Indeed, feminist opposition to the incorporation of women into the military has centred around the argument that integrating women will have the effect of increasing the militarization of society as a whole and so undermine the work of peace movements and women's movements. If masculinity is the central linkage in the militarization process, women will either be relegated to certain subordinate positions in the military or be encouraged to 'kill the woman in them' just as the male soldier is schooled in misogyny to 'kill the woman in him'.[50] The result will be to reaffirm the inferiority of women and women's experience, destroy the feminist tradition of non-violence and increase the militarization of society as a whole.[51]

Furthermore, feminist analysis suggests that what is needed is a fundamental rethink of our whole approach to understanding security. In this process, we need to understand the link between militarism and other forms of domination, including sexism. Radical feminists argue that both militarism and sexism are maintained by a world-view which suggests that men are by nature aggressive and that the social order must be maintained by force. Sexism and militarism need each other. There is a central link between the 'ideal soldier' and the 'ideal wife and mother'; both take orders unquestioningly from men who have power and status and both are expected to sacrifice themselves for those more important.[52] Furthermore, just as sexism is a belief system rooted in a world-view which assigns varying levels of worth to different human beings, militarism is based upon xenophobia and the denial of the full humanity of other peoples. Militarism establishes itself in the lives of citizens as a refusal to recognize the humanity of others, just as the soldier refuses to recognize the humanity of 'alien' peoples.[53] Radical feminists have also argued that there is a link between sexism and other forms of male violence. For this reason, as was noted in chapter 4, feminists have been reluctant to accept the dominant view of war as a discrete phenomenon arranged by diplomats with neat beginnings and endings.

One needs to understand how aggression and violence are related to a cultural emphasis on masculinity and how this relates to other major divisions like race and class. This is a first necessary stage in understanding what kind of social structures can be built which work towards resolving conflicts without violence. The antimilitarist activist has to enlist the struggles against wife abuse because challenging legitimized oppression in personal relations is the most 'theoretically efficient' way to end militarism.[54] The feminist analysis of the causes and consequences of militarization begins with an understanding that it is not simply synonymous with war; nor is it solely the antithesis of peace. Enloe argues that it is only when militarism and war are viewed as processes rather than 'events' that the connections between war, militarism and other processes examined by feminists – such as oppression, colonization, the division of labour, reproduction and liberation – can be understood.[55]

Similarly, it is only when these connections are fully understood that the process of rethinking security in ways that recognize the common humanity and worth of all human beings can begin, and only then will the many ways in which human beings experience violence, oppression and threats to their security be fully understood. Such experiences are, of course, structured not only by gender but also by other social relations such as race and class. As Enloe argues, the very breadth and depth makes it difficult to develop an unambiguously feminist analysis of militarism.[56] However, even if it were not possible to argue conclusively that the social construction of gender is the main *determinant* of militarism, feminist analysis demonstrates that ideas about gender and gender inequality are integral to the way in which militarism works. When an analysis of militarism is combined with the insights derived from the rather less ambitious 'impact-on' approach, it suggests that women as a group might have the most to gain by challenging the forces, processes and ideological beliefs that contribute towards militarism, sexism and xenophobia, and by working to change the discourse of security. To change the discourse is to resist the notion of politics as domination, to problematize violence, to encourage scepticism towards 'the forms and claims of sovereign states'.[57] To challenge the discourse of national security is to 'recognise the powerful sway of received narratives'.[58] That is, argues Elshtain, to recognize that the concepts through which we think about security, war, peace and politics get repeated endlessly, shaping debates, constraining the consideration of alternatives, often reassuring us that things cannot really be different.[59] As such the received narratives of the orthodoxy, 'put our critical faculties to sleep, blinding us to the possibilities that lie within our reach'.[60]

This, however, raises the question of whether there are particular experiences common to women, as a group, which might serve as the point of departure in rethinking security Many feminists, while sceptical of the degree to which values can be seen as essentially male or female, have nevertheless argued that the values of caring and nurturing are symbolically, if problematically, linked to women. Furthermore, while there may be no evidence to support the view that men are *essentially* aggressive and women *naturally* peaceful, there may be good reasons to think that women's particular relationship to the state and the exercise of state-sanctioned violence can serve as a point of departure from which to radically rethink our approach to these areas. As such these values can serve as the basis of a feminist 'standpoint' which challenges the Western narrative of war, politics and militarized conceptions of security: to undermine the 'received narrative' of state security and move feminist discourse to 'centre stage rather than being relegated to the periphery in this alternative story'.[61]

Changing the discourse

If war has historically been associated with men and masculinity, so peace has long historical associations with women and the 'feminine'. Some feminists have argued that women are naturally more peaceful than men. For example, the early suffragettes used the idea of biological difference as an argument in favour of women's suffrage. They argued that women's maternal urges made them different from men, and that women's peacefulness was evidence of moral superiority rather than inferiority.[62] Women peace activists sometimes claim a 'natural' peacefulness on the part of women. Others, while rejecting biological or essentialist accounts of apparent gender differences, have noted the close association with peace and the 'feminine' and have argued that the experience of maternity on the part of the vast majority of women and women's historical exclusion from public power means that women do have a special relationship to peace. This idea has found echoes in the calls by 'moral feminists' in the 1980s and 1990s for the inclusion of women into government elites because the inclusion of women would change the foreign policy of states.[63]

Certainly there is a long history of women's active involvement in peace movements. The Women's International League for Peace and Freedom, a pacifist organization, was founded during the women's peace congress at The Hague in 1915, by feminists from many countries. The League aimed to bring together women of all races, nationalities and social classes to work for disarmament and the abolition of violence as a means of resolving disputes. Members believed that by helping to bring about non-violent social transformation they would also help to bring about social, economic and political equality for all people. Women also act as peacemakers. For example, Nobel Peace Prize winners Betty Williams and Mairead Corrigan were motivated to protest for peace when three small children were killed and the mother seriously injured in Northern Ireland in August 1975.[64] This initiative eventually mushroomed into marches supported by over 100,000 people as the local community 'began to imagine a different way of solving conflict'.[65]

As the discussion in chapter 3 suggested, women's political activities are often closely associated with the domain of their everyday realities. The political actions of 'ordinary women' are often exerted towards 'their life-affirming concerns for the safety of their families and the sustenance of their communities'.[66] Women's anti-war demonstrations typically involve bringing private pain into the public realm. In demonstrations outside Greenham Common in the 1980s, for example, women wove ribbons of life, including photographs of children, and messages around the 'camp of death'.

The association between women and peace has been criticized by some liberal feminists who argue that this association serves to reinforce the stereotype of women as incapable of functioning in the public realm and that this in turn taints obligations of family and childcare as uniquely women's work. Chapkis contends that such essentialist arguments about masculinity and femininity are limited as a basis for organizing opposition to militarism, but also dangerously counter-productive and personally self-defeating.[67] A number of feminist thinkers have criticized the idea that women are specially privileged or situated because they are products of 'women's culture' or 'way of knowing'. Micaela di Leonardo has argued that any reinvigorated image of women as more peaceful will have disastrous consequences for the women's movement.[68] Indeed, Janet Radcliffe Richards has expressed deep concern with the position that women are either by nature or socialization more peaceful than men, because this plays into the hands of those who would keep men and women in separate spheres and limit women's equality.[69] She points out that male chauvinists have always used the idea of 'difference' to discriminate against women. As was discussed at length in chapter 4, many liberal feminists have suggested that the historic women–peace connection should be refused by feminists because it does not help defenceless women.

However, as Dinnerstein has argued, equality and equal rights have never been the sole focus of feminism. Feminist discourse has also emphasized human connectedness, dialogue and cooperation over dominance and violent confrontation.[70] In this view, feminism means mobilizing the wisdom and skills with which female history has equipped women and focusing them to change the world. Dinnerstein argues that equal-rights goals matter because they are to do with psychic growth.[71] Furthermore, women are in fact constantly forced in practice to rediscover the necessity of speaking for peace because they are not represented in places where decisions about war are taken.[72] Therefore, if women do not speak for peace they will be excluded from speaking on all aspects of life and death questions that face the species.[73] Sometimes this leads to the conscious and subversive use of women's traditional place as mother and 'Other', but at the same time demonstrates that women are refusing to stay in their place on the margins. In this way, by taking a more powerful place in the political arena, feminist peace activists are changing the terms in which public discourse is conducted.[74]

Feminist thinking about peace is not necessarily locked into the war–peace dichotomy. Because feminists, generally, start from the conditions of women's lives, and because they see many forms of violence, unhappiness and distress, they define peace as women's achievement of control over their lives. Similarly, non-violence is not just about the absence of war, but a total approach to living, a strategy for change.[75] When wars end it is women who relinquish their freedom. It is women who are expected to repair the damage done to their militarized sons, husbands and lovers. Peace, therefore, is also seen as a process which must reproduce itself.[76] At Greenham Common women learnt how to protest effectively and assertively by confronting the police and military, but at the same time their action was deliberately non-violent. Women also tried to work in supportive ways, sharing tasks, skills and knowledge.[77]

Women drew upon a diverse range of views among the women in the camp as a source of strength and respect, rather than conflict, regarding this way of living and working as a part of 'women's culture and practice'[78] and, as such, a first step in defeating the 'warring patriarchy'.[79] As Enloe notes, women's peace movements in general deliberately avoid forms of organization which are top-down relationships and try to maximize women's ordinary lives, because they see the qualities of equality, spontaneity and connection as the opposites of patriarchy and militarism. Some feminists were unhappy about the female-only peace camps, such as Greenham Common, but women who took part expressed the need to withdraw from what they perceived as a patriarchal system that perpetuated militarism, because it could not be sustained without women's cooperation.[80]

Some feminist thinkers have argued that while not intrinsically feminine, historically the obligation to care threads through women's lives because women have historically performed the mothering role. There is a long history of feminist thinking about war, peace and politics which starts out from the *standpoint* of women's distinctive social experiences. This is associated particularly with the work of Nancy Chodorow,[81] Dorothy Dinnerstein[82] and Carol Gilligan.[83] Carol Gilligan posits that women's experiences, particularly the performance of the mothering role, make women less conflictual and less conflict-orientated. Furthermore, women's psycho-socialization leads them to adopt a moral code which is different from, though not inferior to, the moral code adopted by men. Whereas men are socialized to adopt an ethic of justice or an ethic of rights based on abstract concepts of autonomy and rationality, women adopt an ethic of care or an ethic of responsibility[84] – a mode of reasoning which arises out of attention to concrete particulars, to the specific needs of the concrete, rather than generalized, 'Other'.

A number of feminist thinkers have drawn upon the work of Gilligan to argue that an ethic of responsibility or care provides the basis for women's more peaceful nature. Sara Ruddick's work, perhaps, best exemplifies this school of thought.[85] Ruddick has argued that maternal practices give rise to a preservative love and that when maternal thinking takes upon itself the critical perspective of a feminist standpoint it reveals the contradiction between mothering, war and militarism.[86] According to Gilligan, militarism and caring give rise to different concepts of control. In a sense, both are relationships of power and powerlessness, but whereas the military strive to be superior, in practice most mothers discipline themselves to non-violent strategies. This is not because women are inherently better people, but because they are engaged in a different project. Militarism wishes to create vulnerabilities, while mothers care for human beings who are already vulnerable.

The discourse of security may be changed through a fundamental challenge to dominant conceptions of political community and the ideals of citizenship. Gilligan argues that while the state is not a mother and citizens are not children, nevertheless the ideals of reciprocity inherent in the ethics of care can be used to forge political relationships of mutuality and respect in the midst of particularities, and in so doing provide a fundamentally different conception of community and citizenship.[87]

Rethinking Security

Human-rights approaches

Many liberals take the *individual* as a bearer of *rights* as the fundamental referent of security. Liberals believe that, irrespective of race, gender, class, religion, ethnicity or nationality, human beings have basic *human rights*. Liberals often argue that we cannot achieve truly comprehensive and global security, either in theory or in practice, unless we recognize that security is fundamentally a question of human rights. Indeed in a global age when the nation-state as the basic form of political community is subject to multiple challenges, human rights remains the most fruitful way of approaching security.

States are obliged to uphold and advance human rights. These obligations arise from the UN Charter; notably the provisions of the conventions on civil and political rights and economic and social rights. Liberals believe that all people have a basic right to life, liberty and the pursuit of happiness and so maintain that civil and political rights should also be viewed as basic human rights. Many liberals, though by no means all, would support the view that all human beings need economic and social security and so these things should be recognized as fundamental human rights too. However, while virtually every state in the world has accepted that people do have human rights in principle, just which categories of 'rights' should be recognized as 'human rights' has been the subject of intense political, ideological and, more recently, religious and cultural conflict.

The concept of human rights as a foundation for peace and security has long influenced internationalist and humanitarian approaches to international relations. Article 1 of the United Nations Charter stresses the need to promote respect for human rights. Liberal feminists too have stressed the importance of not only civil and political rights, but also economic and social rights in achieving security, and have argued that women's human rights must be recognized as central to achieving genuine security. Article 1.3 of the UN Charter pledges states to promote human rights without respect to race, ethnicity or sex. In more recent years there have been more systematic attempts to codify the human rights of women. For example, the Declaration on the Elimination of Violence Against Women, and the 1993 World Conference on Human Rights, both recognized gender-based violence in both public and private spheres as a violation of human rights. Many conventions of CEDAW, the Convention on the Elimination of Discrimination against Women, adopted by the UN General Assembly on 18 December 1995 and the Convention on Rights of the Child have implications for the recognition in international law of women's human rights. The preamble to the CEDAW convention notes that 'despite various instruments extensive discrimination against women still exists', while article 16 addresses women's role in the family. Previously the family has been taken as the basic unit in human rights conventions. Arguably the most significant outcome of the Fourth UN Conference on Women, held in Beijing in September 1995, was the shift of emphasis from a concern with women's needs and roles in the development process, to women's human rights.

However, often states refuse to ratify such treaties, enter significant reservations, or ratify but then take no steps to implement the measures. For example, the Declaration on the Elimination of Discriminations Against Women was ratified by 128 states, but both the USA and India refused to ratify the treaty and, significantly, no Islamic states signed up. Where states have ratified treaties and so are obliged to uphold the human rights of women, these are sometimes systematically ignored, thereby obscuring their significance. Furthermore, women's indirect relationship to the state and the inadequacy of the representation of their interests means that women's human rights are not actively addressed within theory, jurisprudence or monitoring.[88]

Liberal feminists have demanded the recognition of the universal and indivisible rights of women. They have argued that women's relationship to the state is mediated by men as husbands, fathers, brothers or sons who at the same time acquire authority over women from the state or traditional political community. From this perspective, the 'modernization' of the state has reduced religious influence, but the relationship of women to the state is still mediated by men.[89] The 'people' of the nation are still perceived to be men. There is a long history of discrimination in the rights tradition which has denied legal personality to women. However, although gender relations appear locked into the private sphere they are 'determined by the modern state through taxation, social security, immigration and nationality law, all of which retain elements of the husband, master legacy'.[90] Where rights have been connected to the ownership of property, a traditional source of European law exported through colonialism, the ramifications for women have been enormous.[91]

Liberal feminists have also entered the growing debate about what should be recognized as a 'human right'. A primary reason why particular forms of violence, for example rape and domestic violence against women, have been kept off the international agenda is because so many governments are opposed to any outside agency being given authority to intervene in the realm of family life. As was noted earlier, until quite recently, in a UN documentation the family was upheld as the basic unit of the sovereign nation-state and thus sacrosanct. Consequently, feminists trying to raise the issue of domestic violence as a violation of human rights faced numerous obstacles. Some government officials still refuse to accept UN jurisdiction in areas regarded as cultural, private or within the jurisdiction of the family.

Liberal feminists have also challenged the view that outside intervention in the areas of family relations or 'cultural practices' is always unjustified. Liberal feminists see an obvious paradox between women's rights and 'cultural rights', because rituals, customs and expressions of nation and community often have negative effects for women and girls.[92] Cultural practices are seen as part of the social glue necessary for society, but frequently they are necessary to the cultural identity of male society. For example, a preference for sons is common to many cultures, and affects the access which girls have to health care, education and food. Liberal feminists have argued that women's right to control their own bodies should be recognized in international law rather than be viewed as a religious or cultural issue.

However, there are a number of objections to the human rights approach to women's security. First, the liberal 'rights' discourse is historically conditioned, culturally specific. Furthermore, the paradigmatic *subject* in human rights discourse has, historically, been male. Indeed, as is apparent from the earlier discussion, many feminist thinkers have rejected conceptions of justice and ethics which are grounded in abstract, so-called 'universal' rights on the grounds that these same concepts are culturally specific and profoundly gendered. One way of meeting these objections is to argue that while the concept of 'human rights' is undoubtedly rooted in a Western liberal discourse, human rights are not 'immutable' and fixed, but open to critical challenge and further development. For example, a number of feminist thinkers have noted that human rights may be gender-specific, in that they have been established by reference empirically to gender-differentiated human rights practices and conceptually by reference to the model of human nature underpinning the rights tradition.[93] However, the response has frequently been to ask whether or not there should be specific 'rights' which recognize the 'otherness' of women, rather than to reject the human rights tradition altogether.

However, many feminists would support the position that the attempts to build global security upon the basis of a bourgeois human rights tradition based upon rational interest, egoism and the defence of property are fundamentally flawed. Indeed, many would argue that non-Western traditions which see the individual as part of the social whole and emphasize human dignity and development are more fruitful starting points for developing alternative conceptions of security. Others[94] have noted affinities between feminist revisions and 'people-centred approaches' which simultaneously argue for the equal importance of all people and their security needs and stress the importance of the collectivities in which people are embedded.

People-centred approaches

Feminists engaged in the project of challenging statecentric and militarized conceptions of security have been able to draw upon a number of quite distinctive approaches which take the specific circumstances of people, rather than 'citizens', as a starting point for thinking about security. This kind of approach does not start out from the *standpoint* of women's lives as such. Nevertheless, people-centred approaches are able to show how when the 'person' is a woman, gender hierarchies and inequalities in power constitute a major source of domination and obstacles to the achievement of genuine security. Feminist calls for a critical reassessment of what constitutes security have taken place in the context of demands for a rethinking of approaches to security in International Relations from critical theorists of all schools. While there are differences in approach and emphasis there are also certain affinities between feminist approaches to security and other critical re-visions. For example, Ken Booth has argued that we cannot have comprehensive security until *people*, rather than citizens, are recognized as the primary subject of security.[95] This approach does not, however, view the individual in abstract terms as the bearer of rights, but rather in social and cultural contexts. Threats to the 'person' are viewed in the context of membership of collectivities that the individual is immersed in. To focus on the person is not to suggest that all people are equally vulnerable, however. Indeed the strength of this approach is that it simultaneously highlights the equal importance of all people and their security needs regardless of race, class, gender or formal political status and highlights the multiple sources of insecurity which particular groups of people face according to their specific circumstances. Threats to security can vary according to the gender, class, race or nationality of the individual in particular historical contexts.

The Women's International Peace Conference in Halifax, Canada, in 1985 defined security in various ways depending on the most immediate threats to the survival of the person. From this perspective 'security' meant freedom from threat of war, but also safe working conditions, freedom from the threat of unemployment or an economic squeeze on foreign debt. Participants also agreed that the security of some could not be built on the insecurities of others. Feminist thinking about security which starts out from the circumstances and needs of people stresses that security is not just the absence of threats or acts of violence, but the enjoyment of economic and social justice.

Approaching security from the perspective of women's security demonstrates the urgent need for new definitions of security which include the elimination of all types of violence, including violence in gender relations. However, people in general and women in particular are vulnerable not only to the threat of direct violence, but also indirect or *structural violence*. Structural violence occurs where the economic insecurity of individuals is such that their life expectancy is reduced. Structural violence consists of the denial of food and economic security to the degree that the health and well-being of the individual is jeopardized. While structural violence affects poor people irrespective of gender, poor women and girls tend to suffer most. In poor countries, when there is a squeeze on already scarce resources, women and girls suffer first.[96]

When security is viewed outside of the nation-state context and in terms of the multiple insecurities that people face, the argument that what is really needed is a *global* perspective on security becomes persuasive. Increasingly International Relations scholars are turning their attention to the security implications of resource depletion, global warming and other ecological 'threats' to the survival of human kind.[97] Constructing global conceptions of security, therefore, involves some engagement with global political economy and development processes. Problems of ecological degradation are inextricably linked to poverty and mal-development. Often environmental degradation and resource depletion are presented as a problem of overpopulation and poverty among 'backward' Third World states. However, the poverty and mal-development of much of the so-called Third World cannot be separated from the wider global political and economic context. Similarly, the achievement of peace, economic justice and ecological sustainability is inseparable from overcoming social relations of domination wherever and however they are manifested.

The Women's International League for Peace and Freedom has suggested that global military activity may be the most serious worldwide polluter and consumer of precious resources. This is compounded by the fact that poverty is induced and increased by high levels of government expenditure on weapons and the arms trade. The debt crisis in the 1980s was in part caused by Third World expenditure on arms, in spite of the desperate need for development. Between 1978 and 1988, collectively poor countries spent about a quarter of all their resources on weaponry.[98] Galbraith has suggested that during that period collectively poor countries spent $30 billion a year on armaments at enormous cost to the world's poorest people.[99] The world's poorest countries collectively spent a larger percentage of GNP on arms than did the rich economies. However, the North contributed enormously to the total global expenditure on armaments. The US military budget in 1987 was $293 billion – equivalent to $1,203 for every man, woman and child in the country, or $280 every minute since the year zero AD.[100]

It seems that in the post-Cold-War world, the much-hoped-for 'peace dividend' has largely failed to materialize. In many cases conflict, of either a civil or interstate kind, is aggravated by economic instability. At the same time the debt burden in the South continues to grow.[101] It is estimated that currently, more than 3 billion people worldwide have insufficient access to the means to live a dignified life.[102] Vickers has argued that the very worst consequences of an insecure and militarized world are felt by that particular group long recognized by the international community to be central to achieving a genuinely secure world: women.[103] Recognition by the international community has taken the form of initiatives like the United Nations' world food programme, which has the declared intention of making food a more effective tool for women's advancement and improved employment prospects and health.[104] According to Vickers, authentic food security depends to a large extent on women who are responsible for 80 per cent of all agricultural production in developing countries, yet own hardly any land, find it difficult to get loans and frequently are overlooked by agricultural advisers and projects.[105] It is precisely in these areas that the UN is concerned to bring about change. Peterson and Runyan also point to UN initiatives as important in recognizing women not as 'victims' but as having a role to play in achieving security through development.[106]

The implications of gender inequality for theorizing security

Inequality, structural violence, militarism, mal-development and human rights abuses are not only relevant to our understanding of the multiple insecurities which people face, but profoundly affect the process of conceptualization and theorization too. When Cynthia Enloe asks, What does it mean to theorize state-sanctioned violence? she reminds us that all too frequently theory is separated from human activity.[107] However, when trying to make sense of security, for example, it is important to look at the implications of theorizing as an activity and not just at the resulting theories. When we think about the activity of theorizing, we understand that hegemonic domination is not just a question of the social relations of inequality and domination, but is also about the production of knowledge and the formulation of concepts and ideas that set the parameters for how we think about 'security'. It is also, crucially, about the ability to be heard.

'Rethinking' security is not just a question of adopting a global, rather than narrowly conceived national perspective. Nor is it simply a question of broadening our definition of security to embrace a range of new issues and concerns. It is also about the capacity of people to articulate their fears and insecurities and present new 'visions'. In this context feminist perspectives do not simply make a contribution to our understanding of security, but are rather central to the 'reconstructive' project. However, as Enloe maintains, women need 'a room of their own' to theorize. Women need space, resources, physical security and, Enloe claims, the more a government is preoccupied with what it calls 'national security', the less women experience the physical security necessary for theorizing.[108] Enloe goes on to say that, similarly, women who question their own subordination are often perceived as 'threats' to national security and it is precisely those women in the world with the most pressing need to discover the underlying causes of war, militarism and peace who have the least capacity to write down their thoughts.[109]

Rethinking security, therefore, involves thinking about militarism and patriarchy, mal-development and environmental degradation. It involves thinking about the relationship between poverty, debt and population growth. It involves thinking about resources and how they are distributed. It is to some of these issues that the discussion now turns.

Chapter 6

The Gender Dimension of Global Political Economy and Development

Chapter 5 concluded with a discussion of new ways of thinking about security which were not framed in terms of the nation-state and nationalist constructions of identity. It was suggested that poverty, inequality, militarism, mal-development and the denial of human rights or at least basic needs – all of which have to be seen in global perspective – were all relevant to understanding how secure or insecure people feel or actually are, according to their specific circumstances. This chapter is concerned to explore further some of these issues through a discussion of critical approaches to global political economy (GPE). However, the chapter is also concerned to explore in some detail gender issues in both the theory and practice of GPE.

The chapter is divided into three broad sections. The first section introduces a number of critical approaches to the study of GPE, before exploring the gender dimension of global political economy in both theory and practice. Section two turns to the development process. This section begins by situating the interest in development in a global context, because the development process in individual countries is profoundly shaped by international institutions and regimes, by trading patterns and global investment flows and also by prevalent ideas about what constitutes 'development'. Section two also outlines, briefly, how development strategies have changed over time, highlighting the gender-specific impact of development strategies and policies. The third section discusses the role the United Nations (UN) has played in 'bringing women into' the development process. Women should not, however, be seen as 'victims' of global economic and political processes, but rather as active participants and potential agents of change in global political economy and development. The final section of the chapter, therefore, considers how women have worked to resist global political and economic practices and advance different conceptions of development.

Global Political Economy

Critical interventions

The study of global political economy has become a dynamic and expanding area within the study of International Relations in recent years. From an initial narrow focus on the relationship between state power and decision-making in the context of the constraints imposed by the economic environment, global political economy has expanded to include the activities of multinational corporations, the influence on state policy of 'military industrial complexes', the role of international organizations in the global economy and the problems of debt and development.

In part the conceptual shift from *international* to *global* political economy is a response to the phenomenon of *globalization*. Global 'restructuring', the increasing influence of transnational corporations, the complex global division of labour, and the intimate relationship between debt, 'development' and environmental degradation, are all integral parts of the ongoing process of interconnectedness characteristic of globalization.[1] While the nature of globalization has been disputed, and its impact is undoubtedly uneven, it can nevertheless be usefully understood as a reordering of time and distance in our lives.[2] Critical approaches to GPE recognize that global processes shape and transform economic activity and that a number of 'actors', both governmental and non-governmental, are agents of economic, social and political change. Political economy can no longer be viewed as an entirely 'internal affair'; it is necessary, therefore, to explore its global dimension while recognizing the specificity of some areas. Furthermore, as was suggested in chapter 3, globalization has encouraged new forms of identification and expressions of solidarity which cut across state boundaries. This concern with the global dimension of social and economic activity has led to considerable criticism of the statecentric assumptions of the orthodoxy in *international* political economy.

However, the recent challenges to the orthodoxy also involve challenging the supposed 'objectivity' of much theory which has obscured the political nature of knowledge claims. Tooze, for example, has argued that there is an 'unwritten preface' to much analysis in global political economy.[3] Scholarship in the field is produced within the mainstream theory of knowledge shared by most social sciences, which combines positivism with empiricism and posits the separation of 'facts' and 'values'. The result is that 'the predominant but often implicit epistemology tends to define the boundaries of legitimate inquiry so as to preclude or discourage consideration of philosophical or epistemological questions both within and outside the mode of knowledge'.[4] That is, it is 'limited in scope, non-reflexive and potentially harmful in the political functions which it serves'.[5] Critical theorists start out from the position that the *subjectivity* of the social science should be recognized and historical modes of analysis and explanation encouraged in the discipline of GPE. In this way, the importance of the *subject*, who positions herself or himself politically, assesses the social and political significance of institutions and practices and infuses her or his own actions with social and political meaning, is made central to our understanding of 'theory'.

Feminist interventions have taken place in the context of a greater degree of self-reflexivity within GPE. Most feminist scholarship in GPE criticizes statecentric analysis and positivism and points to the ideological nature of so-called 'value-free' economic theories. Feminist scholarship in the field has both highlighted the problems of bias and distortion, which occurs when theory is written from the perspective of dominant groups, and challenged the boundaries of 'legitimate' research in the field. Christine Sylvester, for example, has argued that 'there is a hidden gender to the field which affects how we think about empirical political economy'.[6]

For example, in neo-realist analyses, politics dominates economics. Hegemonic states are seen to create and maintain order in the international economy. In this context, transnational corporations and other significant 'actors' are viewed only as instruments of foreign policy or extensions of state power. By concentrating on the impersonal structures of states and markets, it is not possible to see how women's activities have been demoted to the 'private' sphere. One might add that it also impossible to see that women and men enter into the formal economy as bearers of a gender identity. Ann Tickner has argued that ignoring gender distinctions hides a set of social and economic relations characterized by inequalities of power.[7]

Gender is rendered invisible because of the way in which both 'economic' and 'political' activity has conventionally been defined. In capitalist economies the market is viewed as the core of economic activity. Participation in the labour force and the inclusion of production in measurements of global economic activity has been defined only in relation to the market, or to the performance of work for pay or profit. Unremunerated work and the person performing it (usually a woman) is not included because it is not part of the market of paid exchanges for goods or services and so is not viewed as economically significant. This is based on a 'common-sense' view of what constitutes 'economic' activity. GPE has also explored particular kinds of power relationships which underpin economic activity, but the measure of 'power' and what may be construed as 'political' has not been expanded to include areas outside of what is conventionally defined as the 'public sphere'. Much feminist analysis in global political economy is involved in working towards new definitions of 'economic' and 'political' which will reunite what has conventionally been set off as separate.[8]

Dominant, neo-realist approaches to GPE contain another form of gender bias. Ann Tickner has argued that one should be wary of the gender bias of the model of 'rational economic man' which underpins neo-realist analysis.[9] Sylvester similarly claims that the rationality assumption prominent in neo-realism derives from a deep, unexamined cultural expectation that men are supposed to be motivated by calculations of instrumental interests.[10] 'Rational Economic Man' is, then, a construct that extrapolates from behaviour associated with bourgeois man and then uses 'man' to represent humanity as a whole.[11] The first construct of rational economic man was used as the basis for liberal explanations of the workings of the economy which appeared with the rise of capitalism, when a variety of human passions were subordinated to a desire for economic gain. Tickner suggests that this was also a time when definitions of male and female were polarized around the division between 'work' and 'home', and the construction of women as *housewives* placed women's work in the private sphere, as opposed to the public world of the market.[12]

However, feminist scholars have pointed out that much 'critical' scholarship in GPE has also been gender-blind. For example, Marxism offers an alternative view of global political economy and a thoroughgoing critique of both neo-realism and liberal political economy. In this model the key actors are social classes, and economic relations are seen to be structured for the benefit of dominant class interests. Conflicts are, therefore, seen to be either directly or indirectly linked to class conflict. However, the emphasis on the importance of the economic position of the male worker overlooks the fact that the subject has a gender as well as a class identity. Contemporary critical theory, which has its roots in Marxist political economy, emphasizes the intimate connection between theory and practice and the role of ideas and dominant ideologies in perpetuating power relations. It also focuses on the ways in which transnational class alliances cement or legitimize particular dominant economic projects.[13] Neo-Gramscian thinkers, for example, stress the need to develop a 'counter-hegemonic' set of concepts and concerns to deal with the problems of militarism and economic and social inequalities.[14] However, they have largely failed to explore the gender dimension of inequality and forms of resistance which arise in response to the experience of gender inequality.[15] Thus, the gender-specific impact of global restructuring, structural adjustment, debt and the feminization of poverty have long been recognized, but, until recently, not theorized in GPE.[16] It is clear that an exploration of gender relations is needed because ideas about the 'naturalness' of forms of gender inequality are integral to understanding how the global economy functions.

Gender and global restructuring

Since the 1970s, the global economy has been undergoing a process of restructuring. The first phase of global restructuring can be traced to the 1973 oil crisis when big companies in the West resorted to international subcontracting to survive. Initially the knowledge-intensive parts of the production process went to the West, while transnational corporations shifted the labour-intensive parts of the production process to developing countries where cheap female labour was abundant. In the 1980s as big business emphasized the importance of managerial flexibility and decentralized production, corporate strategies in the West sought a more flexible workforce to undermine the power of trade unions.[17]

Global restructuring and the many resistances that it has generated have given rise to profound challenges to the orthodoxy, notably its statecentric predilections. However, neither neorealist, liberal interdependence, nor Marxist-inspired dependency models seem to be able fully to capture this phenomenon, and none are able to elucidate the gender-specific effects of restructuring. Mitter claims that restructuring in the 1980s had a profound effect on the composition of the workforce.[18] The process encouraged the growth of a 'new proletariat' in both the North and South, with women ghettoized in assembly-line work with poor pay and prospects. The 'feminization' of the workforce was a significant phenomenon in many regions of the North previously characterized by heavy industry. Mitter argues that in areas where traditionally unionized industries such as coal and steel had previously thrived, the male workforce frequently had a reputation for radicalism. Employers in growth industries thus preferred to employ the wives and daughters of, for example, ex-miners and ex-steelworkers.

In the 1980s big business also invested more and more in hi-tech research, automation and computer-integrated manufacturing systems. This investment was aimed at replacing skilled labour. However, where labour-intensive and skilled-work aspects of production predominated, it was not always cost-effective to invest heavily in machinery. This was particularly the case where there was a supply of cheap female labour, because women made the most flexible robots of all.[19] In both Europe and North America, in the garment industry, for example, employers who felt threatened by the restructuring of the global economy but who could not relocate abroad moved to feminize their workforce and this resulted in the re-emergence of sweatshops and home-working.[20] This phenomenon was replicated in a number of other industries, including electronics, toy-manufacturing and food-processing. In the West, the official reasons given for preferring women were similar to those offered in the Third World. Employers stressed the 'natural dexterity' and 'nimble fingers' of women workers. However, because women's skills were thus defined in an ideologically biased way – that is, as natural rather than learnt – they were not rewarded.

Furthermore, 'masculinity' continued to be identified with the claims of 'bread-winner' status, and this also provided a justification for paying women less, even though male unemployment was actually increasing. Women were frequently paid between 20 and 50 per cent less than men in comparable jobs.[21] This was justified both by the idea that women and men had innate capabilities and personality traits and on the grounds that men needed to support families but women did not. A further significant aspect of global restructuring in the 1980s was the increasing numbers of part-time and home-workers. The rise in home-working in the West was also a direct manifestation of 'flexible-manning' business strategies. Mitter and van Luijken claim that women constituted and continue to constitute the majority of home-workers, because everywhere women constitute the poorest sections of society.[22] They claim that there is a marked similarity between home-work and housework – both are done by women and both remain invisible. Calling home-working the 'informal sector' of the economy misrepresents the numbers involved. It is not outside or parallel to the formal sector. It is an integral part of the global market economy.[23]

As the least unionized and poorest paid of all workers, women have been particularly vulnerable to the market policies which have continued to characterize global economic restructuring in the 1990s. Where women are encouraged to take up roles in the paid sector – and women now make up some 41 per cent of paid workers in developed countries and 34 per cent worldwide[24] – it is still the case that on average they earn 30–40 per cent less than men for comparable work. Women in general work longer hours than men and make up a disproportionate number of those working in the informal sector, though much of this work is unrecorded and so invisible. Women are concentrated in low-paid jobs. In the developing world, women are still heavily concentrated in Export Production Zones. The centrepiece of recent IMF strategies in the 1980s and 1990s has been export-led growth and structural adjustment. Indebted governments set aside territory specifically for the use of factories producing goods for the global market. In Asia, in the 1980s, women made up 85 per cent of workers in Export Production Zones. In other areas, the figure for women workers was typically around 75 per cent.[25] While there is some evidence that the 1990s have seen a 'remasculinization' of the workplace, women remain concentrated in the lowest-paid jobs.

Elson and Pearson claimed that the provision of women into such jobs was encouraged because it could be viewed as a way of involving women in the development process.[26] World-market factories producing components for the electronics industry, for example, are usually owned or partially owned by subsidiaries of Japanese, North American and European multinationals. These have been particularly important in the development of the global trade in consumer goods. A number of large US and European retailing firms are continuing to place large contracts with world-market factories. When deciding where to locate, a crucial factor remains the availability of a suitable labour force, which is defined in terms of low cost and high productivity. It seems that, as in the 1980s, in the 1990s women remain the cheapest and most productive of all workers. Women's attempts to translate paid employment into financial independence, however, are often thwarted by lack of access to capital, inadequate education and training and because women carry an unequal burden of family responsibilities.

A further aspect of global political economy which has attracted the interest of feminist scholars, is the rapid growth of sex tourism, or prostitution, which is linked to the expansion of the tourist industry. In a number of countries tourism has become an important earner of foreign currency. In Thailand, the Philippines, the Caribbean, West Africa and Brazil, the growing sex industry is linked closely with the expansion of tourism and is inextricably linked to the problems of debt and development strategies.[27] Sex tourism does not just involve women, although it is overwhelmingly women who are drawn into this particular form of prostitution – frequently women who have been displaced as a direct consequence of 'development' strategies. Nor can prostitution be viewed solely from the perspective of tourism. Nevertheless it is conditioned by the demands of a stratified global market and the impact of development policies which are themselves conditioned by global economic processes.[28] Thahn Dan has suggested that prostitution is itself becoming a globally traded commodity. The growing integration of the tourist industry which links countries, hotel chains and package-holiday firms is a crucial enabling factor which allows spare capacity in airline seats and hotel beds to be matched with the demand for esoteric sexual services. With the growing globalization of capital, one finds the spread of prostitution. It is, Thahn Dan claims, no accident that Bangkok and Manila, both major cities which have experienced massive growth in prostitution in recent years are also both major centres for multinational corporations and regional centres for global organizations. Increasingly the issue of prostitution needs a global analysis.[29] Enloe argues that sex tourism is both a part of the global political system and the global economy and the fact 'that it is not taken seriously says more about the ideological construction of seriousness than the politics of tourism'.[30]

Development

Development in global context

The rapid growth and expansion of Export Production Zones, alluded to above, cannot be viewed solely in terms of IMF policy and the related problems of debt and underdevelopment. It must be viewed in the context of a wider process of restructuring. This phenomenon in turn serves to illustrate the degree to which 'development' cannot be viewed in isolation from the global distribution of resources, power and, indeed, from inequalities in access to policy-making bodies at both national and international level. Furthermore, as more is understood about the relationship between development, underdevelopment, debt and environmental degradation, it is coming to be understood that the fate of developed states is closely tied to that of underdeveloped nations. For these reasons, globalization is encouraging new thinking about development.

Early theories of development placed emphasis upon the twin objectives of economic growth and 'modernization'. Modernization is a rather vague and ill-defined concept, but it was usually used in broad terms to describe a process characterized by interconnected economic, technological, industrial, social, cultural and political changes. The process of modernization was held to bring about changes in the social and economic structures and political institutions of developing states. It was assumed that eventually they would become more like 'modern' Western states. Modernization was typically associated with industrialization, technological innovation, consumerism, market economy and increasing population. Modernization was also associated with improved levels of education, an expanding role for the state, the emergence of political pluralism, respect for civil liberties and rights, and democratic, as opposed to authoritarian, forms of government.

In contemporary GPE, rather than imagining the world to consist of a number of separate countries moving in the same direction towards modernization and progress, a single arena of development is now recognized. In recent years, GPE scholars have also argued that historically ideas about what constitutes development, and policies ostensibly designed to achieve modernization, have been conditioned by dominant ideologies which assume that the Western experience provides the model for the 'developing' world. This assumes that growth is both possible and desirable and that it is a relatively unproblematic, linear process. However, the production of knowledge about 'development' is itself a historical process which is conditioned by the socio-political, economic and cultural context in which it takes place. Historically 'development' has been driven by dominant Western perceptions of the needs and circumstances of people in 'under-developed' countries. Knowledge about 'development' and 'modernization' has been largely the affair of Western elites influenced not only by their own particular values but also by dominant ideologies and values systems prevailing at the time. Established views of the needs, circumstances and problems of Third World societies and peoples have been shaped by the historical experiences of subordination to Western economic, political and cultural power and Western perceptions arising from this.[31]

The idea that development was a process which could be encouraged in individual states, and was essentially 'progressive' was challenged by Marxist thinkers in the 1960s and 1970s. For example, Frank argued that the development of rich 'core' countries was inextricably linked with the underdevelopment of poor, 'peripheral' states.[32] While, Wallerstein argued that the capitalist economy had expanded historically and was now one world-system.[33] Wallerstein argued that the modern world-system was 'organized and able to consolidate itself as a capitalist world economy', the guiding principle of which was 'the ceaseless accumulation of capital'.[34] It was characterized by an international division of labour based upon an unequal exchange between 'core' and 'periphery' and 'semi-periphery' countries, but 'governed by a singular logic and set of rules within and through which persons and groups struggle with each other in pursuit of their interests and in accord with their values'.[35]

However, while both dependency theorists and world-systems theorists argued that so-called 'development' and 'modernization' were processes characterized by exploitation and domination, they concentrated largely upon transnational class relations and the role of particular states in supporting and perpetuating capitalism. As will be argued below, both the processes associated with modernization and ideologies of development have been marked with respect to culture, class and gender. Feminists have attempted to address the shortcomings of existing models and theories by incorporating an analysis of gender, or to develop alternative models of GPE which make gender central to understanding development.

Susan George has argued that the principle effect of Third World 'development' has been to impose an economic and political system which actually benefits a small elite.[36] It has been argued that international institutions and development agencies continue to reflect the influence of elites in dominant states. Marianne Marchand suggests that it was no accident that there was no dissent or controversy about development issues and policies during the Reagan era of the early to mid 1980s, for example.[37] During that time approaches to development return to anti-Keynesian economic liberalism. Such strategies promoted free trade, and reasserted a version of modernization theory which saw growth and general improvements in living standards 'trickling down' from the middle class to the poorest groups in society. In more recent years, hand in hand with policies of structural adjustment, has been the notion of 'empowerment', taken to mean the effective harnessing of the energies of local communities involved in development projects. However, this language of participation disguises the real imbalances of power inherent in conditional transfers of money, technology and education.[38]

'Import-led growth' to 'structural adjustment'

Mal-development is undoubtedly one of the most pressing problems facing the world today. As was suggested earlier, since the

late 1950s both development theory and policy have been dominated by the objective of economic growth and modernization,
the best indicator of which was taken to be an increase in per
capita Gross Domestic Product. The underlying assumption has
been that development is an unproblematic, linear process and
that there is a model of development and growth that can be
followed by others. At the end of this process 'emerging' states will
become like rich industrialized countries. However, after nearly
three decades of attempts to promote the development or 'modernization' of the poorest countries of the world, many find that
their relative prosperity has declined. Much of the blame for the
crisis which currently affects many countries has been laid
squarely at the door of previous models of development.

It has been argued that the first models of economic development popular in the late 1950s and 1960s neglected almost everyone but a small elite who were identified as a 'modernizing'
element.[39] Economic growth was measured according to levels of
imports, which were largely consumed by a small middle class.
The theory was that wealth would 'trickle down' from this elite
class to all other sections of society and that this would eventually
eliminate poverty. Notions of 'import-led growth' relied upon
unrestricted consumerism. Loans were made available to some
sections of society – the modernizing elite – to facilitate this.
Often the impact of large increases in imports and easy borrowing
was escalating prices, but the impact of this on vulnerable groups
was not considered. The oil crisis of 1973 encouraged further
Third World borrowing in order to meet the increasing costs of
energy. The world recession which followed the oil crisis resulted
in both deteriorating terms of trade and fewer trading opportunities which further exacerbated the problems of poorer states.
Many Third World states are now so deeply in debt that new loans
are devoted almost entirely to the servicing of old ones. At the
same time the Third World's share of world trade is steadily falling
and in many 'developing states' levels of infant mortality and
malnutrition are rising.[40]

The failure of 'import-led' growth strategies led to important
changes in policy. The failure to halt poverty or improve the
health and nutritional status of the large majority led, in the
1990s, to the inclusion of 'basic-needs' elements in development
strategies. This was designed to meet people's need for adequate
shelter, food and health care. However, since the early 1980s,

development policies have also been dominated by the goal of 'structural adjustment', which relies heavily upon export-led growth, combined with cuts in public expenditure. Structural adjustment is seen as a way of ensuring that states are able to earn enough foreign currency through exports to continue to service existing debts. This is seen as imperative, because default by a major debtor would seriously destabilize the global economy.[41] The IMF offers short-term assistance to countries with balance of payment problems. However, structural adjustment makes receipt of assistance conditional upon the recipient states' willingness to take action to address underlying or 'structural' problems. The IMF makes loans to states in *tranches*, each of which requires stricter and stricter conditions. In return for fresh loans, structural adjustment typically requires states to make drastic cuts in civil spending, cut imports and, at the same time, attempt to increase exports. Indeed, export earnings are put above every other goal. The overriding objective of structural adjustment has been to undermine efforts to provide for basic needs in many poor countries.[42]

The gender-specific impact of debt and structural adjustment

There is considerable evidence that the burden of structural adjustment falls most heavily upon the most vulnerable groups in society, particularly women. In many developing states, agricultural produce is often the first thing singled out for increased exports. Produce grown for export uses land which could be used to grow food for domestic consumption. Therefore, increased *cash-crop* production for export frequently leads to increased domestic food shortages. Since women are usually responsible for providing food for children and adult men, women have to deal with the problems of food shortages.[43] As providers of basic health and social welfare needs, the effects of structural adjustment also fall disproportionately on women whose labour is expected to 'stretch' in order to compensate for cuts in public services. Cuts in social expenditure also result in a disproportionate loss of women's jobs.[44] The burden of debt and economic policies, which are themselves largely conditioned by global constraints, is having particular effects on women in countries throughout the world.

In the Caribbean and Latin America,[45] for example, the impact of the high rates of migration and the drain on resources – both of which have been attributed to structural adjustment – is closely associated with increases in child prostitution, tourist prostitution and sex tourism. While in the Asian Pacific region the negative impact of structural adjustment and migration is also associated with an increase in the trafficking of women.[46] The degree to which women are disproportionally affected by economic restructuring is by no means confined to the 'developing' world or newly industrialized countries. As was noted earlier, this has been a significant phenomenon in the West, while in central and eastern Europe and the former Soviet Union there is evidence that women in particular are losing their jobs as the region 'adjusts' to the rigours of the global marketplace and that they are also taking up the burden of care which results from cuts in the social sectors.[47]

In 1988, in Vienna, a conference on women and the world economic crisis looked specifically at the impact of structural adjustment policies on women and called for alternative approaches,[48] and a report by UNICEF also called for far-reaching changes in IMF policy, notably less emphasis on deflationary measures.[49] This report also called for macro-economic policies which were sensitive to the impact of development on vulnerable groups, and for women from the Third World to be given more real influence in decision-making.[50] The IMF takes the view that it should not involve itself in questions of how the burden of debt is adjusted between different social groups. Similarly, many Western states take the view that to attempt to prescribe what the status or role of women should be is to attack the culture of recipient states. However, the concern of the IMF and many Western states appears rather cynical since in reality development policies are already built upon assumptions about women's single domestic role which ignore the ways in which women already contribute to and are affected by development processes. The consequences of such a stance in practice, and indeed of other development policies which are ostensibly 'gender-blind', are developed further below.

Gender bias in the development process

The problems of bias and distortions resulting from 'gender-blind' policies have been extensively articulated. There is a large feminist literature which explores both the gender bias in dominant theories of development and the gender-specific impact of particular policies.[51] Historically, theories about the nature of economic activity have ignored the contribution which 'women's work' makes to the global economy. As long ago as 1970, Ester Boserup argued that unremunerated work was frequently not included in official statistics, even though in subsistence production it actually had an important weight in the economy.[52] In consequence, Boserup argued the system of underrepresentation of subsistence activities not only made countries seem poorer than they were, but it made their rate of economic growth appear in a more favourable light than was warranted.[53] Boserup argued that the greatest skew in the data appeared in relation to the displacement of women in agriculture through modernization. She suggested that the growing crisis in rural areas from landlessness, low productivity and displacement of jobs which was occurring as countries attempted to 'modernize', and the emphasis on cash crops as a central part of development strategies, had its deepest effects on women. This was because development policies failed to recognize both the female farmer in fact and the role which women played in the production of many other services. Therefore the effect of changes in land ownership was a major source of social disruption rather than development. When 'work' was measured only in terms of the market, a wide range of domestic activities was ignored. In many Third World states women still constitute the main producers of food, and provide a variety of other home-produced goods which make a vital contribution to the overall welfare of families and local communities. Frequently this work is ignored by policy-making elites and this continues to result in serious distortions in the assessment of Gross Domestic Product and National Income of developing states. This distortion has a devastating impact on Third World states generally and on women and children in particular.[54]

It has been argued that development agencies are still largely dominated by white, middle-class men who base their policies on assumptions about households, families and gender relations drawn from Western experience. As such, development strategies frequently reflect ignorance about the role of women in many societies and are not sensitive to how prevailing gender relations both influence and are influenced by the impact of development strategies. For example, as was stated earlier, in recent years the notion of 'trickle down' has once again become popular in the discourse of development. However, in nearly all states, it is women as a group who are at the very bottom of society in terms of wealth, income and access to resources. Women as a group are, therefore, at the bottom in the so-called trickle-down process. In the past, trickle-down strategies have benefited only those at the top of the social ladder.

Furthermore, since women in all states tend to be clustered at the bottom of the socio-economic scale, falling national income tends to disproportionately affect women. In 1992, for example, UNICEF reported that typically a 2–3 per cent fall in national income, resulted in a decrease of between 10 to 15 per cent in the income of the poorest groups.[55] The increased poverty and falling nutritional status of children can further impede development. Some reports have also suggested that in times of crisis the incidence of domestic violence often increases.[56]

When the household is taken to be the basic 'unit', another kind of bias is introduced. Around the world, approximately one-third of all families are supported by women. As was stated earlier, in many cases assumptions about gender relations and the model of the male bread-winner role have served to deprive women of access to land and resources. The idea that women are dependants can serve to deny women access to pension rights or employment. It might also encourage the view that women should be recipients of welfare rather than incorporated into policy-making. Throughout the developing world, but particularly in Africa, women are heavily concentrated in subsistence agriculture. Here, the degree to which women are denied access to land has been highlighted as a significant barrier to women's full participation in economic reconstruction.[57] Even though women are often the main farmers, they are still frequently ignored when development schemes are designed and implemented. It is simply assumed that men, and not women, are farmers. Furthermore, because the value of women's work is overlooked, the introduction of new technologies may not significantly benefit women.

The Western assumption of a harmonious family unit also disguises the fact that conflicts of interest can exist within the family group. This may in itself result in women being displaced from their land and so deprive many communities of their source of food. Men may have very different interests in cash-crop production, for example, and so be willing to sell the rights to forest land to timber merchants. This can deprive women of not only the means to grow food but also the means to provide for their energy requirements.[58] It has been claimed that a major cause of the current crisis in food self-sufficiency which affects many Third World states is a consequence of the neglect of the needs and interests of the majority of women farmers. It is often the case that 'progressive' farmers are selected for schemes and real farmers are disadvantaged. Since subsistence farmers are often also small traders who produce a surplus for sale, when they are forced out of production the local community loses a vital source of food supply which had previously helped to meet seasonal and regional shortfalls.[59] In Africa, poor economic performance and high population growth rates have left the majority of the population in a marginal position with respect to mainstream development processes. In the name of development, African states have been encouraged to move to the production of cash crops. This has particular implications for rural women who constitute the major part of the labour force in African peasant agricultural production. In part, then, the reluctance of women farmers to invest can be explained by cultural practices. However, it is clear that the widespread hunger which exists in many parts of Africa is not simply a consequence of the failure of crops, or cultural practices, but connected to the global power structures and global economic processes.

The UN Decade for Women

From its inception, the United Nations (UN) has seen itself as having a role to play in promoting development. Similarly the UN has a long history of promoting the status of women throughout the world. Until quite recently most of the UN's work in this area had concentrated on promoting women's status through the development process. In 1973 the United States Foreign Assistance Act led to the setting up of USAID. This act required women to be involved in decision-making bodies which dealt with aid and development issues. This measure prompted UN agencies, including the International Bank for Reconstruction and Development, UNESCO,[60] the ILO[61] and FAO[62] to set up special offices that concentrated on women's role in the development process. Shortly afterwards, in 1975, the First United Nations Conference on Women was held in Mexico to mark the beginning of International Women's Year. At the Mexico conference, delegates adopted a Plan of Action which aimed to improve the status of women, and 1976–85 was duly designated as the United Nations Decade for the Advancement of Women. In 1976 INSTRAW[63] and the Voluntary Fund for the UN Decade for Women (UNIFEM) were set up. The midway point in the UN Decade for Women was marked by the Second United Nations Conference on Women, held in Copenhagen in 1980.

In some respects the very existence of the UN Decade for Women was an important step forward. Up until that point, women had not really figured in debates about development at all. For the first time attempts were made to assess women's contribution to development, particularly in the crucial area of subsistence agriculture. The UN initiative required the attention of governments and gave women some access to policy-making by insisting that women's offices were set up within development agencies. It also led to the first real attempts to look at how technologies could be developed and applied which would help to reduce the drudgery characteristic of much women's work. In addition, it also helped to legitimize the women's movement as an international actor.[64] The so-called 'Women in Development' (WID) approach that underpinned various initiatives was also important in terms of facilitating the inclusion of women in workshops and seminars, by facilitating networking amongst women and by disseminating information through the WIDlink newsletter. The WID literature produced in the 1970s put the issue of women firmly on the political agenda, highlighted the inequalities of opportunity and the disproportionate contribution which women made to the development process. Furthermore, while the special offices set up to deal with women and development were often poorly funded, they did at least allow women to travel and meet and challenged the idea that men were the bread-winners in all societies.[65]

However, since 1985, the WID approach has been subjected to considerable criticism. At the end of the UN Decade for Women, surveys suggested the relative status and position of women throughout the world had declined in the previous ten years.[66] To some extent, the failure of the UN Decade can be explained by the failure on the part of many states to implement UN recommendations. In the 1980s a survey conducted by INSTRAW found that out of ninety-six countries, only six included women's issues as central issues in their development plans.[67] However, the failure was also attributed to the underlying assumptions of the WID approach. During the UN Decade, development policies were based on the underlying belief that the problems of Third World women were related to insufficient participation in the process of development. It has been argued that WID rested on a liberal feminist view that the problems of sexual inequality could be largely overcome if women were integrated into the public sphere. The aim of WID was to 'bring in' women, but women were already involved in the development process. According to Ashworth and Allison, the WID idea also contained the seeds of its own failure, because it recognized as visible producers only those whose commodities could be traded. The economic role of women as subsistence farmers, providers and full-time carers, which is the cornerstone of economic life, remained uncounted and unrewarded.[68]

Furthermore, the possibility that increasing poverty amongst women, and the relative decline of women to men during the decade, were the direct result of previous development policies was not considered. However, as was argued earlier, many development strategies which made reform and restructuring of agriculture production a priority had led directly to the displacement of women from the land that they had traditionally farmed. Critics argued that WID policy documents avoided and obscured issues of inequalities and power by presenting the issue of assistance to women as a purely technical exercise. It did not address the broader redistributional issues that assisting women raised. The WID approach ignored the broader context in which women-specific projects were inscribed. Increases in the productivity of women were not matched by relief from reproductive tasks. Women were too often regarded as 'victims' in need of assistance, rather than farmers, workers, investors and trade unionists. Ashworth, Allison and Redcliffe have argued that the central issue of gender inequalities in development policies ignored the fact that men and women could not benefit equally from aid and development initiatives if they had different political rights, burdens of time, and expectations and if the laws of inheritance and ownership discriminated against women and they could not get access to credit.[69]

Criticisms of the assumptions that guided the WID approach led to widespread calls for a different approach, which placed less emphasis on access and more on recognition of the degree to which women were already involved in the development process. The term 'gender and development' (GAD) was coined to describe an approach which was sensitive to the specificity of gender relations in particular countries and localities, rather than simply centred on women. Here 'the technical project of access, as numerical inclusion' was seen as insufficient to challenge the unequal allocation of values which sustained oppressive gender relations.[70] The stress on gender, rather than women, was a reminder that men must also be the target of attempts to redress gender inequalities and that their interests are also socially constructed and amenable to change.[71]

Gender and development approaches also highlighted the degree to which the neutrality and autonomy of the state, the focus of the liberal feminist strategies typical of WID, could not simply be taken for granted. As feminists have long argued, 'part of the definition of the state and the delimitation of the state's proper sphere involves the active codification and policing of the boundaries of the public and the private'.[72] Furthermore, 'in many states those boundaries also 'delineate gendered spheres of activity, where the paradigmatic subject of the public and economic arena is male and that of the private and domestic is female'.[73] In this way, according to Goetz, by confirming and institutionalizing the arrangements that distinguish the public from the private, states are involved in the social and political institutionalization of gendered power differences. For example, states set the parameters for women's structurally unequal position in families and markets by condoning gender-differential terms in inheritance rights and legal adulthood, by tacitly condoning domestic and sexual violence, or by sanctioning differential wages for equal or comparable work.[74]

Increasingly, the environment has come to be seen by many as another victim of so-called 'development' policies. Dominant models of development which emphasize economic growth as the main indicator of 'progress' have neglected almost entirely the resources that the local environment can provide and the skills which local people have. Neo-classical approaches to growth, which have become popular again in the 1980s and 1990s, emphasize the efficacy of the market in generating economic activity and distributing resources. Such approaches emphasize the importance of enterprise which encourages economic growth, the benefits of which trickle down to poorer members of society. This approach has been criticized not only on the aforementioned grounds that it may in reality benefit only a small elite, but also because it fails to recognize the environmental consequences of development and the inherent limits to growth.[75]

Challenges to the notion that development means economic growth and 'progress' by emulating the development pattern of Western states have been given a boost in recent years by a growing awareness of environmental issues. When nature is viewed as a resource which is there to be exploited, growth is frequently accompanied by environmental destruction. For example, the dash to growth in many countries has resulted in massive deforestation through commercial exploitation and cash-crop production. Deforestation leads to soil erosion which in turn affects rivers and local water supplies. The exploitation of the earth's resources continues to fuel economic expansion in the West where nations comprise 22 per cent of the world's population, but use 70 per cent of its energy and are responsible for two-thirds of carbon emissions and 90 per cent of chlorofluorocarbons.[76] Development strategies that rely on energy intensive modes of production and transportation are spreading throughout the world.

By the end of 1994 the world's population reached an estimated 5.7 billion and the figure will increase by 93 million by the end of the 1990s.[77] The enormous growth in the world's population will put enormous pressure on the world's resources and on the environment. Population size and the need for fertility control are all important gender issues, of course, and are recognized as central to combating global environmental degradation.[78] However, the real issues which need to be addressed are poverty and inequality. In more recent debates, the emphasis has shifted from WID and GAD, to WED – women, environment and development.[79] A growing number of commentators and activists interested in the gender-specific impact of development have called for a new approach which challenges dominant conceptions of development and calls for a greater understanding of the crucial role that women play in managing the environment.

'Mainstreaming' gender issues

Since the UN Decade for Women, there have been calls to 'mainstream' gender issues in development strategies. Mainstreaming means incorporating gender concerns into development strategies and policies as a matter of course rather than as 'add ons'. Although, as debates about gender and development have shifted from an emphasis on bringing women in, to an analysis of gender relations, to understanding the gender dimension of environmental concerns, 'mainstreaming' in common usage, has also come to mean highlighting gender issues in other areas within the remit of the UN, such as human rights provision.

The Third UN Conference on Women, held in Nairobi in 1985 at the end of the UN Decade for Women, produced an important document called *Forward Looking Strategies for the Advancement of Women to the Year 2000* (FLSAW). The strategies outlined in the document aimed to promote women's interests in health, employment, family life, political life, and also promote women's human rights. Since the UN Decade for Women in 1976, UN development agencies have included sections that are specifically charged to advance the interests of women. These sections have pushed for a greater degree of gender sensitivity in government policies, for awareness of the problems of women's double burden, for equal access to and control over land and property, and for equal access to credit. The United Nations has long recognized the need to include the contribution which women make to the economy in order to undertake effective planning and estimate potential output. More accurate data enables more effective policies to be formulated in areas ranging from employment and income distribution to social security provision and welfare. Thus, the FLSAW document pressed for the inclusion of unpaid work in national accounts and in social and economic indicators. It also pressed for the allocation of social and economic benefits to take into account this broader definition of work. Redefining work in the global economy effectively means recognizing both waged and unwaged work as essential to the social and economic well-being of countries.

The Fourth UN Conference on Women, held in Beijing in 1995, took place after the Commission on the Status of Women had met in 1990 to review the progress of the FLSAW since 1985. The Commission decided that not enough progress had been made. The Fourth UN Conference on Women was the largest UN conference to date. The Draft Platform for Action which was negotiated at Beijing echoed many of the key themes and objectives of the FLSAW, identifying eleven specific areas of concern:

poverty, access to education, inequality in health-care provision, violence against women, the needs of women refugees, access to participation in economic decision-making structures, greater participation in public life and the political process, improvements in monitoring mechanisms, improvements in the awareness on the part of women of the commitments made by member states, the representation of women in the media, and, finally, women's contribution to managing natural resources and safeguarding the environment. The conference 'Platform of Action' made explicit linkages between the empowerment of women, access to reproductive health care, equality and women's human rights.

Challenging the discourse of 'development'

Since the end of the UN Decade for Women, there have been a number of challenges to dominant models of development. These have been couched not only in terms of questions of *inclusion*, but have rather challenged the entire strategy of development and modernization imposed by Western states and Western-dominated institutions on the so called developing world.[80] This critique has spilled over into a critique of the WID/GAD discourse too. It has been argued that Women in Development approaches implicitly assume that First World women are more advanced than Third World women. In many respects, the status of women has in fact been used as a measure of progress, a barometer of civilization, in modernization theory.[81] The WID approach appears to accept implicitly that 'modernization' involved not only economic growth, but a change in social structures, institutions and cultural practices in so-called Third World countries which disadvantage women. WID, therefore, seems to accept that the basis of development lay in a diffusion of capital, technology and values from the West.[82]

Gender and Development approaches emphasize the importance of understanding the role that women already play in development and stresses the importance of understanding how socially constructed ideas about gender and gender relations affect and are affected by development strategies. Therefore GAD implicitly, if not always explicitly, points to the importance of historical modes of analysis which are sensitive to the cultural specificity of gender relations. However, in recent years, postcolonial and postmodern feminist scholars have also challenged many of the assumptions of GAD too. Gender and Development approaches are derived from Marxist feminism and, as such, often rest on an unstated commitment to an emancipatory politics, which critics argue is implicitly grounded in a Western discourse of universalism, 'progress' and 'liberation'.

In order fully to appreciate the basis of the critique of both WID and GAD which has come from postmodern and postcolonial feminist thinkers in more recent years, it is necessary at this juncture to both revisit some of the themes in feminist thought which were set out in chapter 1, and to explain more fully how these have been played out in debates about women, gender and development.

At the heart of both historical and contemporary debates in feminism are issues of identity and difference. In liberal, radical and Marxist feminism discussions of 'difference' have been largely concerned with the difference between women and men. As was suggested in chapter 1, the emergence of postcolonial feminism in the 1980s and 1990s expanded the debate about 'difference' considerably by raising important issues about race and ethnicity in feminist thinking and exposing the pretence of homogeneity of 'women's experience'. Furthermore, postmodern feminism not only problematized the binary opposition between women and men, but also used the notion of difference to problematize the category of 'woman'. In this way, postmodern feminists argued that 'difference described the human condition' and that 'women were many not one'.[83]

Postmodern feminism is not located in the 'experiences of women'. Rather, postmodern feminists focus on gender as discourse and the relationship between discourse and social practices. Some feminists have drawn upon postmodernism because it is useful in understanding the political, theoretical, self-analysing practices by which the relations of the *subject* can be rearticulated from the historical experience of women. All women can and do think about, criticize and alter discourse, and thus subjectivity can be reconstructed through the process of reflective practice. Similarly, individual 'identity' is constituted by a historical process of consciousness. This is a process in which one's history is interpreted or reconstructed within the horizons of meaning and knowledge available in given historical moments, horizons that also include modes of political commitment and struggle. Such an approach formulates the subjectivity of women in ways which give agency to individual women while at the same time placing them within particular discursive configurations.[84]

Much postmodern feminist scholarship in the broad field of global political economy and development in the 1980s and 1990s was, therefore, characterized by a move from grand theory to local studies and from cross-cultural analysis of patriarchy to the complex and historical interplay of sex, race and class, and from notions of a female identity or the interests of women towards the instability of female identity and the active creation and recreation of women's needs or concerns.[85]

In 1984, shortly before the end of the UN Decade for Women, at the Third UN Conference on Women, held in Nairobi, the movement 'Development Alternatives for Women in a New Age' (DAWN) was set up by women from the developing world. DAWN called for an entirely different approach to development which aimed at economic and social sufficiency. Inspired by initiatives like DAWN, postmodern feminist thinkers criticized much previous feminist theorizing about development and global political economy, arguing that it had been equally guilty of privileging Western experience and was built upon the same kind of universalizing Enlightenment concepts of modernization and progress.

Both postmodern and postcolonial feminists recognize the existence of gender inequalities, but are sceptical of the degree to which the specific problems of particular groups of women can and should be addressed in a forum like the UN. The influential postcolonial feminist thinker Spivak, for example, has adopted a rather cynical perspective on the 'significance' of events like Beijing and other 'women's' conferences. She argues that the Platform of Action, ostensibly concerned to address problems of female poverty and inequality, accepted the underlying logic of the free market as the best distributor of resources and 'life chances'. In this view the Beijing conference, and women's conferences in general, can be seen as 'tremendously well organized ideological apparatus', used ostensibly to demonstrate the unity of North and South, when 'the North organizes the South'.[86]

Gender issues in global perspective

Postmodern feminist thinkers have argued that grand theories of gender and development or gender and global political economy should be abandoned. Instead, research should concentrate on the historically and culturally specific experiences of different groups of women. Many feminists believe that such an approach will merely produce empirical studies and have nothing to say about how existing power structures can be challenged. They also believe that the emphasis on difference threatens to undermine the very notion of feminist theorizing and cannot be reconciled with the urgent need for collective action to challenge and change gender inequalities.

The suggestion underlying criticisms of postmodern feminism is that it implies nihilism, cynicism and political quietism. This is in itself something of a caricature, and has been challenged by those who argued that a distinction should be made between oppositional and non-oppositional postmodernism.[87] Postmodern feminism clearly falls into the first category. Postmodern feminism, it is argued, refines our sensitivity to differences and our ability to tolerate the incommensurable.

Postmodern feminists argue that the deconstruction of identity, or scepticism towards the usefulness of 'woman' as a category of analysis, does not mean the deconstruction of feminist politics, although it does involve redefining feminist politics outside of the binary and sexual difference upon which it had been built historically. The deconstruction of binary oppositions characteristic of postmodern thought does not, however, necessarily imply the rejection of all values. Postmodern feminists rather resist the notion that 'truth' is only that which could be demonstrated within an accepted theoretical framework. Feminism can take this insight on board by resisting the notion that political strategies must entail the mobilization of a homogeneous group with a common interest in realizing common goals.

Postmodern feminists are more likely to advocate a politics of dissent which disrupts the theory and practice of specific power regimes,[88] than an *emancipatory* politics. They might also argue that feminism offers 'sites of resistance' to hegemonic discourse and provides spaces for women to be heard.[89] In this view, feminist politics required complex and shifting alliances.

Nevertheless, it is clear from contemporary debates in feminist theory[90] that many feminists continue to regard postmodern feminism with not a little suspicion and argue that the most productive way forward for feminism in coming to terms with the implications of cultural and historical specificity and questions of difference is through the construction of a feminist critical theory. These debates and their implications for International Relations are discussed at greater length in chapter 7. Furthermore, some commentators see the UN, for example, as playing a valuable role in facilitating networking, providing the 'web that links NGOs, social movements and groups across national borders'.[91] For example, in preparation for the Beijing conference, women met in a number of regional forums to discuss the major concerns for women in those particular regions. However, the stress was on the need to view the problems of women in a local, national, regional and global context.

In much contemporary feminist analysis the still striking disparities between North and South, rural and urban and rich and poor are emphasized. Western feminists acknowledge explicitly that concern with gender inequalities has to be seen in the context of broad inequalities not only between states and regions, but between women of colour and women of different social groups. For example, the 'expert report' on the ECE region, in preparation for Beijing,[92] explicitly recognized that issues of women's rights and sustainable development could not be seriously addressed unless the consumption and production patterns in the ECE region changed. Significantly European feminists have also cited the problems of racism in Europe, noting that women of colour in the region are particularly affected by global restructuring processes and make a particular contribution to unwaged and low-waged work. Women in Europe have, therefore, joined women in Latin America and in the Asia Pacific region in rejecting dominant economic paradigms and arguing that the deep contradictions in economic policies of restructuring and globalization are resulting in economic and social policies which are detrimental to the rights of women. They have called for gender-sensitive and socially responsible government policies. And they have also demanded that governments make multinational, and transnational corporations abide by standards which promote women's equality, that commercial advertising be made accountable and that images of women no longer be used in advertising which, by perpetuating notions of consumerism as the route to personal fulfilment, promotes overconsumption in the West.[93]

Feminist scholarship in GPE and Development Studies has demonstrated that one cannot analyse the characteristics of the global economy in terms of class and national struggles alone; gender must be incorporated into the analysis. It has also demonstrated the need for the inclusion of areas which have been conventionally set off from the main/malestream in GPE and development analysis. However, it has demonstrated too that there has never been a single feminist theory or approach. Given the importance of other forms of social inequality revolving around race or class, one might argue that what is needed is a feminist analysis which is sensitive to how dimensions such as class and race cut across gender historically. The concluding chapter of this book now turns to the challenges of thinking about gender and feminism in a global context.

Chapter 7

Reconstructions and Resistances

The book has focused on gender, feminism and International Relations in order to rework the main concerns of the discipline. However, in so doing, it has also critiqued mainstream approaches to theorizing in International Relations and suggested ways in which feminist perspectives encourage a radical rethinking of key concepts and categories in International Relations. In so doing, it has drawn selectively from feminist scholarship from International Relations and other fields of study. The book has not aspired to construct a 'feminist International Relations'. It has drawn upon many feminisms and approaches which view gender in terms of social *structures* and *processes* and approaches which concentrate on *discourses* of gender and *social practices.*

Nevertheless, both the notion of 'feminist lenses' introduced in chapter 1 and feminist critiques of the kind undertaken in chapter 2 do rather imply that there are other ways of 'seeing', 'knowing' and 'being in the world' which could give rise to different standpoints or perspectives. Similarly, addressing issues of gender and conceptions of political space and identity and looking through feminist lenses at war, the nature of the state, the military and citizenship, security, global political economy and development necessarily raises questions about the so-called 'reconstructive' project in International Relations. That is, how can approaches to studying the international/global realm be developed which avoid the reductionism and silences of the orthodoxy?

This concluding chapter is divided into two broad sections. The first section moves from critique to '*reconstruction*'. This section does not attempt to construct a coherent feminist 'world-view', for reasons that will become clear. Rather it explores the potential for, first, incorporating gender into established liberal and Marxist paradigms in International Relations and, second, for constructing International Relations from a feminist *standpoint*. In chapter 1 feminist scholarship in International Relations was situated within the context of broader theoretical challenges that have emerged from the 'third debate', and some of the overlapping concerns of feminism, critical theory and postmodernism were highlighted. The second section, entitled *resistances*, revisits this debate. Resistances is chosen as the organizing theme for this section because feminist critical theorists are inclined to view feminist movements as 'counter-hegemonic forces' which can be marshalled in the cause of an emancipatory politics; while postmodernists see feminist discourses as *sites of resistance* or point to feminist movements as examples of 'critical social movements' which resist dominant discourses and political projects in international politics. However, postmodern feminists also resist the closures and totalizing imperatives of 'reconstructive' projects.

Reconstructions

Feminist readings of International Relations texts highlight issues of bias and exclusion. In so doing, they necessarily raise questions about whether it is possible to develop less biased approaches to understanding the international/global realm and so achieve more theoretical inclusivity. Feminist theories are not only valuable, therefore, in developing critiques of mainstream/male-stream theories, but also as a potentially rich source to mine in the search for alternative concepts which will assist in this task. However, as was apparent from the discussion of the uses of critique in chapter 2, in the process of 'deconstructing' the *text* of International Relations, the category 'woman' has been used as the 'other' – that which exposes the presuppositions and distortions of the orthodoxy rather than as a lived experience. Similarly, while feminist scholars have had a great deal to say about issues and areas conventionally defined as International Relations and, indeed, have argued forcibly for the inclusion of areas which have been conventionally set off from the main/malestream, there has never been a single feminist approach or one feminist theory.

Indeed, the very possibility of 'woman', no less, is at the heart of contemporary debates in feminist theory.

As was suggested in chapter 1, contemporary feminist theory can be divided into two broad schools: those who remain committed to articulating the experiences and aspirations of women, but at the same time recognize the need to develop approaches to both theory and practice which allow some historical and cultural specificity, and those who argue that the whole process of theorizing is a form of domination whereby the theorist comprehends and *appropriates* the objects of knowledge. Similarly, feminists are broadly divided amongst those who insist that gender can be understood in terms of social structures, and those who emphasize the importance of discourse in understanding how gender is constructed. Given what appears to be, at first sight at least, fairly fundamental divisions in contemporary feminist thought, one might ask whether it is possible to move beyond critique and develop gender-sensitive and/or feminist approaches to International Relations.

Furthermore, 'feminist International Relations' could describe a number of quite different projects. For example, it could be an approach to understanding and analysing aspects of international relations from a feminist *standpoint*. In contrast, it could centre on women as actors in international politics, or highlight the economic, social and political status of women throughout the world. Alternatively, 'a feminist International Relations' might focus on the gendered nature of hegemonic power structures and economic and social processes and attempt to view their operation and impact in a global context.

In the light of the emphasis which has been placed on the rich diversity of feminist thought throughout this text, the reader will not be surprised to find that there is no one feminist theory of International Relations. There are a number of approaches to gender/feminism, each of which is itself informed by particular assumptions.

'Bringing in women': liberal feminism

While liberal feminists point to the silences and biases in existing International Relations, they remain committed to the possibility of 'objective' analysis based upon sound empirical research. From a liberal feminist perspective, the shortcomings of existing International Relations can be remedied by 'bringing in' more women. *Feminist empiricism* is closely associated with the liberal feminist strategy of 'bringing women in'. The absence or under-representation of women in positions of power and influence is itself a major obstacle to pushing women's interests and concerns onto the agenda of international politics. Feminist empiricism thus seeks to raise levels of awareness of women in international relations and argues for more research on women in International Relations. Liberal feminists focus on *women* in international relations and are primarily concerned with the empirical dimension of women's inequality, the economic and social status of women around the world, the suppression of women's human rights and the denial of justice to women. However, liberal feminists are also concerned about the underrepresentation of women in the academy, because this in itself is likely to mean inadequate levels of empirical research on women. Feminist empiricism also concentrates on the way in which false beliefs and prejudices distort the findings of research and seek an enlarged perspective, arguing that bringing more women in as researchers will result in a less biased, partial and distorted view of the world.[1]

Feminist empiricism has been dismissed as an 'add women and stir' approach, because it assumes that the issue of male bias can simply be addressed by including more women both as researchers and by more 'woman-centred' research. Feminist empiricism rests firmly with the mainstream theories of knowledge characterized by the separation of 'facts' and 'values' and of subject and object. As such, it does not fundamentally challenge the basic epistemological foundations of positivism. However, as Sandra Harding has argued, it would be a mistake to dismiss the value of feminist empiricism outright, because taking women's lives seriously has great transformative potential. It is an argument for more resources, more research, putting women's concerns onto foreign policy agendas, attacking the usual tendency to view women and their lives as insignificant or irrelevant. Furthermore, Sandra Harding suggests that feminist empiricism has the potential radically to undercut the assumptions of traditional empiricism by attacking the androcentric biases which operate when research projects are identified and formulated and by demonstrating how dominant research methods and norms contribute to androcentric results. In this way, feminist empiricism

undermines the *male subject as human* case and opens up a space
for a deeper analysis of the ways in which a culture's best beliefs,
what it calls knowledge, are socially situated.[2] It also reveals how
women's situation in a gender-stratified society can be used as a
resource in feminist research and how research directed by social
values and political agendas can nevertheless produce empirically
and theoretical preferable results.[3]

As was noted in chapters 1 and 2, while realism has dominated
the discipline of International Relations, there has been an
equally long history of liberal thought about international relations. Contemporary 'liberal-pluralists' conceptualize international relations as a dense network of transnational linkages and
point to the increasing number of 'actors' – including transnational movements – and issues that pepper the agenda of world
politics. It is possible, therefore, to focus on gender issues and
feminist politics within a broadly liberal framework which stresses
the importance of transnational 'legitimized' relationships. Women's human rights advocate Georgina Ashworth, for example,
has highlighted the solidarities between women which cut across
national boundaries.[4] Global gender issues are finding their way
onto the agenda of international politics due to effective lobbying
by women's groups, some of which have achieved institutional
status.

Since the end of the UN Decade for Women in 1985, a number
of UN-sponsored conferences have been organized which have
attracted an ever-increasing number of participants, both at the
intergovernmental level and in NGO forums. Lobbying on behalf
of women takes many forms, from direct pressure-group activity,
for example, to the 'women's section' of intergovernmental organizations. Kathleen Newland has described the interactions of
women's groups as part of a dense web of transnational relationships that emerged out of the Women in Development movement
in the 1970s and 1980s and, as such, provide a prime example
of transnational movements in action.[5] Newland argues that the
study of women in international relations, therefore, fits neatly
within the world-society paradigm popularized by John Burton.[6]
In the 1990s, women have continued to play a major role in
shaping debates and organizing effectively to be major players in
international forums such as the United Nations and have continued to further legitimize the women's movement as an actor

through participation in the NGO forums that have accompanied major UN conferences.

In some respects, liberal pluralism represents a radical challenge to statecentric views in International Relations. It breaks down the hierarchy of 'high' and 'low' politics characteristic of realism and casts doubt upon what are usually considered to be the 'big issues' in International Relations. Furthermore, while much of this work has concentrated on transnational *linkages*, it raises interesting questions about expressions of collective identity. However, arguably liberals do not go far enough in drawing out the deeper implications of their empirical observations. Furthermore, liberal feminist research about *women* does not cast any light upon the way in which gender relations are structured. Nor does it address the implication of power relations in the construction of knowledge. As was noted in the early discussion of gender and development issues, for example, liberal feminists have been criticized because they frequently advocate strategies for the 'advancement' and 'equality' of women which are profoundly shaped by Western ideas of what constitutes human freedom and progress.

Liberal feminists who lobby for the advancement of women are frequently accused of 'interfering with culture' or even 'cultural imperialism' by nationalist men from Third World countries. Attempts to use international organizations to improve the status of women are often resisted on the same grounds. For example, the IMF takes the view that it should not be involved in questions of how the burden of debt is adjusted between various social groups in recipient states in apparent deference to indigenous culture and tradition. Liberal feminists respond to such criticisms by arguing that gender inequality cannot be seen purely in the context of the particularism of local customs or cultural practices.[7] For example, historically development policies have been built upon neo-colonialist assumptions about the status of women as dependants and men as bread-winners, assumptions that have often served to deprive women of traditional rights.[8] Today Western ideologies, values, technologies and commercialism all interfere with indigenous culture and beliefs, powerful gendered images are decimated by telecommunications and the global media, and 'the intrusion of education systems brings alternative value systems and the introduction of fertility control techniques also poses fundamental challenges to indigenous cultural values and traditional practices'.[9] Furthermore, international processes create the conditions for feminist politics in the Third World, as in the West.

However, while it is undoubtedly the case that 'the language of culture and tradition disguise the politics of colonisation, nationalism and gender relations',[10] liberal feminists have largely failed to take seriously the issue of power, and consequently have attracted criticism. Liberals see the United Nations, for example, as playing a positive role in challenging traditional cultural beliefs and prejudices, often reinforced in law, which have assigned women to lower social status and which have been seen as hindering progress in improving the status of women. However, liberals have not seriously addressed the degree to which this has been a Western-led agenda or the ways in which women from the South have in practice had little opportunity to articulate their own specific concerns and aspirations. All too frequently women in the Third World have been portrayed as the helpless victims of 'backward' cultural practices. Western feminists have been attacked for implicit racism inherent in calls for the 'advancement' of Third World women by postcolonial feminist thinkers. Thus, Mohanty has castigated Western feminists for naively positing the existence of a 'global sisterhood',[11] while Spivak has recently criticized the way in which NGOs are put together in the South to exclude the poorest women as self-critical agents. In her view, NGO forums, such as those that accompany UN conferences, afford diaspora the opportunity to represent the 'South' and women from the 'North' the opportunity to matronize women from the 'South'. According to Spivak, 'serious activists' stay away because 'the real work is to be done elsewhere'.[12]

Patriarchy and capitalism: Marxist feminism

In contrast, Marxist feminists have a great deal to say about gender and power. Rather than focusing on the exclusion of women and questions of bias, Marxist feminists concentrate on gender as a specific form of social inequality. From a Marxist feminist perspective gender is not natural, but constructed and when 'gender is viewed as essentially an inequality constructed as a socially relevant difference in order to keep that inequality in place, then gender itself can be seen as an outcome of social processes of subordination and the issue of gender in International Relations can be treated as a question of systemic dominance'.[13] Marxist feminists see gender as a form of social inequality which is rooted in the 'privatization' of women's productive and reproductive labour power, the control of women's sexuality and the subordination of women to male authority through a range of patriarchal institutions.

There is a long history of Marxist feminist theorizing about gender which is integrated into and informed by an analysis of the changing global economy. Perhaps the most systematic account of gender oppression and global political economy has come from feminist thinkers who have significantly developed and expanded Immanuel Wallerstein's 'world-systems theory',[14] which was discussed briefly in chapter 6. A number of feminist thinkers have found Wallerstein's basic framework a useful starting point for thinking about gender inequality and oppression in global context. In an influential book entitled *Patriarchy and Accumulation on a World Scale*, Maria Mies, for example, adapted a basically world-systems framework to trace out the emergence of two world-systems, patriarchy and capitalism.[15] Mies argued that capitalism could not function without patriarchy; indeed, of the two 'world-systems', patriarchy was the older. The sixteenth-century capitalist revolution was also a patriarchal revolution in which practices such as witch-burning asserted male control over women.

According to Mies, women's inequality was neither natural nor cultural, but a part of production relations. Historically, as capitalism expanded across the world, violence was used to define women and colonial people as 'property', rather than as free citizens. The freedom of the male citizen was, therefore, predicated on the unfreedom of women and colonial peoples. In recent years Wallerstein's own work has included a more systematic account of racism and sexism in the capitalist world-system. Notably, he has been concerned to show how bourgeois revolutions, while ostensibly ushering in an age of democratization and universal values, changed relatively little in the economic structures of the world-system because the 'response of the powerful to dangers of democratization' was 'the invention of ideologies, the reconstruction of the knowledge system and the triumph of scientism' and the 'taming of anti-systemic movements'.[16] According to Wallerstein, a truly free market or democratic state would soon make unviable the underlying *raison d'être* of the capitalist world economy, which is capitalist accumulation. Similarly, universalism sweeps away the justification for hierarchy in both the workplace and in the political system. The answer to the 'problem' was, therefore, to institutionalize racism and sexism. Racism ensured that so-called 'universal values' only applied to the 'in group' defined by race, while women were excluded on the grounds of their 'essential difference'. Sexism also served to restrict women to certain modes of production and define women's work as 'non-work' through the concept of the 'housewife'. According to Mies, in the contemporary global economy, the coercion of women as 'housewives' remains essential for a system which allowed male workers to be free citizens.

Mies argues that as capitalism developed Third World women were encouraged to enter income-generating export production sectors and increasingly women who were involved in non-household production defined themselves as 'consumers'. In this way the extension of the 'housewife' ideology from the West to the Third World and from richer to poorer classes helped to isolate and atomize women workers and mystify the process of labour control. There was therefore a parallel between housewifization and colonization, in effect the coercion of women in the home and the coercion of 'underdeveloped' communities in the periphery.[17] The notion that women are first 'housewives' and 'consumers' enabled capitalism to devalue women's work, and renumerate women less when they became paid labourers. In this way, wages in large sectors of the world economy were significantly reduced.[18]

While not all Marxist feminists have explicitly employed the notion of a capitalist world-system, the sexual division of labour is generally seen as the root of female subordination. Gender inequality, therefore, can only be understood in terms of the intersection of two sets of social forces, capitalism and patriarchy. Mackintosh, for example, argues that feminists are interested in the sexual division of labour because it appears to express and embody and further perpetuate female subordination.[19] The sexual division of labour is not natural because only in a society where men and women constitute unequal genders would there be any reason why gender should be an important organizing principle of the social division of labour, except for the physical process of childbearing. For this reason, the search for a material understanding of women's subordination must involve the study of 'reproductive' work. The gender-typing of particular social roles is likely to be most rigid in areas crucial to social relations – which she calls relations of human reproduction – and which generally incorporate male dominance and control of women's sexuality. In this way, Mackintosh suggests that in developed capitalism, the household becomes a kind of mediating institution, mediating two sets of social relations: marriage and filiation. This works to constitute the household and determine the content of much childcare and the wider economic relations of society. There are close links between the organization of production and the operation of sexual relations which have been traced by feminists in areas such as inheritance and economic relations within marriage. Men acquire a vested interest in women's services in the home and generally in their relatively favourable position in the economic structure.

Once the sexual division of labour is established it takes on a life of its own and creates a national division of labour between men and women which can be exploited by employers. According to Mackintosh, the increase in the part-time and flexible work which is an integral part of the global economy reflects the constraints of women's domestic role and so is an economic expression of the marriage contract. Swasti Mitter similarly argues that the patriarchal values of the state and family in both North and South place women in a position of subjugation.[20] Thus if gender hierarchy and subordination are rooted in the institution of marriage or the privatization of the 'household', they become embedded features of the wider economic structure and, so, the global economy.

The *specific* form taken by the sexual division of labour is perpetually being transformed and recreated as economic and social change occurs, but it is hard to challenge. Many states support an unequal sexual division of labour or turn a blind eye when women are paid below the minimum wage. In the meantime women working in the textile and electronics industries in world-market factories, for example, constitute a super-flexible workforce which can be readily exploited by transnational corporations. Paid employment takes women out of the home, of course, and gives women some measure of independence. However, studies show that where women do work or earn money income, it does not necessarily create the same sort of power in the household. Allocation mechanisms within the household embody important ideologies which render non-comparable the work that men and women do and the income that they earn. Pearson and Elson argue that women's role in the family is socially constructed as a subordinate role.[21] Females do the work which is required to nurture children and men, work which appears private and personal, while it is the male role to represent women and children in the wider society. It is this representative role which confers social power.[22] The gendering of the bread-winner role as essentially male means that it is also easier to dismiss women workers in times of crisis. In this way, a number of Marxist feminists have argued, capitalism benefits from a 'reserve army of labour', flexible workers who are absorbed in phases of expansion and are then thrown back into dependency when crisis sets in. Women are the cheapest and most vulnerable of the waged labour force and are thus open to high levels of exploitation. The material divisions which emerge in the workforce between men and women, differences in pay, competition for jobs in situations of unemployment allow capital to divide and rule. Historically as wage-work has spread, capital has seized upon the division between men and women and incorporated that division within the workforce to its own advantage.[23] Thus, historically the organization of global production has depended upon a multifaceted power structure and the profitability of mobile global capital continues to thrive on the politics of class and gender.[24]

Feminist standpoint

Both liberal feminist and Marxist feminist perspectives highlight particular aspects of sexual inequality and in their own distinctive ways suggest a basis for solidarity among women. However, while liberal feminist research is driven by social values, has a political agenda and may indeed have transformative *potential*, liberals remain committed to the ideal of objective, impartial analysis. Marxist feminism is both reflexive and historical. However, much Marxist feminist scholarship is primarily concerned with the structures and social practices that support and perpetuate gender relations and rarely extends to a discussion of epistemological issues. In chapter 1 it was suggested that contemporary debates in feminist theory have raised central issues of the subject and the epistemological claims of feminism. Feminism is not only concerned with analysing the structures and processes which underpin gender inequality. The stress on the importance of the political subject goes beyond the aim of 'bringing in' women, or making visible gender inequalities. It involves moving women 'from the margin to the centre' as the *subjects of knowledge.*

Feminist standpoint is very much a *postpositivist* approach to theorizing, in that it starts out from the position that the 'reality' that positivist theories claim to address is made 'real' by the power of particular groups to impose definitions. In adopting a feminist standpoint the first aim is to reverse the usual understanding of events, and reveal hidden assumptions in dominant theories or common-sense views of the world.[25] Feminists argue that representations of the 'human' are those devised by men and are about the male world as seen by men. It is a world in which women are defined through an androcentric lens, as mother, nurturer, caretaker and helpmate. Standpoint thinkers have, for example, noted the failure of social scientists to address issues of sexuality, procreation, childrearing and socialization practices as definitively human problematics and argued that this failure reflects the 'male as norm' standpoint The lack of men's awareness of this particular bias reflects their privileged position. The implication of this kind of critique is that women occupy radically different life worlds and, as such, feminist critiques, particularly those which draw upon psychoanalytic and radical feminist thought, raise questions which are both ontological and epistemological. But what is it precisely about 'women's experiences' which can serve as a vantage point from which to construct knowledge of the world? How can the ontological and epistemological claims of feminist standpoint be substantiated?

As was noted in chapter 1, some radical feminists argue that women are essentially different from men and that this difference is rooted in women's *biology*. Other radical feminists, while rejecting such essentialist or deterministic accounts of women's 'nature', have nevertheless insisted that women's *socialization* or the experience of mothering on the part of the vast majority of women give rise to a distinctly female experience. Other feminist standpoint theorists have drawn upon psychoanalytic feminist thought that locates gender difference in childrearing practices and take seriously the idea that the process of *psychic and social development* produces differences in views of the self as either fundamentally separate or connected. Nancy Hartsock, for example, has combined a basically Marxist historical materialism, which posits that groups who share socially and politically significant characteristics also share a standpoint, with object-relations theory to argue that women's material life activity has important epistemological and ontological implications.[26]

A number of contemporary feminist scholars in International Relations, notably Ann Tickner, have drawn upon object-relations theory and feminist standpoint to provide a set of concepts with which to construct a very different kind of International Relations.[27] Standpoint theorists frequently argue that a girl's gradual oedipal period takes place in such a way that empathy is built into their primary definition of self. A more complex relational world is then reinforced by the process of socialization. Taking the profound socio-sexual processes involved in the construction of boundaries between self and other as a starting point leads to a critique of rigid notions of autonomy and separation in the construction of identities and boundaries, emphasizing instead the processes of interdependence and connections. From this perspective, our sense of place and identity is understood not in terms of rigid separation between 'inside' and 'outside', 'domestic' and 'foreign', but in terms of interconnections. Boundaries are not viewed as 'enclosures', because identity is not viewed as being constructed by the counterpoising of 'inside' and 'outside'. Rather, linkages to the outside are seen as constituting our very same sense of place and identity. This alternative conception moves away from ideas of 'autonomy', 'vulnerability' and 'penetrability' which make outsiders unwelcome.[28] Such an approach can give rise to a conception of inter-national relations as a series of complex relationships and interdependencies.

Since power is an essentially contested concept and because alternative theorizations of power can be expected to rest on alternative epistemological and ontological bases, it is possible to argue that the different life experiences of men and women give rise to different conceptions of power. Thus Hartsock argues that 'helping another to grow and develop, avoiding excessive control and gradually relinquishing control are all important features of women's work'.[29] Women are positioned in particular kinds of power relationships, but nevertheless have a different understanding of power. Hartsock suggests that the different accounts of power produced by women and men can be taken to be indications of systematic and significant differences in life activity. Women's experiences thus provide a related but more adequate epistemological terrain for understanding power. The theorization of power is, therefore, a second area in which feminist-standpoint theory has proved useful to feminist scholars in International Relations. A number of feminist thinkers have identified a separate tradition of theorizing power which is found in the work of women's writing. While few women have theorized power, those that have bear a striking similarity. Many make distinctions between 'power over' and 'power with', or 'coercive' and 'co-active' power and view power as a capacity, energy and competence, rather than as dominance.[30] This view of power also challenges the view of international relations as primarily characterized by force and domination in favour of a more interdependent and cooperative vision.[31]

As was noted in previous chapters, the notion of a feminist standpoint has been criticized from a number of quite distinctive positions. One of the main objections, however, is the very idea that there is an 'authentic woman's experience' which can serve as a basis for identification, political action and knowledge claims. It has been argued that feminist reformulations often offer alternatives which are themselves based on the idea of an ahistorical 'other' as if we take it for granted that there are distinct realities to which 'male' and 'female' refer behind the social masks.[32] Furthermore, one might recognize that men construct their identity around conceptions of 'abstract masculinity', but a feminist reconstruction cannot be carried out in the name of an authentic self, because to do so is to reassert the dichotomy.[33] It is important to distinguish, therefore, between the category 'women' that can be usefully employed in the process of deconstruction or critique and the experiences of real women who are material subjects of their own history.[34]

Standpoint feminists have attempted to address such criticisms by arguing that one's world-view is fundamentally shaped by social position and experience. Thus to make a standpoint claim is not to universalize 'womanhood', but to draw out the implications of the public/private dichotomy and the implication of gender difference in the social world on identity formation. Standpoint thinkers insist that feminist theory must be able to show how women are positioned in relation to dominant power structures and how this forges a sense of identity and a politics of resistance and to suggest ways in which both theory and practice can be

directed in liberatory directions. If material life is structured differently for different groups, not only will the vision available to
each represent an inversion of others in systems of domination,[35]
but a standpoint will also suggest ways of moving beyond these
relations. To overcome female subordination involves real struggle which involves far-reaching social transformations. A *feminist*
standpoint is not the world-view of all *women*, but an 'engaged'
position, an achievement, a claim to *know* which is struggled for.[36]
Standpoint theorists thus recognize the historical and political
nature of all knowledge as power and understand that theory is
inexorably linked to practice. The theory/practice relationship
here is explicitly linked to an emancipatory politics. However, it is
a view of emancipation that does not depend upon the scientific
discovery and application of universal laws but on social practice
associated with critical reflection on dominant knowledge/power
relations.

The *political subject* of feminism has been integral to debates
about feminism and identity politics. Indeed, feminism has
understood 'the subject in terms of identity; the political subject is
that which remains identical to itself in the face of contradiction'.[37] Debates within contemporary feminist theory have
centred on the possibility of combining identity politics with a
conception of the subject as non-essentialized and emergent from
historical experience, retaining gender as a point of departure.
Some of the positions taken in this debate parallel debates
which have taken place between standpoint feminist thinkers
and their critics. For example, some feminists insist that one's
identity is taken as a point of departure, as a motivation for action
and as delineation of one's politics.[38] Here the concept 'woman'
is not understood as a set of particular characteristics or
attributes, but a particular position. Women then use their
positional perspective as a place from which values are interpreted and constructed. Such an approach does not construct
women as the passive 'victims' of patriarchy but as self-
determining agents who are capable of challenging and resisting
structures of domination and in so doing of constructing new
identities for themselves.

However, some feminist standpoint thinkers have recently acknowledged that there can be no one feminist standpoint. Similarly, some standpoint thinkers have seemingly abandoned the
claim that knowledge constructed from a feminist standpoint is

'less partial', 'less distorted' and so 'more objective'[39] and make the less ambitious claim that feminist standpoints produce partial truths, partial understandings of the world, which are nevertheless valid.[40] Many standpoint theorists have conceded that because 'masculinity' and 'femininity' are always categories within every race, class and culture there can only be feminisms and feminist standpoints. Once the historical and cultural specificity of gender is acknowledged, the *subject* of knowledge has to be seen as multiple and, perhaps, contradictory.

Resistances

Feminist critical theory

The challenge of developing approaches to understanding gender in global context, which allow for some historical, social and cultural specificity and which start out from the insight that knowledge is not transcendent but a *moment* of emancipation, provides an opportunity to look again at feminist critical theory. Feminist critical theorizing involves constructing 'knowledge' about the world, not in the interests of social and political control, but in the service of an emancipatory politics. Thus feminist critical theorists claim that knowledge is a *moment* of emancipation. Feminist critical theorists insist that power cannot be understood as an instrument of policy but that it extends to social relations. Feminist critical theory sees the absence of particular issues or the invisibility of major social inequalities in any body of social and political thought as a powerful form of exclusion. Feminists have pointed to the marginalization of gender in International Relations. Furthermore, feminist critical theory explains these silences in terms of the dominance of positivism within the discipline and attempts to develop approaches to theory which recognize the links between knowledge, power and interests.

In some respects, feminist critical theory can be viewed as an approach which fuses elements of standpoint – in so far as it seeks to empower women as subjects – with a broadly Marxist feminist analysis of hegemonic structures of power and institutions, particularly in the global economy. Critical theorists working in global political economy are interested in exploring the emancipatory potential of groups which emerge with the expansion of the global production process and which struggle to challenge existing power relations and resist the political projects of dominant social groups. The growth of global capitalism transforms social orders. Transnational corporations and giant multinationals located in global cities roam the world looking for cheap labour and organize economic and social relations across state boundaries. In this way global capitalism generates 'counter-hegemonic forces'.[41] Critical theorists concentrate on the role played by dominant and oppositional forces in either supporting or challenging the status quo. Critical theorists have, perhaps, in practice been guilty of ignoring or marginalizing gender in their work, preferring to concentrate on social class. Nevertheless such an approach could examine the social and economic position of women in relation to the globalization of these same forces. Feminists have campaigned against the damaging effects on women and children of the activities of transnational corporations, the concentration of women in export production zones and the use of ideas about gender to legitimize low wages and the feminization of poverty, for example. As was argued in chapter 6, the expansion of global capitalism has profoundly affected the social and economic position of women in specific societies and encouraged the growth of groups which, while sometimes reluctant to adopt the label 'feminist' nevertheless organize around gender interests.

It is by no means certain that the expansion of capitalism is giving birth to a 'global sisterhood'. There are a whole range of factors that shape identities and foster cooperation across national boundaries. Division between women in the North and South, between rural women and urban women and between women of different social classes and races in the contemporary world remain highly significant. Nevertheless, while there are also factors which limit the possibilities for transnational alliances, critical analysis of the social and economic forces associated with globalization is a particularly promising starting point for thinking about the complexities of gender identification and feminist politics in a global context.[42]

Feminist critical theory attempts a complex analysis of why and how the construction of gender has served to legitimize the subordination of women and of how hegemonic structures are imbued with patriarchal ideology. It draws out the global dimensions of gender inequalities, highlights the ways in which ideologies of gender play a role in producing and reproducing power relations and how these relations are structured and transformed. Sandra Whitworth argues that we need to view men and women as gendered agents and explore the ways in which ideas about 'masculinity' or 'femininity' allow men, even the most disadvantaged, to assert control over women.[43] Whitworth argues that the focus should be on gender relations rather than women because this forces us to think about how gender relations which operate in different situations are affected by both international and internal factors. However, at the same time it allows an analysis of the changing social relations between women and men in specific social and historical contexts.

Clearly, the problems and interests of women have to be viewed in local, national, regional and global contexts. Broad disparities between the 'North' and 'South', between rural and urban, rich and poor are highly significant in understanding the limits of 'global sisterhood' and the relationship between gender inequalities and other forms of inequality based on class or race or ethnic group. Nevertheless, feminist critical analysis challenges the common-sense view that gender subordination can only be seen in the context of particular cultural practices by demonstrating the degree to which gender relations are constantly amended by global and local processes. Gender, therefore, has to be understood in terms of both local and specific practices and global power relations.

It was suggested earlier that nationalist movements often present feminism as a product of decadent Western capitalism, based on a foreign culture and of no relevance to women in the non-Western world. It is also clear that sometimes the term 'feminist' is equated with Western imperialism. However, Jayawardena contends that feminism is no more or less 'alien' than other ideologies, such as socialism and, indeed, nationalism, which have influenced both the internal social and economic structure of states and their external politics.[44] In a study of the impact of both feminism and nationalism in the Third World Jayawardena argues that feminism was not imposed on Third World women, but rather historical circumstances produced changes that affected women through the impact of imperialism and nationalism. Historically, Western thought has been a significant element in the development of feminism in many parts of Asia, but Jayawardena claims that movements for women's emancipation took place against a background of nationalist struggle in which the assertion of national and cultural identity was coupled with reforms which promoted education, scientific and cultural advance.

This analysis suggests that resistance to imperialism and foreign domination was coupled with opposition to feudal structures and traditional forms of patriarchal authority. The growth of capitalism thus changed the social order and gave birth to new structures. However, women's movements did not occur in a vacuum but were informed by wider social movements in which they played a role. Indeed, as Tohidi has argued, one fundamental challenge for global feminism is that the conception, objectives and strategy of feminism in different nations and regions have become intertwined with very different economic, socio-cultural and political conditions.[45]

Much contemporary feminist theory is explicitly concerned with the problem of developing concepts which allow some specificity whilst providing cross-cultural reference points urgently needed in feminist work. For example, if we see the sex/gender system as a product of the specific social relations which organize it, it allows historically and culturally specific analysis but points to the relative autonomy of the sexual realm. It enables the subordination of women to be seen as a product of the relationships by which sex and gender are organized and produced. Thus to account for the development of specific forms of sex/gender system reference must be made not just to modes of production but also to the totality of specific social formations within which each system develops.[46]

What is clear from the above discussion is that the challenges involved in developing a feminist critical theory are not rooted in the contested status and knowledge claims of feminism as such, nor in the complexity of gendered structures, institutions and practices, but rather in the dangers inherent in falsely universalizing the conditions of women's oppression and attempting to interpret and represent the experiences of women. Feminist critical theory must recognize other significant divisions besides gender, and be able to allow the articulation of different experiences of gender oppression. Similarly a feminist politics must recognize the need for different strategies to challenge forms of gender inequality and build upon the many sites of feminist struggle.

Postmodern feminism

The concept of woman has been central to feminist theory. However, what recent debates in feminist theory have demonstrated is that it is a concept that has been difficult to formulate precisely. For postmodern feminists the concept of woman is, itself, 'a problem',[47] because employing 'woman' as a category of analysis presupposes that all people of the same gender across classes and cultures are somehow socially constituted as a homogeneous group identifiable prior to the process of analysis.[48] In this way the discursive consensual homogeneity of 'women' is mistaken for the specific material reality of groups of women.[49] Postmodern feminists not only reject the notion of fixed identity as a starting point for feminist praxis, but also the notion that race or class, for example, can be 'added' to gender, because they are, rather, constitutive of it. Gender relations, then, have to be viewed in the context of the nuances and complexities of social relations, culture and power. A woman's place in human social life is not in any direct sense a product of the things she does, still less a function of what she is biologically, but rather of the meanings her activities acquire through *concrete* interactions. It is necessary, therefore, to examine what women do in particular societies and how, for example, their access to resources is limited within specific definitions of femininity.[50]

This argument has been echoed by postcolonial feminist thinkers, such as Mohanty, who argue that the 'hegemonic white women's movement has colonized and appropriated the experiences of third world women'. 'Third World Women' has been produced as a single monolithic subject, while the point of reference for women's emancipation has been a feminist interest as articulated in the West.[51] All too often, the specific material and ideological context which renders women powerless has been overlooked. Furthermore, Mohanty has argued that while feminist discourse may serve as an ideological mode of intervention into hegemonic discourse and political praxis which counters and resists the totalizing imperatives of age old legitimate and scientific bodies of knowledge, there is no universal patriarchal framework which feminist scholarship attempts to counter.[52] She claims that racism ensures that black men do not have the same relations to patriarchal/capitalist hierarchies as white men, while white women stand in a particular power relation as oppressors of black women.[53]

Postmodern feminists argue that difference has to be dealt with without retreating into the totalizing ideals of the Enlightenment. This does not necessarily imply nihilism or relativism, because it is legitimate to accept that there might be different forms of knowledge, different value systems, and to engage in debate about which are preferable. Similarly, feminist politics has to be seen outside the binary and sexual difference upon which until now it has been built. This means resisting the notion that emancipatory discourse must always attribute the universal to one particular social group. A distinction should be made between oppositional[54] or 'affirmative'[55] postmodernism and sceptical or non-oppositional postmodernism. Postmodern feminism clearly falls into the first category. Thus postmodern feminists argue that while there is a need to *decentre* the white middle-class heterosexual woman who has been taken as the model of 'woman' in much Western feminism, feminist critique, analysis and politics are still possible.

It is sometimes suggested that postmodern thinkers reject the notion of a coherent unified *subject* as a concrete reference point. As was noted earlier, many feminists argue that because, in the final analysis, postmodernism even in its 'affirmative' or 'oppositional' modes, rejects the notion of a subject with a voice, it undermines the notion of a 'woman's perspective'. This is at the very historical moment that women are constituting themselves as empowered subjects.[56] However, some postmodernists are sympathetic to human-centred analysis and seek to retain or salvage something of the humanist tradition characteristic of the Enlightenment.[57] The idea of the subject as 'master of the universe' is rejected, however, and the subject is, in a sense, viewed as conscious of his or her 'own fictionality'.[58]

Some feminists argue that postmodern ideas are useful in understanding subjectivity, not as a product of external ideas, values or material causes, but as experience grounded in one's personal, subjective engagement in the practices, discourses and institutions that lend significance to events in the world. Such an approach locates feminist theory in the political, theoretical, self-analysing practices by which the relations of the subject in social reality can be rearticulated from the historical experience of women.[59] Postmodern feminists concentrate on the dynamic ways 'in which the subject is constructed through practices of liberation and subjection'.[60] Subjectivity is formulated in a way which gives agency to the individual while at the same time placing her within 'particular discursive configurations'. Subjectivity may thus become imbued with race, class and gender without being subject to an overdetermination that erases agency. This allows a degree of agency and self-determination to individuals without resorting to essentialist views of the subject. The subjectivity of women can be seen in terms other than those of the passive victims of patriarchy.[61] Women have not slipped passively into ascribed gender roles, but have resisted, challenged and changed socially proscribed standards and roles.[62] All women can, and do, think about, criticize and alter discourse and thus subjectivity can be reconstructed through the process of reflective practice.

The deconstruction of identity does not, therefore, necessarily mean the deconstruction of feminist politics. Rather than taking gender identity as a point of departure, in the sense of being a given thing, gender is seen as a construct formalized through a matrix of habits, practices and discourses. Individual 'identity' is constituted through a historical process of consciousness in which one's history is interpreted or reconstructed by each of us within the horizons of meaning and knowledge available at given historical moments, a horizon that also includes modes of political commitment and struggle. Gender 'identity' is not stamped on to the individual, but is rather infused through the process through which gender is constructed with emancipatory potential.[63]

While postmodern feminists reject *metanarratives* – privileged discourses which inevitably silence competing discourses and deny the possibility of other forms of knowledge – feminist discourses can still offer *sites of resistance* to hegemonic discourse and power and provide a space for the voices of women to be heard. Political strategies do not, however, entail the mobilization of a homogeneous group with a common interest in realizing common goals. Women are not a homogeneous group by virtue of their womanhood or their 'dependency'. Marianne Marchand has pointed out that in Latin America feminism is often associated with Western imperialism.[64] Nevertheless, in Latin America the 'sites' of resistance to the orthodoxy of development theory often come from women's organizations. Furthermore, these movements are mobilized around what are perceived to be 'women's issues'. These movements are not overtly 'feminist' and see themselves as resisting imperialism rather than developing a deeper analysis of forms of patriarchal dominance. Nevertheless, women's movements do constitute forms of 'political resistance' and, as Marchand suggests, there are also organizations which are explicitly feminist in orientation. Women can become a strategic group when they enter into a common struggle against class, race, gender and imperialist hierarchies. Indeed, feminists who view the world from a non-Western perspective have recognized the urgent political need to form strategic alliances across class, race and national boundaries, but have pointed out that the analytical principles of Western feminist discourse may in themselves limit the possibilities of coalitions amongst white Western feminists, working-class women and women of colour.

Postmodern thinkers seldom use the term 'emancipatory' politics to describe the projects of resistance. The notion of 'emancipation' is too closely tied to the language of old ideologies such as Marxism and socialist national liberation movements which have, in practice, 'produced little of consequence where they succeeded in gaining power'[65] and have frequently engaged in repression. Furthermore, emancipation 'implies a general prescription, a coherent plan'.[66] However, 'affirmative' postmodernists 'support a range of new political movements, organized around everything from peace/ecology/environment, feminism, green politics, nationalism, popularism, and anarchism'.[67] Such movements are seen as 'communities of resistance'.[68] Some commentators have pointed explicitly to feminist movements as examples of *critical social movements.*[69] Critical social movements are composed of people who 'struggle in particular circumstances' and 'yet recognize new forms of interaction between people, new forms of human community and solidarity that cut across social and territorial categories'.[70] Critical social movements might also develop 'patterns of common affinity and even identity on the basis of shared commitments',[71] bring a radical dimension to the discourse of world affairs and undertake new forms of political action in support of particular values.[72] Feminist movements have played an important role in changing the discourse of 'development', for example, and security. A critical social movement comprises people who strive to make sense of the world in which they live and change affirmatively. From this perspective, the feminist groups can indeed be properly viewed as a critical social movement and, as such, a part of a broader alliance of critical social movements involved in an ongoing struggle to transform oppressive relations in all their complex and diverse manifestations.

As was noted earlier, many feminists argue that the postmodern rejection of truth claims and value judgements cannot be reconciled with the feminist desire to overcome the subordination of women; a desire which in the final analysis is based upon a metanarrative of equality, freedom and emancipation. However, postmodern thinkers see feminist discourse as a celebration of all that has been excluded or marginalized in the name of 'universalism'. Postmodern feminism affirms the importance of the private and emotional aspects of human life, and values the experience of women as a group in so far as women's position in the existing order and the ways in which they engage in the world are shaped by these experiences. Feminism can then be viewed as an example of the 'otherness' that the universalizing tendency of Enlightenment projects cannot tolerate.

Postmodern feminists argue that there is no Archimedean vantage point from which to construct or reconstruct International Relations. To move beyond the orthodoxy is to recognize that because there is no one objective reality out there, only intersubjective understanding, knowledge can only be constructed on the basis of ongoing critique, continual critical reappraisal, negotiation and dialogue. Postmodern scholars are attempting to find ways of moving beyond critique and deconstruction and find ways in which postmodernism can actually further our understanding of a range of human problems. Indeed, many see spaces within modernist discourses of 'emancipation' which allow for critical engagement and negotiation.[73]

Sylvester argues that postmodern feminism and feminist 'standpoint' are not incommensurable since both recognize the many faces of feminism, the many identities of women and affirm the possibility of coherent knowledge.[74] Feminist 'theory', in this view, involves an ongoing dialogue between feminists who consciously reject theoretical projects which universalize the condition of women's experience. It is an approach which emphasizes the importance of dialogue and the need to *listen* to the voices of marginalized women and understand the way in which they make sense of their own lives and define their own priorities and concerns, rather than attempt to articulate the 'interests of women' on the basis of a priori assumptions or in abstract terms.

Furthermore, increasingly feminist theorists are recognizing the necessity of negotiation, because 'the political is best understood as the realm of continual negotiation; the 'space of the contested with regard to the social'.[75] In this way, the foundations of a feminist politics grounded in stable subjects or identities – instances of negotiations limited by the political models of identity or rights which precede them[76] – become increasingly shaky. However, this in itself makes possible a cooperative negotiation of knowledge.[77] Thus negotiation should be distinguished from a relativism, 'a refusal to cooperate or engage in negotiation in the name of tolerance denying that the invented "other" to whom one gives space could possibly have anything in common with one's fixed sense of self'.[78]

A concluding thought

This concluding chapter has concentrated on the ways in which different approaches lead to a rather different understanding of what is involved in analysing gender and constructing feminist knowledge in an International Relations context. Having outlined some of the ways in which one could move from critique to 'reconstruction', one might ask how we decide which approach is 'correct' or at least most satisfactory. Conclusions frequently – all too frequently perhaps – also aspire to deliver the decisive blow by offering conclusive 'evidence' or 'proof', or to settle an argument by appeals to reason or the power of logical argument alone. Given the emphasis which has been placed throughout on the value of drawing upon a number of feminist approaches in International Relations and on the intimate connection between theory/practice and between knowledge, interests and power, it would, perhaps, be perverse at this stage to resort to an accepted theoretical framework in order to demonstrate the 'truth' of an argument.

The collapse of the 'old world order' has increased dissatisfaction with the 'orthodoxy' and given fresh impetus to the search for new conceptual and theoretical tools of analysis in International Relations. These historical developments have contributed towards a general climate which, in some quarters at least, welcomes dialogue. Perhaps the 'feminist project' in International Relations should not be seen as an attempt to 'reconstruct' *the discipline*, but rather as opening up spaces for critical engagement and dialogue. In this way, feminist scholarship in International Relations is central to the project of understanding a complex social and political world.

Notes

Introduction
---

1 The interest in gender issues in International Relations, in the UK
at least, is usually dated from the symposium held at the London
School of Economics in 1988 on 'Women in International Relations'. A special edition of *Millennium: Journal of International Studies*
was subsequently published. See Special Edition 'Women and International Relations', *Millennium: Journal of International Studies*, vol.
17, no. 3, 1988. There is now a growing literature, however, including: Grant, R. and Newland, K. *Gender and International Relations*,
Milton Keynes, Open University Press, 1991; Peterson, V. S. and
Runyan, A. *Global Gender Issues*, Boulder, CO, Westview Press, 1993;
Pettman, J. J. *Worlding Women: A Feminist International Politics*, Lon-
don, Routledge, 1996; Whitworth, S. *Feminist Theory and International
Relations*, Basingstoke, Macmillan, 1994; Tickner, A. *Gender in Inter-
national Relations*, New York, Columbia University Press, 1992;
Sylvester, C. *Feminist Theory and International Relations in a Postmodern
Era*, Cambridge, Cambridge University Press, 1994; Peterson, V. S.
Gendered States: Feminist (Re)Visions of International Theory, Boulder,
CO, Lynne Rienner, 1992. See also: Zalewski, M. 'Feminist Theory
and International Relations', in Bowker, M. and Brown, R. (eds)
From Cold War to Collapse: Theory and World Politics in the 1980s,
Cambridge, Cambridge University Press, 1993; True, J. 'Feminism',
in Linklater, A. and Burchill, S. (eds) *Theories of International Rela-
tions*, Basingstoke, Macmillan, 1996; Williams, A. 'On the Outside
Looking In; Or, Without a Look In: A Feminist Perspective on the
Individual in IR', *Oxford International Review*, May, 1993; Elshtain, J.
'Reflections on War and Political Discourse: Realism, Just War and
Feminism in a Nuclear Age', in Smith, M. and Little, R. *Perspectives*

on World Politics, Milton Keynes, Open University Press, 1994; Hutchins, K. 'The Personal Is International: Feminist Epistemology and the Case of International Relations', in Whitford, M. and Lennon, K. (eds) *Objectivity, the Knowing Subject and Difference*, London, Routledge, 1993; *The Fletcher Forum of World Affairs*, Special Edition, 'Gender and International Relations', vol. 7, no. 2, 1993; *Alternatives Special Edition, Feminists Write International Relations*, vol. 18, no. 1, 1993; Laurien, A. 'Genderizing International Studies: Revisioning Concepts and Curriculum', *International Studies Notes*, vol. 14, no. 1, 1989. While Cynthia Enloe has, of course, been writing 'feminist IR' and encouraging and supporting others in their efforts for some considerable time. See, for example, Enloe, C. *Bananas, Beaches and Bases: Making Feminist Sense of International Relations*, London, Pandora, 1989, and *The Morning After: Sexual Politics after the Cold War*, Berkeley, University of California Press, 1993.

2 There is, however, some debate about whether or not feminism is transforming the discipline or, like other critical approaches, merely 'expanding the margins'. See, for example, Peterson, V. Spike 'Transgressing the Boundaries: Theories of Knowledge, Gender and IR', *Millennium: Journal of International Studies*, vol. 21, no. 2, 1992, pp. 183–206.

3 To borrow from Cynthia Enloe, see Enloe *Bananas*.

4 See, for example, Zalewski, M. and Enloe, C. 'Questions about Identity', in Booth, K. and Smith, S. *International Relations Theory Today*, Cambridge, Polity Press, 1995; Krause, J. 'Gendered Identities in International Relations', in Krause, J. and Renwick, N. *Identities in International Relations*, Basingstoke, Macmillan, 1996; Peterson, V. S. 'Security and Sovereign States: What Is at Stake in Taking Feminism Seriously', in Peterson, V. S., 'Transgressing' and Pettman, J. J. *Worlding Women*, pp. 15–24; Tickner, A. 'Hans Morgenthau's Six Principles of Political Realism: A Feminist Reformulation', in Grant and Newland *Gender*; Tickner *Gender*; Peterson *Transgressing*; Grant, R. 'The Quagmire of Gender and International Security', in Peterson *Transgressing*; Tickner, A. 'On the Fringes of the Global Economy', in Tooze, R. and Murphy, C. *The New International Political Economy*, Boulder, CO, Lynne Rienner, 1992; Sylvester, C. *The Emperor's Theories and Transformations: Looking at the Field through Feminist Lenses*, in Sylvester, C. and Pirages, D. *Transformations in Global Political Economy*, London, Macmillan, 1990; Whitworth, S. *Theory as Exclusion: Gender and International Political Economy*; Stubbs, R. and Underhill, G. *Political Economy and the Changing Global Order*, Basingstoke, Macmillan, 1994; Krause, J. 'The International Dimensions of Gender Inequality and Feminist

Politics', in MacMillan, J. and Linklater, A. *Boundaries in Question: New Directions in International Relations*, London, Pinter, 1995. See, for example, Parpart, J. and Marchand, M. (eds) *Feminism, Postmodernism, Development*, London, Routledge, 1995.

5 This is an extensive literature. See, for example, Coole, D. *Women in Political Theory: From Ancient Misogyny to Contemporary Feminism*, London, Harvester Wheatsheaf, 1993; Di Stefano, C. 'Masculinity as Ideology: Hobbesian Man Considered', *Women's Studies International Forum*, vol. 6, 1983; Elshtain, J. *Public Man/Private Woman*, Princeton, Princeton University Press, 1981; Evans, J. (ed.) *Feminism as Political Theory*, Beverley Hills, CA, Sage Publications, 1986; Okin, S. *Women in Western Political Thought*, Princeton, Princeton University Press, 1979; Pateman, C. *The Problem of Political Obligation*, Cambridge, Polity Press, and Berkeley, University of California Press, 1985; Sunstein, C. *Feminism and Political Theory*, Chicago, University of Chicago Press, 1990.

6 See for example, Grant, R. 'The Sources of Gender Bias in International Relations Theory', in Grant and Newland *Gender*.

7 Youngs, G. '"Beyond Inside"/"Outside"', in Krause and Renwick *Identities in International Relations*.

8 Grant 'The Sources of Gender Bias'.

9 In this sense 'critical theories', or 'critical theorists', is used to refer to feminists, postmodern thinkers and those whose work is more closely related to a Gramscian or Frankfurt School tradition. Contemporary debates in feminist theory have raised issues of identity and difference, the subject of feminism and ontological and epistemological issues. In this way some of the debates in feminist theory have echoed debates in critical theory and postmodernism.

10 See, for example, Turpin, J. and Lorentzen, L. A. *The Gendered New World Order*, London, Routledge, 1996.

11 To give but one example, increasingly as the problems of environmental degradation, poverty, population growth and sustainable development have found their way onto the agenda of world politics, it is coming to be recognized that the fate of women is a global concern. Women work longer hours than men, though their work is frequently rendered invisible. It is women who perform hours of unpaid work in bearing and rearing children. Women are not only usually the main providers of food, fuel and water in many societies, but often the main sustainers and developers of whole communities. The fate of women is a crucial determinant of the fate of whole societies and, indeed, countries. However, women across the world are more likely than men to be trapped in a cycle of poverty and low pay. In every area of the world there are 'women's' and 'men's' jobs, and everywhere women's jobs are lower paid and lower status. The

degree to which women have control over income and resources is also a major factor in understanding the relative nutritional status of children throughout the world. See Seagar, J. and Olson, A. *Women in the World: An International Atlas*, New York, Simon & Schuster, 1986.

12 See Bryson, V. 'Adjusting the Lenses: Feminist Analyses and Marxism at the End of the Twentieth Century', *Contemporary Politics*, vol. 1, no. 1, Spring 1995. See also Jagger, A. and Rothenberg, P. (eds) *Feminist Frameworks*, New York, Praeger, 1993.

13 See Peterson and Runyan, *Global Gender Issues*.

14 Benedict Anderson's notion of nations as 'imagined communities' has been influential in debates about identities in International Relations. See Anderson, B. *Imagined Communities*, London, Verso Books, 1983.

15 Pettman *Worlding Women*.

16 Youngs, 'Beyond "Inside"/"Outside"'.

17 Ibid., p. 27.

18 Ibid., p. 28.

19 Ibid, p. 30.

20 The third being standpoint feminism, the best examples of which are found in Ann Tickner's work. See, for example, Tickner *Gender*.

1   Gender, Feminism and International Relations

1 See discussion in Connell, R. *Gender and Power*, Cambridge, Polity Press, 1995.

2 Ibid.

3 Ibid.

4 See Delphy, C. *Close to Home: A Materialist Analysis of Women's Oppression*, London, Hutchinson, 1984.

5 Connell *Gender and Power*, p. 34.

6 See Millett, K. *Sexual Politics*, London, Virago, 1977.

7 Connell *Gender and Power*.

8 See McNay, L. *Foucault and Feminism*, Cambridge, Polity, 1992.

9 See Butler, J. *Gender Trouble: Feminism and the Subversion of Identity*, London, Routledge, 1996.

10 See McNay *Foucault and Feminism*.

11 Connell *Gender and Power*, p. 80.

12 Ibid.

13 Ibid., p. 85.

14 The term 'feminist movement' is being used loosely here to describe a number of groups ranging from the women's liberation

movement to feminist movements which organized within liberal or Marxist organizations.

15 Alcoff, L. 'Cultural Feminism and Poststructuralism: The Identity Crisis in Feminist Theory', *Signs*, vol. 13, no. 3, 1988.

16 Tong, R. *Feminist Thought: A Comprehensive Introduction*, London, Unwin Hyman, 1989.

17 For a detailed discussion of liberal feminism see: Tong *Feminist Thought*; Eisenstein, H. *Contemporary Feminist Thought*, London, G. K. Hall, 1983; Gatens, M. *Feminism and Philosophy: Perspectives on Equality and Difference*, London, Routledge, 1989; Lovell, T. *British Feminist Thought: A Reader*, Oxford, Blackwell, 1990; Rossi, A. S. (ed.) *John Stuart Mill and Harriet Taylor Mill: Essays on Sex Equality*, Chicago, Chicago University Press, 1970; Phillips, A. *Feminism and Equality*, New York, New York University Press, 1987; Barrett, M. and Phillips, A. *Destabilizing Theory: Contemporary Feminist Debates*, Cambridge, Polity Press, 1992; Eisenstein, Z. *The Radical Future of Liberal Feminism*, London, Longman, 1981; Mitchell, J. and Oakley, A. *What Is Feminism?*, Oxford, Blackwell, 1986.

18 With the notable exception of J. S. Mill, perhaps, early Liberal thinkers assumed that the human subject was male.

19 Wollstonecraft, M. *A Vindication of the Rights of Woman*, Harmondsworth, Penguin, 1985.

20 See Eisenstein *Radical Future*.

21 For a detailed discussion of Marxist feminism see: Hamilton, R. *The Liberation of Women*, London, George Allen & Unwin, 1978; Tong *Feminist Thought*; Barrett, M. *Women's Oppression Today: Problems in Marxist Feminist Analysis*, London, Verso, 1980; Barrett, M. 'The Concept of Difference', *Feminist Review*, no. 26, 1987, pp. 45–53; Eisenstein *Contemporary Feminist Thought*; Hamilton, R. and Barrett, M. *The Politics of Diversity; Feminism, Marxism and Nationalism*, Cambridge, Polity Press, 1986; Hartmann, H. 'The Unhappy Marriage of Marxism and Feminism: Towards a More Progressive Union', in Sargeant, L. (ed.) *Women and Revolution*, London, South End Press, 1981, pp. 1–41; Landry, D. and Maclean, G. *Materialist Feminism*, Oxford, Blackwell, 1993; Lovell *British Feminist Thought*; MacKinnon, C. 'Feminism, Marxism, Method and the State: An Agenda for Change', *Signs*, vol. 7, no. 3, 1982, pp. 515–44; Mitchell and Oakley *What Is Feminism?*

22 Engels, F. *The Origins of the Family, Private Property and the State*, London, Lawrence & Wishart, 1972.

23 Hamilton *Liberation of Women*.

24 Tong *Feminist Thought*, p. 34.

25 Ibid.

26 For a detailed discussion of radical feminism see: Daly, M. *Beyond*

God the Father. Towards a Philosophy of Women's Liberation, Boston, Beacon Press, 1977; Daly, M. *Gyn/Ecology: The Metaethics of Radical Feminism*, London, The Women's Press, 1979; Eisenstein *Contemporary Feminist Thought*; Tong *Feminist Thought*; Gatens, M. *Feminism and Philosophy: Perspectives on Difference and Equality*, Cambridge, Polity Press, 1990; Lovell *British Feminist Thought*; Mitchell and Oakley *What Is Feminism?*

27 Daly *Beyond God the Father* and *Gyn/Ecology*.
28 Regretfully, it is not possible to give a detailed review of socialist-feminist thought in this text. The reader who is interested in reading more about the work of socialist-feminists might find the following texts useful: Barrett, M. and McIntosh, M. 'Ethnocentrism and Socialist Feminist Theory', *Feminist Review*, no. 20, pp. 23–47; Barrett and Phillips *Destabilizing Theory*; Mitchell, J. *Women's Estate*, Harmondsworth, Penguin, 1977; Eisenstein, *Contemporary Feminist Thought*; Eisenstein, Z. (ed.) *Capitalist Patriarchy and the Case for Socialist Feminism*, Boston Monthly Review Press, 1979; Landry and Maclean *Materialist Feminism*; Lovell *British Feminist Thought*; Rowbotham, S. *Woman's Consciousness, Man's World*, Harmondsworth, Penguin, 1973.
29 Tong *Feminist Thought*.
30 A term associated particularly with the work of Juliet Mitchell. See Mitchell, *Women's Estate*.
31 Tong *Feminist Thought*.
32 Ibid.
33 Once again, there is insufficient space to undertake a detailed discussion of psychoanalytic or existential feminist thought. The reader will find a more thorough and detailed treatment in the following texts: Tong *Feminist Thought*; Chodorow, N. *The Reproduction of Mothering*, Berkeley, University of California Press, 1978; Rich, A. *Of Woman Born: Motherhood as Experience and Institution*, W. W. Norton, 1976.
34 For a more detailed discussion of object-relations theory see Chodorow *Reproduction*, and Hirschmann, N. *Rethinking Obligation: A Feminist Method for Political Theory*, Ithaca, Cornell University Press, 1992.
35 Chodorow *Reproduction*.
36 Nancy Hartsock has identified a separate tradition of theorizing power which is found in women's writing. She draws from this that different accounts of power produced by women and men are indicative of systematic and significant differences in life activity. Alternative theorizations of power can be expected to rest on alternative epistemological and ontological bases, perhaps in the different life experiences of men and women. See Hartsock, N. *Money, Sex*

and Power: Towards a Feminist Historical Materialism, Boston, Northeastern University Press, 1983.

37 Ibid.
38 See, for example, Tickner, A. 'Hans Morganthau's Six Principles of Political Realism', *Millennium: Journal of International Studies*, vol. 17, no. 3, 1988.
39 De Beauvoir, S. *The Second Sex*, Harmondsworth, Penguin, 1987.
40 Ibid., pp. 16–29.
41 Ibid.
42 For a more detailed discussion of postmodern feminism see: Nicholson, L. *Feminism/Postmodernism*, London, Routledge, 1990; Benhabib, S., Butler, J. and Fraser, N. 'An Exchange on Feminism and Postmodernism', in *Praxis International*, no. 11, 2 July, 1991, pp. 137–65; Bordo, S. 'Feminism, Postmodernism and Gender', in Nicholson *Feminism, Postmodernism*; Butler *Gender Trouble*; Butler, J. and Scott, J. W. (eds) *Feminists Theorise the Political*, London, Routledge, 1992; Di Stefano, C. 'Dilemmas of Difference; Feminism, Modernity and Postmodernism', in Nicholson *Feminism/Postmodernism*; Flax, J. 'Postmodernism and Gender Relations in Feminist Theory', in Nicholson *Feminism/Postmodernism*; Fraser, N. *Unruly Practices: Power, Discourse and Gender in Contemporary Social Theory*, Cambridge, Polity Press, 1989; Gatens *Feminism and Philosophy*; Hekman, S. *Gender and Knowledge: Elements of a Postmodern Feminism*, Cambridge, Polity Press, 1990; Hirsch, M. and Fox Keller, E. (eds) *Conflicts in Feminism*, London, Routledge, 1990.
43 The term 'postmodernism' is used broadly in this text to describe a variety of distinctive critical positions which are anti-foundationalist.
44 See also Horkheimer, M. and Adorno, T. *Dialectic of the Enlightenment*, New York, Herder & Herder, 1972.
45 Tong *Feminist Thought*.
46 Associated particularly with the work of Jacques Derrida. See Derrida, J. *Of Grammatology*, Baltimore, Johns Hopkins University Press, 1976; *Speech and Phenomena, and Other Essays on Husserl's Theory of Signs*, Evaston, Northwestern University Press, 1973; *Writing and Difference*, London, Routledge, 1978.
47 Bordo, S. 'Feminism, Postmodern and Gender Scepticism', in Nicholson *Feminism/Postmodernism*.
48 Mohanty, C., Rosso, A. and Torress, L. (eds) *Third World Women and the Politics of Feminism*, Indiana University Press, 1991.
49 For a more detailed discussion of postcolonial feminism see: Mohanty, Rosso and Torress *Third World Women*; Amos, V. and Parmar, P. 'Challenging Imperial Feminism', *Feminist Review*, no. 17, 1984, pp. 13–19; Carby, H. *The Empire Strikes Back: Race and Racism in 70s Britain*, London, Hutchinson, 1982.

50 See: Ramazanoglu, C. *Feminism and the Contradictions of Oppression*, London, Routledge, 1989; Amos and Parmar 'Challenging Imperial Feminism'; hooks, b. and Watkin, G. *Aint I a Woman? Black Women and Feminism*, London, South End Press, 1981; hooks, b. *Yearning: Race, Gender and Cultural Politics*, London, South End Press, 1990.

51 See *Feminist Review*, no. 17, 1984, p. 93.

52 Indeed, as Alcoff suggests, for many contemporary feminists the concept of woman itself became a problem. While woman as both a social and analytical category had been central to feminist theory, it was a category which was impossible to formulate precisely. See Alcoff 'Cultural Feminism'.

53 Ibid., p. 141.

54 George, J. *Discourses of Global Politics: A Critical (Re)Introduction to International Relations*, Boulder, CO, Lynne Rienner, 1994.

55 Ibid.

56 Lorde, A. *Sister Outsider*, Boston, Crossing Press Feminist Series, 1984.

57 See Foucault on specific and general intellectuals. See 'Intellectuals and Power: A Conversation between Michel Foucault and Gilles Deleuze', in Foucault, M. *Language, Counter-Memory, Practice*, Oxford, Blackwell, 1977.

58 Bryson, V. 'Adjusting the Lenses: Feminist Analysis and Marxism at the End of the Twentieth Century', *Contemporary Politics*, vol. 1, no. 1, Spring 1995, p. 5.

59 George *Discourses of Global Politics*.

60 Habermas, J. *Knowledge and Human Interests*, London, Heinemann, 1972.

61 See Held, D. *Introduction to Critical Theory*, Cambridge, Polity Press, 1986.

62 An idea which has been central to the work of Robert Cox. See, for example, Cox, R. *Production, Power and World Order*, New York, Columbia University Press, 1987, or 'Social Forces, States and World Order: Beyond International Theory', *Millennium: Journal of International Studies*, vol. 10, no. 2, pp. 126–55.

63 See Sassoon, A. Showstack *Approaches to Gramsci*, London, Writers and Readers, 1992.

64 Ibid.

65 According to Gill a counter-hegemony might come together and form an historic bloc with a congruence to fit between prevailing ideas and conceptions of society and forces of production embodied in politics, parties, trade unions and associations. See Gill, S. 'Knowledge Politics and Neo-Liberal Political Economy', in Stubbs, R. and Underhill, G. *The International Political Economy*, London,

Routledge, 1990. See also Gill, S. and Law, D. *Global Political Economy*, Hemel Hempstead, Harvester Wheatsheaf, 1988.

66 See discussions by Marchand, M. and Runyan, A. in 'Part Three: Trading Places or Gendering the Global', in Youngs, G. and Kofman, E. *Globalisation: Theory and Practice*, London, Pinter, 1996.

67 Schnieder, M. *Feminism: The Essential Historical Writings*, London, Vintage, 1972, pp. xii–xiii.

68 Fraser, N. 'What's Critical about Critical Theory? The Case of Habermas and Gender', in Fraser, N. and Benhabib, S. *Feminism as Critique*, Cambridge, Polity Press, 1987, p. 31.

69 Ibid. See Marx, K. Letter to A. Ruge, September 1843, in McLellan, D. *Karl Marx: Selected Writings*, Oxford, Oxford University Press, 1977.

70 Ibid., p. 31.

71 Ibid., p. 15.

72 Grimshaw, J. *Feminist Philosophers*, Hemel Hempstead, Harvester Wheatsheaf, 1987.

73 See discussion in Disch, L. 'Towards a Feminist Conception of Politics', *The Political Science Teacher*, September 1991.

74 For a discussion of feminist critical theory and the analysis of gender relations and institutional contexts, see ibid.

75 See, for example, Whitworth, S. *Feminist Theory and International Relations*, Basingstoke, Macmillan, 1994.

76 Ibid.

77 See discussion of the implication of the third debate for critical theorists in Hoffman, M. 'Critical Theory and the Inter-paradigm Debate', *Millennium: Journal of International Studies*, vol. 16, 1987, pp. 231–49.

78 For a general discussion of the various phases of International Relations theory and the debates which have shaped the discipline see, Groom, A. J. R. and Olson, W. *International Relations Then and Now*, London, HarperCollins, 1991.

79 Banks, M. 'The Inter-paradigm Debate', in Groom, A. J. R. and Light, M. *International Relations: A Handbook of Current Theory*, London, Pinter, 1985.

80 Lapid, Y. 'Quo Vadis International Relations? Further Reflections on the "Next Stage" of International Theory', *Millennium: Journal of International Studies*, vol. 18, no. 1, 1989, pp. 77–88.

81 Hoffman 'Critical Theory and the Inter-paradigm Debate'.

82 Whitworth, S. 'Gender in the Inter-paradigm Debate', *Millennium: Journal of International Studies*, vol. 18, no. 2, 1989, pp. 265–72.

83 The work of Sandra Harding has been particularly important here. See, for example, Harding, S. *Whose Science? Whose Knowledge? Thinking from Women's Lives*, Milton Keynes, Open University Press, 1991.

84 Walker, R. *Inside/Outside: International Relations as Political Theory*, Cambridge, Cambridge University Press, 1993.

85 Peterson, V. S. 'Transgressing the Boundaries; Theories of Knowledge, Gender and IR', *Millennium: Journal of International Studies*, vol. 21, no. 2, 1992, pp. 183–206.

86 Walker, R. 'Gender and Feminist Critique', in Peterson, V. S. *Gendered States: Feminist (Re)Visions of International Theory*, Boulder, CO, Lynne Rienner, 1992.

87 See, for example, Peterson, V. S. and Runyan, A. *Global Gender Issues*, Boulder, CO, Westview Press, 1993; Pettman, J. J. *Worlding Women: A Feminist International Politics*, London, Routledge, 1996; Whitworth, S. *Feminist Theory and International Relations*, Basingstoke, Macmillan, 1994; Tickner, A. *Gender in International Relations*, New York, Columbia University Press, 1992; Sylvester, C. *Feminist Theory and International Relations in a Postmodern Era*, Cambridge, Cambridge University Press, 1994; Peterson 'Transgressing'; Zalewski, M. 'Feminist Theory and International Relations', in Bowker, M. and Brown, R. (eds) *From Cold War to Collapse: Theory and World Politics in the 1980s*, Cambridge, Cambridge University Press, 1993; Enloe, C. *Bananas, Beaches and Bases: Making Feminist Sense of International Relations*, London, Pandora, 1989 and *The Morning After: Sexual Politics after the Cold War*, Berkeley, University of California Press, 1993; Weber, C. 'Good Girls, Bad Girls and Little Girls', *Millennium: Journal of International Studies*, 1993; Marchand, M. 'Latin American Voices of Resistance: Women's Movements and Development Debates', in Rostow, S., Rupert, M. and Samatur, A. *The Global Economy as Political Space: Essays in Critical Theory and International Political Economy*, Cambridge, Cambridge University Press, 1995.

2 Feminism and Critiques of the 'Orthodoxy'

1 See for example Banks, M. 'The Inter-paradigm Debate', in Light, M. and Groom, A. J. R. *International Relations: A Handbook of Current Theory*, London, Pinter, 1985.

2 Waltz, however, locates the problem of conflict in the anarchical nature of the international system. See, for example, Waltz, K. *Theory of International Politics*, Reading, Addison-Wesley, 1980. See also Vincent, J. 'The Hobbesian Tradition in Twentieth Century International Thought', *Millennium: Journal of International Studies*, vol. 10, no. 2, 1981, pp. 91–9.

3 Carr, E. H. *The Twenty Years' Crisis 1919–1939: An Introduction to the Study of International Relations*, London, Macmillan, 1939.

4 Ibid., pp. 3–15.

5 Morgenthau, H. J. *Politics among Nations: The Struggle for Power and Peace*, Alfred A. Knopf, New York, 1948.
6 See Vasquez, J. *The Power of Power Politics*, London, Pinter, 1983; Groom, A. J. R. and Olson, W. *International Relations Then and Now: Origins and Trends in Interpretation*, HarperCollins, London, 1991, pp. 109–10.
7 Kuhn, T. *The Structure of Scientific Revolutions*, Chicago, Chicago University Press, 1962.
8 See the discussion of the impact of Kuhn's work and its implications for International Relations theory in Vasquez *Power of Power Politics*.
9 Ibid.
10 Ibid.
11 Indeed, some moved closer to it. See, for example, Keohane, R. *After Hegemony*, Princeton, Princeton University Press, 1984.
12 Vasquez *Power of Power Politics*.
13 Ibid.
14 Rosenau, J. *The Scientific Study of Foreign Policy*, London, Frances Pinter, 1980, is perhaps a good example.
15 Vasquez *Power of Power Politics*.
16 See Ashley, R. 'The Poverty of Neo-Realism', in Keohane, R. *Neo-Realism and its Critics*, New York, Columbia University Press, 1986.
17 See, for example, Morgenthau *Politics among Nations*, pp. 4–5.
18 See discussion in Maclean, J. 'Political Theory, International Theory and Problems of Ideology', *Millennium: Journal of International Studies*, vol. 10, no. 2, 1981, pp. 102–25.
19 Held, D. *Introduction to Critical Theory: Horkheimer to Habermas*, Cambridge, Polity Press, 1980, p. 22.
20 Ibid.
21 Ibid., p. 22.
22 Ibid.
23 Ibid.
24 See for example, Cox, R. 'Social Forces, States and World Order, Beyond International Relations Theory', *Millennium: Journal of International Studies*, vol. 10, no. 2, 1981, pp. 126–55.
25 Martin Wight, for example, questioned how far the behaviour of non-Western people could be understood on the basis of a series of generalizations drawn from the West. See discussion in Potter, B. 'Patterns of Thought and Practice: Martin Wight's International Theory', in Donalan, M. *The Reason of States: A Study in International Political Theory*, London, Allen and Unwin, 1978.
26 Maclean 'Political Theory'.
27 Ibid.
28 Stanley, L. and Wise, S. *Breaking Out: Feminist Consciousness and Feminist Research*, London, Routledge, 1983.

29 Foucault, M. *Power/Knowledge: Selected Interviews and Other Writings, 1972–1977* (ed. C. Gordon), Brighton, Harvester Wheatsheaf, 1980.
30 Bourdieu, P. *Outline of a Theory of Practice*, Cambridge University Press, Cambridge, 1977.
31 Ibid., pp. 78–86.
32 Ibid., p. 82.
33 Ibid., p. 86.
34 Maclean 'Political Theory'.
35 Ibid.
36 Bourdieu *Outline*, pp. 159–71.
37 Hutchins, K. 'The Personal Is International: Feminist Epistemology and the Case of International Relations', in Whitford, M. and Lennon, K. (eds) *Objectivity, the Knowing Subject and Difference*, London, Routledge, 1993.
38 Ibid.
39 See also Runyan, A. 'The "State" of Nature: A Garden Unfit for Women and Other Living Things', in Peterson, V. S. *Gendered States: Feminist (Re)Visions of International Relations Theory*, Boulder, CO, Lynne Rienner, 1992; Sylvester, C. 'Feminists and Realists View Autonomy and Obligation in International Relations', in Peterson *Gendered States*; Peterson, V. S. and Runyan, A. 'The Radical Future of Realism: Feminist Subversions of IR Theory', *Alternatives*, vol. 16, no. 1, 1991, pp. 67–106.
40 Ashley, R. 'Untying the Sovereign State: A Double Reading of the Anarchy Problematique', *Millennium: Journal of International Studies*, vol. 17, no. 2, 1988, pp. 256–7.
41 See Tickner, A. 'Hans Morgenthau's Six Principles of Political Realism: A Feminist Reformulation', in Grant, R. and Newland, K. *Gender and International Relations*, Milton Keynes, Open University Press, 1991.
42 Grant, R. 'The Sources of Gender Bias in International Relations Theory', in Grant and Newland *Gender*, p. 9.
43 Ashley, R. 'Untying'.
44 See discussion in Groom and Olson *International Relations*, p. 7.
45 See Krause, J. 'Power, Autonomy and Gender in Realist Theory', in Pfetsch, F. (ed.) *International Relations and Pan-Europe*, Hamburg, Lit Verlag, 1994.
46 See Machiavelli *The Prince* (trans. G. Bull), Harmondsworth, Penguin, 1961.
47 See the discussion in Kelly, J. *Women, History and Theory*, Chicago, Chicago University Press, 1984.
48 See Pitkin, H. *Fortuna Is a Woman: Gender and Politics in the Thought of Niccolo Machiavelli*, Berkeley, University of California Press, 1984.
49 Ibid., pp. 80–105.

50 Ibid., p. 25.
51 Ibid., pp. 55–79.
52 Ibid.
53 Ibid.
54 Carr *Twenty Years' Crisis*, p. 159.
55 Ibid., p. 159.
56 Ibid., p. 25.
57 Morgenthau *Politics among Nations*.
58 Ibid., p. 103.
59 Ibid., p. 103, my emphasis.
60 Hobbes, T., (1651) *Leviathan*, Oxford, Oxford University Press, 1952.
61 Benhabib, S. 'The Generalised and Concrete Other', in Benhabib, S. and Cornell, D. *Feminism as Critique*, Cambridge, Polity Press, 1987, p. 85.
62 See discussion in Coole, D. *Women in Political Theory: From Ancient Misogyny to Contemporary Feminism*, Hemel Hempstead, Harvester Wheatsheaf, 1989.
63 Ibid.
64 Ibid.
65 Morgenthau *Politics among Nations*.
66 Ibid.
67 Ibid.
68 Ibid.
69 Ibid.
70 Claude, I. *Power and International Relations*, New York, Random House, 1962.
71 Ibid., p. 55.
72 Ashley 'Poverty of Neo-Realism'.
73 Hirschmann, N. *Rethinking Obligation: A Feminist Method for Political Theory*, New York, Cornell University Press, 1992.
74 Ibid.
75 Ibid., p. 166.
76 Ibid., p. 167.
77 Pitkin *Fortuna*.
78 Ibid.
79 Ibid.
80 Navari, C. 'Knowledge, the State and the State of Nature', in Donalan *Reason of States*, p. 102.
81 Ibid.
82 Lloyd, G. *The Man of Reason: Male and Female in Western Philosophy*, London, Methuen, 1984.
83 Peterson, V. Spike 'Whose Rights? A Critique of the "Givens" in Human Rights Discourse', *Alternatives*, vol. 15, no. 3, pp. 183–206.

84 Ibid.
85 Ibid.
86 Di Stefano, 'Masculinity as Ideology in Political Theory: Hobbesian Man Considered', *Women's Studies International Forum*, vol. 6, no. 6, pp. 633–44.
87 Ibid.
88 Ibid.
89 Ibid.
90 Ibid.
91 Hartsock, N. 'The Barracks Community in Western Political Thought', *The Women's Studies International Forum*, vol. 5, no. 3/4, 1982, pp. 283–6.
92 Hirschmann *Rethinking Obligation*.
93 Hartsock 'Barracks Community'.
94 Brittan, A. *Masculinity and Power*, Oxford, Basil Blackwell, 1989.
95 Ibid.

——3 States, Nationalisms and Gendered Identities——

Part of this chapter was published as 'Gendered Identities in International Relations', in Krause, J. and Renwick, N. *Identities in International Relations*, Basingstoke, Macmillan, 1996.

1 Kratochwil, F. 'Citizenship: On the Border of Order', in Lapid, J. and Kratochwil, F. *The Return of Culture and Identity in IR Theory*, London, Lynne Rienner, 1996. See also Linklater, A. 'Citizenship and Sovereignty in the Post Westaphalian State', *European Journal of International Relations*, vol. 2, no. 1, March 1996, pp. 77–103.
2 Kratochwil 'Citizenship', p. 182.
3 Krause, J. and Renwick, N. 'Concluding Thoughts', in Krause and Renwick *Identities*, p. 213.
4 Farrands, C. 'Society, Modernity and Social Change: Approaches to Nationalism and Identity', in Krause and Renwick *Identities*.
5 Krause and Renwick *Identities*, p. 214.
6 See, for example, Buzan, B. *People, States and Fear: An Agenda for International Security Studies in the Post-Cold War Era*, Hemel Hempstead, Harvester Wheatsheaf, 1991.
7 Krause and Renwick *Identities*.
8 Ibid., p. 213.
9 Zalewski, M. and Enloe, C. 'Questions of Identity', in K. Booth and Smith, S. *International Relations Theory Today*, Cambridge, Polity Press, 1995, p. 281.
10 See for example, Seager, J. and Olson, A. *Women in the World: An International Atlas*, New York, Simon & Schuster, 1993; Peterson,

V. S. and Runyan, A. *Global Gender Issues*, Boulder, CO, Westview Press, 1993.

11 Scholte, J. A. 'Globalization and Collective Identities', in Krause and Renwick *Identities*, p. 38.

12 Ibid.

13 Ibid.

14 Parker, A., Russo, M., Sommer, D. and Yaeger, P. *Nationalisms and Sexualities*, London, Routledge, 1992.

15 Anderson, B. *Imagined Communities*, London, Verso Books, 1983.

16 Yuval Davis, N. and Anthias, F. 'Introduction', *Woman, Nation, State*, Basingstoke, Macmillan, 1989. See also discussion of Yuval Davis's work in Kandiyoti, D. 'Identity and its Discontents', *Millennium: Journal of International Studies*, vol. 20, no. 3, 1992.

17 See Callaway, H. and Ridd, R. *Caught Up in Conflict*: Women's Responses to Political Strife, Basingstoke, Macmillan, 1986.

18 Kandiyoti 'Identity', p. 429.

19 Jayawardena, K. *Feminism and Nationalism in the Third World*, London, Zed Books, 1986.

20 Kandiyoti 'Identity', p. 431.

21 Parker, A. et al. *Nationalisms*.

22 Mosse, G. *Nationalism and Sexuality: Middle Class Morality and Sexual Norms in Modern Europe*, Madison, University of Wisconsin Press, 1985.

23 Kandiyoti 'Identity', p. 429.

24 Ibid.

25 Parker et al. *Nationalisms*.

26 Kandiyoti 'Identity'.

27 Massey, D. and Jess, P. (eds) *A Place in the World? Places, Cultures and Globalization*, Milton Keynes, Open University Press, 1995, p. 65.

28 Ibid.

29 Ibid.

30 Ibid.

31 Kandiyoti 'Identity', p. 435.

32 Ibid., p. 429.

33 See discussion in Parker et al. *Nationalisms*, p. 6.

34 Yuval Davis and Anthias *Woman, Nation, State*.

35 Ibid.

36 Obbo, C. 'Sexuality and Economic Domination in Uganda', in Yuval Davis and Anthias *Woman, Nation, State*.

37 Kriger, N. J. *Zimbabwe's Guerilla War: Peasant Voices*, Cambridge, Cambridge University Press, 1992.

38 Ibid.

39 See O'Barr, J. 'African Women in Politics', in Hay, M and Stichter, S. *African Women South of the Sahara*, London, Zed Books, 1984.

40 Callaway and Ridd *Caught up in Conflict*.

41 Harris, H. 'Women and War: The Case of Nicaragua', in Isaksson, E. (ed.) *Women in the Military System*, Brighton, Harvester Wheatsheaf, 1988.
42 Ibid.
43 Frente Sandinista para la Liberación National.
44 Harris 'Women and War'.
45 Jayawardena *Feminism and Nationalism*.
46 Ibid.
47 Callaway and Ridd *Caught up in Conflict*.
48 Ibid.
49 Harris 'Women and War'. For a discussion of the relative neglect of gender issues on the part of the Sandinista regime see Pettiford, L. 'Identities and the Nicaraguan Revolution', in Krause and Renwick *Identities*.
50 Ibid.
51 Chatterjee, P. 'Whose Imagined Communities?', *Millennium: Journal of International Studies*, vol. 20, no. 3, 1991.
52 Helie-Lucas, M. A. 'The Role of Women During the Algerian Liberation Struggle and After: Nationalism as a Concept and as a Practice towards both the Power of the Army and the Militarization of the People', in Isaksson *Women in the Military System*, p. 173.
53 Ibid., p. 175.
54 Ibid., p. 176.
55 Ibid.
56 See Callaway, H. 'Survival and Support: Women's Forms of Political Action', in Callaway and Ridd *Caught up in Conflict*.
57 Westwood, S. and Radcliffe, S. (eds) *'Viva': Women and Popular Protest in Latin America*, London, Routledge, 1993.
58 Ibid.
59 Ibid.
60 Callaway and Ridd *Caught up in Conflict*.
61 Ibid.
62 Molyneux, M. 'Mobilisation without Emancipation? Women's Interests, State and Revolution in Nicaragua', *Feminist Studies*, vol. 11, no. 2, Summer 1985.
63 Callaway and Ridd *Caught up in Conflict*.
64 Chatterjee, P. 'Whose Imagined Communities?'.
65 The work of Homi Bhabha is central here. See, for example, *Black Skin, White Masks*, Harmondsworth, Penguin, 1986.
66 Massey, D. 'A Global Sense of Place', *Marxism Today*, June 1991, p. 29.
67 Giddens, A. *The Consequences of Modernity*, Cambridge, Polity Press, 1990.
68 Ibid.

69 Scholte 'Globalization'.
70 Rutherford, J. *Identity, Community, Culture and Difference*, London, Lawrence & Wishart, 1990.
71 The best example of this work in an IR context is probably Jan Aart Scholte. See, for example, Scholte, J. 'Globalization and Collective Identities', in Krause and Renwick *Identities*.
72 Ibid., p. 39.
73 Walker, R. J. B. 'Gender and Critique in the Theory of International Relations', in Peterson, V. S. and Runyan, A. S. *Gendered States: Feminist (Re)Visions of International Theory*, Boulder CO, Lynne Rienner, 1992, p. 180.
74 Ibid.
75 See discussion in chapter 6. Also see Krause, J. 'Gender Issues and Feminist Politics in Global Perspective', in Kofman, E. and Youngs, G. *Globalization: Theory and Practice*, London, Pinter, 1996.

——4 The 'Warrior Hero' and the Patriarchal State——

1 Hartsock, N. *Money, Sex and Power: Towards a Feminist Historical Materialism*, Boston, Northeastern University Press, 1983, pp. 187–90, and Hartsock, N. 'The Barracks Community in Western Political Thought: Prolegomena to a Feminist Critique of War and Politics', *Women's Studies International Forum*, vol. 5, no. 4, 1982, pp. 283–6.
2 Mann, M. *The Sources of Social Power*, Cambridge, Cambridge University Press, 1986.
3 See, for example, Phillips, A. *Engendering Democracy*, Cambridge, Polity, 1991.
4 See Fraser, N. 'What's Critical About Critical Theory', in Cornel, D. and Benhabib, S. *Feminism as Critique*, Cambridge, Polity Press, 1987; Peterson, V. S. 'Security and Sovereign States', in Peterson, V. S. *Gendered States: Feminist (Re)Visions of International Relations Theory*, Boulder, CO, Lynne Rienner, 1992; and Elshtain, J. 'Reflections on War and Political Discourse', *Political Theory*, vol. 13, no. 1, 1985, pp. 39–57.
5 Epstein, C. Fuchs 'In Praise of Women Warriors', *Dissent*, vol. 38, 1991, pp. 421–2.
6 Stiehm, J. H. 'The Protector, The Protected and The Defender', *Women's Studies International Forum*, vol. 5, no. 3/4, 1982, pp. 367–76.
7 Epstein 'In praise'. See also Chapkis, W. (ed.) *Loaded Questions: Women in the Military*, Amsterdam, Transnational Institute, 1981.
8 Connell R. 'The State, Gender and Sexual Politics: Theory and Appraisal', *Theory and Society*, vol. 19, 1990, p. 530.
9 Ibid.

10 Ibid.
11 Ibid.
12 Epstein 'In Praise'.
13 Hartsock 'Barracks Community' and *Money, Sex and Power.*
14 Ibid.
15 Pierson, R. 'Beautiful Soul or Just Warrior: Gender and War', *Gender and History*, vol. 1, no. 1, 1989, p. 78. See also Elshtain, J. *Women and War*, New York, Basic Books, 1987.
16 Elshtain 'Reflections', p. 43.
17 Ibid.
18 See the discussion in Connell 'The State, Gender and Sexual Politics'.
19 MacKinnon, C. *Towards a Feminist Theory of the State*, Cambridge, MA, Harvard University Press, 1989, p. 157.
20 See the discussion in Yuval-Davis, N. and Athias, F. *Woman, Nation, State*, Basingstoke, Macmillan, 1987, pp. 1–14.
21 McIntosh, M. 'The State as Oppressor of Women', in Kuhn, A. and Wolfe, A. (eds) *Feminism and Materialism. Women and Modes of Production*, London, Routledge, 1985.
22 Dalerup, D. 'Confusing Concepts – Confusing Reality: A Theoretical Discussion of the Patriarchal State', in Sassoon, A. Showstack (ed.) *Women and the State*, London, Hutchinson, 1987.
23 Standt, K. 'Women, Development and the State: On the Theoretical Impasse', *Development and Change*, vol. 17, 1986, pp. 325–33.
24 Connell 'The State, Gender and Sexual Politics', p. 351.
25 Ibid.
26 Ibid.
27 Connell, R. *Gender and Power*, Cambridge, Polity Press, 1995.
28 Ibid.
29 Ibid., p. 109.
30 Cohn 'Wars, Wimps and Women', in Cooke, M. and Woollacott, A. *Gendering War Talk*, Princeton, Princeton University Press, 1993.
31 Ibid.
32 Ruddick, S. 'Notes Towards a Feminist Peace Politics', in Cooke, M. and Woollacott, A. *Gendering War Talk*, Princeton, Princeton University Press, 1993.
33 Enloe, C. 'Thinking about War, Militarism and Peace', in Hess, B. and Feree, M. (eds) *Analysing Gender: A Handbook of Social Science Research*, Beverley Hills, Sage, 1987.
34 Ibid.
35 Ruddick 'Notes'.
36 Cohn 'Wars, Wimps and Women. See also Cohn, C. 'Sex and Death in the Rational World of Defence Intellectuals', *Signs*, vol. 12, no. 4, 1987, pp. 687–718.

37 Cooke and Woollacott *Gendering War Talk.*
38 See Connell, 'The State, Gender and Sexual Politics'.
39 Connell *Gender and Power*, p. 130.
40 Hacker, B. 'From Military Revolution to Industrial Revolution: Armies, Women and Political Economy in Early Modern Europe', in Isaksson, E. *Women in the Military System*, Brighton, Harvester Wheatsheaf, 1988.
41 Roberts, M. *The Military Revolution*, Belfast, 1956. See also discussion in Hacker 'From Military Revolution'.
42 Beevor, A. *Inside the British Army*, London, Hamish Hamilton, 1994, p. 59.
43 Ibid., p. 72.
44 Ibid., p. 74.
45 Enloe, C. *Does Khaki Become You? The Militarisation of Women's Lives*, London, Pandora, 1988.
46 Hacker 'From Military Revolution'.
47 Braydon, G. and Summerfield, P. *Out of the Cage: Women's Experiences in Two World Wars*, London, Pandora, 1987.
48 Ibid.
49 Ibid.
50 Ibid.
51 Ibid.
52 Ruddick, S. 'Mothers and Men's Wars', in Harris, A. and King, Y. *Rocking the Ship of State: Towards a Feminist Peace Politics*, Boulder, CO, Westview, 1989.
53 Ibid.
54 Ibid.
55 Ibid.
56 Ibid.
57 Ibid.
58 Ibid.
59 Connell *Gender and Power.*
60 Ruddick 'Mothers and Men's Wars'.
61 Beevor *Inside the British Army.*
62 Ibid.
63 Ruddick 'Mothers and Men's Wars'.
64 Connell 'The State, Gender and Sexual Politics'.
65 Ibid.
66 Ibid.
67 Enloe *Does Khaki Become You?*
68 Ibid.
69 See Brock-Utne, B. *Educating for Peace*, Oxford, Pergamon, 1985, and Reardon, B. *Sexism and the Military System*, New York, Teachers College Press, 1985.
70 Stiehm 'The Protector'.

71 Stiehm, J. *Women's and Men's Wars*, Oxford, Pergamon Press, 1984.
72 Stiehm 'The Protector'.
73 Beevor *Inside the British Army*.
74 See discussion in Cock, J. 'Keeping the Home Fires Burning: Militarism and the Politics of Gender in South Africa', *Review of African Political Economy*, vol. 5, no. 2, 1989, pp. 50–64.
75 Beevor *Inside the British Army*.
76 Yuval-Davis, N. 'Front and Rear: The Sexual Division of Labour in the Israeli Army', *Feminist Studies*, vol. 11, no. 3, 1985, pp. 649–75.
77 Stiehm, J. *Arms and the Enlisted Woman*, Philadelphia, Temple University Press, 1989.
78 Yuval-Davis 'Front and Rear'.
79 Ibid.
80 Beevor *Inside the British Army*.
81 Enloe *Does Khaki Become You?*, p. 218.
82 Beevor *Inside the British Army*.
83 Pierson, R. 'They're Still Women After All: Wartime Jitters over Femininity', in Isaksson *Women in the Military*.
84 Ibid.
85 Ibid., p. 43.
86 South African Defence Force.
87 Cock 'Keeping the Home Fires'.
88 Yuval-Davis 'Front and Rear'.
89 Cock 'Keeping the Home Fires'.
90 Beevor *Inside the British Army*.
91 Stiehm *Arms and the Enlisted Woman*.
92 Evans, G. and Newnham, J. *The Dictionary of World Politics*, Hemel Hempstead, Harvester Wheatsheaf, 1990.
93 Clausewitz *On War* (ed. A. Rapaport), Harmondsworth, Penguin, 1986.
94 See Clausewitz *On War*.
95 Vickers, J. *Women and War*, London, Zed Books, 1993.
96 Pettman, J. *Worlding Women: A Feminist International Politics*, London, Routledge, 1996.
97 Stiehm 'The Protector'.
98 Pettman *Worlding Women*, p. 100.
99 In recent years, women in Korea have demanded and received reparation from the Japanese government and an apology for the 100,000 women who during the war between Korea and Japan in 1930–40, were forced to the Pacific Islands into sexual slavery.
100 *Peace News*, Summer, 1995.
101 See discussion in Connell 'The State, Gender and Sexual Politics'.
102 Hartsock 'Barracks Community'.
103 Ibid.
104 Connell 'The State, Gender and Sexual Politics'.

105 Elshtain 'Reflections', p. 43.
106 Hartsock 'Barracks Community'.

───────────5   Feminist Perspectives on Security───────────

1 Scruton, R. *A Dictionary of Political Thought*, London, Pan, 1983.
2 Buzan, B. *People, States and Fear: An Agenda for International Security in a Post Cold War Era*, Hemel Hempstead, Harvester Wheatsheaf, 1991.
3 Ibid.
4 Scruton *A Dictionary*.
5 Ibid.
6 Tickner, J. A. 'Revisioning Security', in Booth, K. and Smith, S. *International Relations Theory Today*, Cambridge, Polity, 1995.
7 Buzan *People, States and Fear*.
8 Ibid., p. 177.
9 Ibid., p. 39.
10 Ibid., p. 38.
11 Ibid., p. 188.
12 Jervis, R. 'The Spiral of International Insecurity', in Smith, M., Shackleton, M. and Little, R. *Perspectives on World Politics*, Milton Keynes, Open University Press, 1981.
13 Buzan *People, States and Fear*.
14 See, for example, Waltz, K. *Man, the State and War*, New York, Columbia University Press, 1959.
15 Youngs, G. 'Beyond the Inside/Outside Divide', in Krause, J. and Renwick, N. *Identities in International Relations*, Basingstoke, Macmillan, 1996.
16 Linklater, A. 'The Question of the Next Stage in International Relations Theory: A Critical Theoretical Point of View', *Millennium: Journal of International Studies*, vol. 21, 1992.
17 Ibid.
18 Campbell, D. *Writing Security: United States Foreign Policy and the Politics of Identity*, Manchester, Manchester University Press, 1992. See also discussion in Tickner 'Revisioning Security'.
19 Elshtain, J. 'Reflections on War and Political Discourse: Realism, Just War and Feminism in a Nuclear Age', *Political Theory*, vol. 13, no. 1, 1985, pp. 39–57. Elshtain is, however, drawing upon the work of Michel Foucault. See *Discipline and Punish*, New York, Vintage Books, 1979.
20 Elshtain 'Reflections'.
21 Ibid., p. 40.
22 Hartsock, N. 'The Barracks Community in Western Political

Thought', *Women's Studies International Forum,* vol. 5, no. 3/4, 1982, pp. 283–6.

23 Ibid.

24 Ibid.

25 Tickner, J. A. *Gender and International Relations,* New York, Cornell University Press, 1992.

26 Beneria, L. and Blank, R. 'Women and the Economics of Military Spending', in Harris, A. and King, Y. *Rocking the Ship of State: Towards a Feminist Peace Politics,* Boulder, CO, Westview Press, 1989.

27 Ibid.

28 Ibid.

29 Ibid.

30 Ibid.

31 Enloe, C. 'Feminist Thinking about War, Militarism and Peace', in Hess, B. and Ferree, M. *Analysing Gender: A Handbook of Social Science Research,* Beverley Hills, Sage, 1987.

32 See the discussion in Beneria and Blank 'Women and the Economics of Military Spending'.

33 Ibid.

34 Ibid.

35 Enloe 'Feminist Thinking'. See also Enloe, C. *Does Khaki Become You? The Militarisation of Women's Lives,* London, Pandora, 1988.

36 Enloe 'Feminist Thinking'.

37 Ibid.

38 See discussion in Cock, J. 'Keeping the Home Fires Burning: Militarism and the Politics of Gender in South Africa', *Review of African Political Economy,* vol. 5, no. 2, 1989, p. 51.

39 Ibid.

40 Enloe *Does Khaki Become You?* See also, for example, Eide, A. and Thee, M. *Problems of Contemporary Militarism,* London, St Martins Press, 1980.

41 Enloe 'Feminist Thinking', p. 220.

42 Ibid.

43 Ibid.

44 Ibid.

45 Connell, R. *Gender and Power,* Cambridge, Polity, 1995.

46 Ibid.

47 Ibid.

48 Enloe C. *Does Khaki Become You?*

49 Cock 'Keeping the Home Fires'.

50 Brock-Utne, B. *Educating for Peace,* Oxford, Pergamon, 1985.

51 Reardon, B. *Sexism and the War System,* New York, Teachers College Press, 1985.

52 Brock-Utne, B. *Educating for Peace.*

53 Ibid.
54 Enloe 'Feminist Thinking'.
55 Ibid.
56 Ibid.
57 Elshtain 'Reflections'.
58 Ibid., p. 54.
59 Ibid.
60 Ibid.
61 Ibid.
62 See discussion in McGlenn, N. and Sarkees, M. *Women in Foreign Policy: The Insiders*, London, Routledge, 1993, pp. 1–15.
63 Ibid.
64 See discussion in Callaway, H. 'Survival and Support: Women's Forms of Political Action', in Callaway, H. and Ridd, R. *Caught Up in Conflict: Women's Responses to Political Strife*, Basingstoke, Macmillan, 1986, p. 224.
65 Ibid., p. 76.
66 Ibid.
67 Chapkis, W. *Loaded Questions: Women in the Military*, Amsterdam, Transnational Institute, 1981.
68 Di Leonardo, M. 'Morals, Mothers and Militarism; Anti-Militarism and Feminist Theory', *Feminist Studies*, vol. 11, no. 3, 1985.
69 Richards, Radcliffe J. 'Why the Pursuit of Peace Is no Part of Feminism', in Elshtain, J. and Tobias, S. (eds) *Women, Militarism and War: Essays in History, Politics and Social Theory*, Savage, Rowmann & Littlefield, 1990.
70 Dinnerstein, D. 'What Does Feminism Mean?', in Harris and King *Rocking the Ship of State.*
71 Ibid.
72 Ibid.
73 Ibid.
74 Ibid.
75 Ibid.
76 Ibid.
77 Ibid.
78 Ibid.
79 Ibid.
80 Ibid.
81 Chodorow, N. *The Reproduction of Mothering: Psychoanalysis and the Sociology of Gender*, Berkeley, University of California Press, 1978.
82 Dinnerstein, D. *The Rocking of the Cradle and the Ruling of the World*, New York, Harper & Row, 1976.
83 Gilligan, C. *In a Different Voice: Psychological Theory and Women's Development*, Cambridge, MA, Harvard University Press, 1982.

84 Ibid.
85 Ruddick, S. *Maternal Thinking: Towards a Politics of Peace*, Boston, Beacon Press, 1989.
86 Ruddick, S. 'Notes towards a Feminist Peace Politics', in Cooke, M. and Woollacott, A. *Gendering War Talk*, Princeton, Princeton University Press, 1993.
87 Ibid.
88 Ashworth, G. *Changing the Discourse: A Guide to Women and Human Rights*, London, Change Publications, 1993.
89 Ibid., pp. 13–14.
90 Ibid., p. 14.
91 Ibid.
92 See, for example, Ashworth *Changing the Discourse.*
93 Peterson, V. S. 'Whose Rights? A Critique of the "Givens" in Human Rights Discourse', *Alternatives*, vol. 15, no. 3, 1990, pp. 303–44.
94 Tickner 'Revisioning Security'.
95 Ibid.
96 Brock-Utne *Educating for Peace.*
97 See, for example, *World Women's Conference for a Healthy Planet*, Official Report, Miami, November, 1991, published by WEDO, New York. See also Commission on Environment and Development, *Our Common Future*, Oxford, Oxford University Press, 1987.
98 See Vickers, J. *Women and War*, London, Zed Books, 1993.
99 Galbraith, J. K. 'Weapons and World Welfare', *Development Forum*, vol. XV, no. 3, 1987.
100 Vickers *Women and War.*
101 George, S. *The Debt Boomerang*, London, Pluto, 1992.
102 Ibid.
103 Vickers *Women and War.*
104 Ibid.
105 Ibid.
106 Peterson, V. S. and Runyan, A. *Global Gender Issues*, Boulder, CO, Westview, 1993.
107 Enloe 'Feminist Thinking'.
108 Ibid.
109 Ibid.

6 The Gender Dimension of Global Political Economy and Development

1 Giddens, A. *The Consequences of Modernity*, Cambridge, Polity Press, 1990.
2 Ibid.

3 Tooze, R. 'The Unwritten Preface', *Millennium: Journal of International Studies*, vol. 17, no. 2, 1988.
4 Ibid., p. 291.
5 Ibid., p. 291.
6 Sylvester, C. 'The Emperor's Theories and Transformations: Looking at the Field through Feminist Lenses', in Sylvester, C. and Pirages, D. *Transformations in Global Political Economy*, London, Macmillan, p. 230.
7 Tickner, A. 'On the Fringes of the Global Economy', in Tooze, R. and Murphy, C. *The New International Political Economy*, Boulder, CO, Lynne Rienner, 1992.
8 Sylvester 'Emperor's Theories'.
9 Tickner 'On the Fringes'.
10 Sylvester 'Emperor's Theories'.
11 A critique derived from Marx. See, for example, McLennan, D. *Karl Marx Collected Writings*, Oxford, Oxford University Press, 1977.
12 Tickner 'On the Fringes'.
13 See, for example, Cox, R. 'Social Forces, States and World Order: Beyond International Theory, *Millennium: Journal of International Studies*, vol. 10, no. 2, 1981, pp. 126–55.
14 Ibid.
15 For a fuller discussion of the relationship between feminist IPE and critical theory see Whitworth, S. 'Gender in the Inter-Paradigm Debate', *Millennium: Journal of International Studies*, vol. 18, no. 2, 1989.
16 See discussion in Krause, J. 'The International Dimension of Gender Inequalities and Feminist Politics: A "New Direction" for International Political Economy', in MacMillan, J. and Linklater, A. *Boundaries in Question: New Directions in International Relations*, London, Pinter, 1995.
17 Mitter, S. *Common Fate, Common Bond: Women in the Global Economy*, London, Pluto, 1986.
18 Ibid.
19 Ibid.
20 Mitter, S. and Luijken, A. *The Unseen Phenomenon: The Rise of Homeworking*, London, Change Publications, 1989.
21 See discussion in Ashworth, G. and May, N. *Of Conjuring and Caring*, London, Change Publications, 1990.
22 Mitter and Luijken *The Unseen Phenomenon*.
23 Ibid.
24 Hooper, E. *Report on the UN ECE Regional Preparatory Meeting for the Fourth World Conference on Women*, Geneva, 1994.
25 See Mitter *Common Fate*, and Elson, D. and Pearson, R. 'The Situa-

tion of Women and the Internationalisation of Factory Production', in Young, K., Wolkowitz, C. and McCullagh, R. *Of Marriage and the Market: The Subordination of Women Internationally and its Lessons,* London, Routledge, 1991.

26 Elson and Pearson 'Situation of Women'.

27 Umfreville, M. *$£XONOMIC$: An Introduction to the Political Economy of Sex, Time and Gender,* London, Change Publications, 1990.

28 Thahn Dan, T. 'The Dynamics of Sex Tourism: The Case of South East Asia' *Development and Change,* vol. 14, pp. 533–53.

29 Ibid.

30 Enloe, C. *Bananas, Beaches and Bases: Making Feminist Sense of International Politics,* London, Pandora, 1989, p. 40.

31 De Groot, J. 'Conceptions and Misconceptions: The Historical and Cultural Context of Discussions of Women in Development', in Ashfar, H. *Women, Development and Survival in the Third World,* London, Longman, 1991.

32 Frank, G. *The Development of Underdevelopment,* New York, Monthly Review Press, 1966, and *Latin America: Underdevelopment or Revolution,* New York, Monthly Review Press, 1967.

33 Wallerstein, I. *The Capitalist World Economy,* Cambridge, Cambridge University Press, 1979.

34 Wallerstein, I. 'The Inter-State Structure of the Modern World-System', in Smith, S., Booth, K. and Zalewski, M. *International Theory: Positivism and Beyond,* Cambridge, Cambridge University Press, 1996, p. 87.

35 Ibid.

36 George, S. *A Fate Worse Than Debt,* Harmondsworth, Penguin, 1989, and George, S. *The Debt Boomerang,* London, Pluto, 1992.

37 Marchand, M. 'Latin American Voices of Resistance; Women's Movements and Development Debates', in Rostow, S., Rupert, M. and Samatur, A. *The Global Economy as Political Space: Essays in Critical Theory and International Political Economy,* Cambridge, Cambridge University Press, 1995.

38 Simmonds, P. 'Women in Development. A Threat to Liberation', *The Ecologist,* vol. 22, no. 1, 1992.

39 George *A Fate Worse Than Debt.*

40 Ibid.

41 Ibid.

42 Ibid.

43 Moser, C. 'Adjustment from Below: Low Income Women, Time and the Triple Role in Guayaygil', in Westwood, S. and Radcliffe, S. (eds) *'Viva': Women and Popular Protest in Latin America,* London, Routledge, 1993.

44 Ibid.
45 Hooper, E. *Report on the UN LAC Regional Preparatory Meeting for the Fourth World Conference on Women*, La Plata, 1994.
46 Hooper, E. *Report on the UN ESCAP Regional Preparatory Meeting for the Fourth World Conference on Women*, Jakarta, 1994.
47 See Hooper, *Report UN ECE*. See also Special Edition of *Feminist Review*, no. 39, 1991, pp. 16–36.
48 See Vickers, J. *Women in the World Economic Crisis*, London, Zed Books, 1991.
49 Cornia, G., Jolly, R. and Stewart, F. *Adjustment with a Human Face: Protecting the Vulnerable and Promoting Growth, A Study by UNICEF*, Oxford, Oxford University Press, 1987.
50 Ibid.
51 The discussion of gender and development in this chapter is necessarily brief and selective. It cannot hope to reflect the enormous literature in this area. However, see for example: Afshar, H. *Women, Development and Survival*; Banderage, A. 'Women in Development: Liberalism, Marxism and Marxist-Feminism', *Development and Change*, vol. 15, no. 4, 1984; Beneria, L. and Sen, G. 'Accumulation, Reproduction and Women's Role in Economic Development: Boserup Revisited', *Signs*, vol. 7, no. 2, 1981; Buvinic, M., Lycette, A. and McGreevey, P. (eds) *Women and Poverty in the Third World*, Baltimore, Johns Hopkins University Press, 1983; Development Alternatives with Women for a New Era, *Alternatives*, vol. 1, and vol. 2, Rio de Janeiro, Editora Rosa dos Tempos, 1991; Elson, D. *Male Bias in the Development Process*, Manchester, Manchester University Press, 1991; Joekes, S. *Women in the World Economy, An INSTRAW Study*, Oxford, Oxford University Press, 1987; Kardam, N. *Bringing Women In: Women's Issues in International Development Programs*, Boulder, CO, Lynne Rienner, 1990; Leacock, E., Safa, H. et al. *Women's Work: Development and the Division of Labour by Gender*, South Hadley, Bergin & Garvey, 1986; Marchand, M. and Parpart, J. (eds) *Feminism, Postmodernism, Development*, London, Routledge, 1995; Mies, M. *Patriarchy and Accumulation on a World Scale*, London, Zed Books, 1986; Momsen, J. H. *Women and Development in the Third World*, London, Routledge, 1996; Nash, J. and Fernandez-Kelly, M. P. (eds) *Women, Men and the International Division of Labour*, New York, State University of New York Press, 1983; Sen, A. K. *Resources, Values and Development*, Oxford, Blackwell, 1984; Sen, G. and Grown, C. *Development, Crisis and Alternative Visions: Third World Women's Perspectives*, New Delhi, DAWN, 1985; Shiva, V. *Staying Alive: Women, Ecology and Development*, London, Zed Books, 1989; Staudt, K. (ed.) *Women, International Development and Politics: The Bureaucratic Mire*, Philadelphia, Temple University Press, 1990; Tinker, I. *Persistent Inequalities:*

Women and World Development, Oxford; Oxford University Press, 1990; Ward, K. B. *Women Workers and Global Restructuring*, Ithaca, ILR Press, 1990; Waring, M. *If Women Counted: A New Feminist Economics*, San Francisco, Harper & Row, 1988.

52 Boserup, E. *Women's Role in Economic Development*, London, Earthscan Publications, 1989.

53 Ibid. See also Beneria, L. 'Conceptualizing the Labour Force: The Underestimation of Women's Economic Activities', in Nelson, N. (ed.) *African Women in Development*, London, Frank Cass, 1981, and Waring *If Women Counted*.

54 Ibid.

55 Ibid.

56 Moser 'Adjustment from Below'.

57 Vickers *Women in the World*.

58 Ibid.

59 Muntemba, S. (ed.) *Rural Development and Women: Lessons from the Field*, vols. I and II, ILO, 1986.

60 United Nations Educational, Scientific and Cultural Organization.

61 International Labour Organization.

62 Food and Agriculture Organization.

63 The United Nations' International Research and Training Institute for the Advancement of Women.

64 For a fuller discussion see Tinker, I. and Jaquette, J. 'UN Decade for Women: Its Impact and Legacy', *World Development*, vol. 15, no. 3, 1987, pp. 419–27; Vickers *Women in the World*.

65 Tinker and Jaquette 'UN Decade'.

66 Ibid.

67 Ibid.

68 Boserup *Women's Role*.

69 Allison, H., Ashworth, G. and Redcliffe, N. *Hardcash: Man Made Development and its Consequences; A Feminist Perspective on Aid*, London, Change Publications, 1980.

70 Ibid.

71 Ibid.

72 Goetz, A. M. *The Politics of Integrating Gender to State Development Processes: Trends, Opportunities and Constraints in Bangladesh, Chile, Jamaica, Mali, Morocco and Uganda*, United Nations Research Institute for Social Development, Geneva, 1995, p. 8.

73 Ibid.

74 Ibid., p. 3.

75 See *The Ecologist*, Special Edition, Women in Development. vol. 22, no. 1, Jan/Feb 1992, and Dankelman, I. and Davidson, J. *Women and the Environment in the Third World: Alliance for the Future*, Earthscan Publications, 1994.

76 See UNIFEM *World Survey of the Role of Women in Development,* New York, United Nations Publications, 1989, and UNIFEM Newsletter, vol. 2, no. 1, New York, United Nations Publications, February 1994.
77 UNIFEM, 1989, op. cit.
78 See, for example, Shiva *Staying Alive.*
79 Regrettably, there is not space in the text for an expanded discussion of the Women, Environment and Development movement. Nor is it possible to discuss at any length the important contribution which eco-feminist thought has made to debates about the relationship between environmental degradation, mal-development and women's oppression. The interested reader might like to consult Jackson, C. 'Women/Nature or Gender/History', *Journal of Peasant Studies,* vol. 20, no. 3, 1993, pp. 389–419, or *The Ecologist,* vol. 22, no. 1, 1992, or Dankelman and Davidson *Women and the Environment.*
80 See Jaquette, J. 'Women and Modernization Theory: A Decade of Feminist Criticism', *World Politics,* vol. 34, no. 2, 1982.
81 See Jayawardena, K. *Feminism and Nationalism in the Third World,* London, Zed Books, 1986.
82 See also Ashworth, G. and Bonnerjea, L. *The Invisible Decade: UK Women and the UN Decade for Women,* London, Gower, 1985.
83 Kourany, J., Sterba, J. P. and Tong, R. (eds) *Feminist Philosophies,* Hemel Hempstead, Harvester Wheatsheaf, 1993.
84 See MacNay, L. *Foucault and Feminism,* Cambridge, Polity Press, 1994.
85 Indeed, as Alcoff suggests, for many contemporary feminists concept of woman itself became a problem. While woman as both a social and analytical category had been central to feminist theory, it was a category which was impossible to formulate precisely. See Alcoff, L. 'Cultural Feminism and Poststructuralism: The Identity Crisis in Feminist Theory', *Signs,* vol. 13, no. 3, 1988.
86 Spivak, G. ' "Woman" as Theatre: United Nations Conference on Women, Beijing, 1995', *Radical Philosophy,* no. 75, January/February 1996, p. 2.
87 See also Rosenau, P. *Postmodernism and the Social Sciences,* Princeton, Princeton University Press, 1994.
88 Ibid.
89 Mohanty has similarly argued that there is urgent political necessity of forming strategic alliances across class, race and national boundaries. The analytical principles of Western feminist discourse limit the possibilities of coalitions amongst white Western feminists, working-class women and women of colour around the world. Feminist scholarship is not 'objective' knowledge about certain subjects; it is discursive practice, purposeful and ideological, a mode of intervention into hegemonic discourse and political praxis which

counters and resists the totalizing imperatives of age-old legitimate and scientific bodies of knowledge. See 'Under Western Eyes: Feminist Scholarship and Colonial Discourse', *Feminist Review*, no. 30, 1988, pp. 61–88.

90 See, for example, the various papers in Nicholson, L. *Feminism/Postmodernism*, London, Routledge, 1990.
91 Tickner 'On the Fringes'; Vickers *Women in the World*.
92 Hooper *Report UN ECE*.
93 Ibid.

7 Reconstructions and Resistances

1 See the discussion in Harding, S. *Whose Science? Whose Knowledge?*, Milton Keynes, Open University Press, 1991, pp. 111–18. See also Harding, S. 'Is There a Feminist Method', in Harding, S. (ed.) *Feminism and Methodology*, Milton Keynes, Open University Press, 1987.
2 Ibid.
3 Ibid.
4 Ashworth, G. 'An Elf among Gnomes: A Feminist in North–South Relations', *Millennium: Journal of International Studies*, vol. 17, no. 3, 1988, pp. 497–537.
5 Newland, K. 'From Transnational Relationships to International Relations: Women in Development and the International Decade for Women', in Grant, R. and Newland, K. *Gender and International Relations*, Milton Keynes, Open University Press, 1991.
6 Ibid., p. 122.
7 Ashworth, G. and May, N. *Of Conjuring and Caring*, London, Change Publications, 1990, p. 1.
8 Ibid.
9 Ibid.
10 Pettman, J. J. *Worlding Women: A Feminist International Politics*, London, Routledge, 1996, p. 54.
11 Mohanty, C. 'Under Western Eyes: Feminist Scholarship and Colonial Discourse', *Feminist Review*, no. 30, 1988, pp. 61–88.
12 Spivak, G. '"Woman" as Theatre: United Nations Conference on Women, Beijing, 1995', *Radical Philosophy*, no. 75, January/February 1996, pp. 2–3.
13 Brown, S. 'Feminism, International Theory and International Relations of Gender Inequality', *Millennium: Journal of International Studies*, vol. 17, no. 3, p. 471.
14 Wallerstein, I. *The Capitalist World Economy*, Cambridge, Cambridge University Press, 1979.

15 Mies, M. *Patriarchy and Accumulation on a World Scale*, London, Zed Books, 1986.
16 Wallerstein, I. 'The Inter-state Structure of the Modern World-System', in Smith, S., Booth, B. and Zalewski, M. *International Theory: Positivism and Beyond*, Cambridge, Cambridge University Press, 1996, p. 95.
17 Mies *Patriarchy*.
18 Ibid.
19 Mackintosh, M. 'Gender and Economics: The Sexual Division of Labour and the Subordination of Women', in Young, K., Wolkowitz, C. and McCullagh, R. *Of Marriage and the Market*, London, Routledge, 1984.
20 Mitter, S. *Common Fate, Common Bond: Women in the Global Economy*, London, Pluto, 1986.
21 Pearson, R. and Elson, D. 'The Subordination of Women and the Internationalisation of Factory Production', in Young, Wolkowitz and McCullagh *Of Marriage and the Market*.
22 Ibid.
23 Mackintosh 'Gender and Economics'.
24 Mitter *Common Fate*.
25 Hartsock, N. *Money, Sex and Power: Towards a Feminist Historical Materialism*, Boston, Northeastern University Press, 1983.
26 Ibid.
27 See for example, Tickner, A. 'Hans Morgenthau's Principles of Political Realism', in Grant and Newland *Gender and International Relations*; or Tickner, A. *Gender in International Relations: Feminist Perspectives on Achieving Global Security*, New York, Columbia University Press, 1992.
28 See particularly the discussion in Massey, D. and Jess, P. (eds) *A Place in the World? Places, Cultures and Globalization*, Milton Keynes, Open University Press, 1995, pp. 66–9.
29 Hartsock *Money, Sex and Power*, p. 236.
30 Hartsock *Money, Sex and Power*.
31 A number of writers could be cited here but see, for example, Hartsock *Money, Sex and Power*; or Hirschman, N. *Rethinking Obligation: A Feminist Method for Political Theory*, London, Cornell University Press, 1992.
32 Brittan, A. *Masculinity and Power*, Oxford, Basil Blackwell, 1989, p. 14.
33 Grimshaw, J., *Feminist Philosophers: Women's Perspectives on Philosophical Traditions*, London, Harvester Wheatsheaf, 1986.
34 Mohanty 'Under Western Eyes'.
35 Hartsock *Money, Sex and Power*, p. 208.
36 Harding, S. 'Feminism, Science and the Anti- Enlightenment Cri-

tiques', in Nicholson, L. *Feminism/Postmodernism*, London, Routledge, 1990, p. 90.

37 Elam, D. *Feminism and Deconstruction: Ms. en Abyme*, London, Routledge, 1994, p. 71.

38 Alcoff, L. 'The Identity Crisis in Feminist Theory, *Signs*, vol. 13, no. 3.

39 Harding argues that standpoint does not imply judgemental or epistemological relativism. Indeed it represents the logical complement to the judgemental absolutism characteristic of Eurocentric thought. Harding suggests that 'value-free' objectivity, which requires a faulty theory of the ideal agent or subject of knowledge, must be rejected, but one can nevertheless accept that knowledge is both socially located and objective. Harding introduces the notion of 'strong objectivity' which requires a commitment to acknowledging the historical character of every belief, but which is nevertheless less partial, less distorted and therefore, more objective. See discussion of 'strong objectivity' in Harding *Whose Science*, pp. 138–63.

40 See Harding's discussion in Nicholson *Feminism/Postmodernism*.

41 The term 'counter-hegemonic' group or force is associated particularly with the work of Robert Cox. See, for example, 'Social Forces, States and World Orders: Beyond International Relations Theory', *Millennium: Journal of International Studies*, vol. 10, no. 2, pp. 126–55.

42 See Krause, J. 'Gender in Global Perspective' in Youngs, G. and Kofman, E. *Globalization: Theory and Practice*, London, Pinter, 1996.

43 Whitworth, S. 'Gender in the Inter-paradigm Debate', *Millennium: Journal of International Studies*, vol. 18, no. 2, 1993. See also Whitworth, S. *Feminist Theory and International Relations*, Basingstoke, Macmillan, 1994.

44 Jayawardena, K. *Feminism and Nationalism in the Third World*, London, Zed Books, 1986.

45 Tohidi, N. 'Modernity, Islamisation and Women in Iran', in Moghadam, V. *Gender and National Identity: Women and Politics in Muslim Societies*, London, Zed Books, 1994.

46 For a discussion of feminist critical theory and the analysis of gender relations and institutional contexts, see Disch, L. 'Towards a Feminist Conception of Politics', *The Political Science Teacher*, September 1991.

47 Alcoff 'Identity Crisis'.

48 Mohanty 'Under Western Eyes'.

49 Ibid.

50 Rosalda M. Z. 'The Use and Abuse of Anthropology: Reflections on Feminism and Cross Cultural Understanding', *Signs*, vol. 5, no. 3, 1980.

51 Mohanty 'Under Western Eyes'.

52 Ibid., p. 67.

53 Ibid.
54 White, S. K. *Political Theory and Postmodernism*, Cambridge, Cambridge University Press, 1991, pp. 1–2.
55 Rosenau, P. *Postmodernism and the Social Sciences: Insights, Inroads and Intrusions*, Princeton, Princeton University Press, 1992, pp. 14–17, 174.
56 See the discussion in Elam *Feminism and Deconstruction*, pp. 69–72.
57 Rosenau *Postmodernism*.
58 Ibid., p. 45.
59 McNay, L. *Foucault and Feminism*, Cambridge, Polity Press, 1992.
60 Ibid., p. 7.
61 Ibid.
62 Ibid., p. 41.
63 Ibid.
64 Marchand, M. 'Latin American Voices of Resistance: Women's Movements and Development Debates', in Rosow, S., Inayatullah, N. and Rupert, M. (eds) *The Global Economy as Political Space*, Boulder, CO, Lynne Rienner, 1994.
65 Rosenau, *Postmodernism*, pp. 146–7.
66 Ibid., p. 146.
67 Ibid., p. 144.
68 Ibid.
69 See, for example, Pettman, R. *International Politics*, London, Longman, 1991, and Walker, R. J. B. *One World, Many Worlds*, Boulder, CO, Lynne Rienner, 1988.
70 Walker *One World, Many Worlds*, p. 115.
71 Ibid.
72 Ibid.
73 Meisenholder, 'Habermas and Feminism', in Wallace, R. (ed.) *Feminism and Sociological Theory*, Ithaca, Cornell University Press, 1989.
74 Ibid.
75 Elam *Feminism and Deconstruction*, p. 82.
76 Ibid.
77 Sylvester 'Empathetic Communication', *Millennium: Journal of International Studies*, vol. 23, no. 1, 1994, pp. 407–24.
78 Ibid., p. 328.

Index